BANK MANAGEMENT AND SUPERVISION IN DEVELOPING FINANCIAL MARKETS

Also by Wilbert O. Bascom

THE ECONOMICS OF FINANCIAL REFORM IN DEVELOPING COUNTRIES

Bank Management and Supervision in Developing Financial Markets

Wilbert O. Bascom

President and Chief Executive Officer
First Equity Corporation, Investment Bankers
State of Florida

First published in Great Britain 1997 by
MACMILLAN PRESS LTD
Houndmills, Basingstoke, Hampshire RG21 6XS and London
Companies and representatives throughout the world

A catalogue record for this book is available from the British Library.

ISBN 0–333–63387–3

First published in the United States of America 1997 by
ST. MARTIN'S PRESS, INC.,
Scholarly and Reference Division,
175 Fifth Avenue, New York, N.Y. 10010

ISBN 0–312–17701–1

Library of Congress Cataloging-in-Publication Data
Bascom, Wilbert O.
Bank management and supervision in developing financial markets /
Wilbert O. Bascom.
p.   cm.
Includes bibliographical references and index.
ISBN 0–312–17701–1 (cloth)
1. Bank management.   2. Banks and banking—State supervision.
3. Bank management—Developing countries.   4. Banks and banking–
–Developing countries—State supervision.   I. Title.
HG1615.B374 1997
332.1'068—dc21   97–18983
                                                          CIP

This book is printed on paper suitable for recycling and made from fully managed and
sustained forest sources.

10   9   8   7   6   5   4   3   2   1
06   05   04   03   02   01   00   99   98   97

Printed and bound in Great Britain by
Antony Rowe Ltd, Chippenham, Wiltshire

To my children

Wilbert, Richard, Jessica and Jacqueline

Contents

List of Illustrations

Boxes

x

Figures

Tables

Preface

As financial markets are liberalized, bank management and bank supervisors are faced with new and complex challenges. Bank management is faced with the challenge of managing their banks in a competitive and volatile market environment – an environment with high levels of unaccustomed risks that must be identified, monitored and controlled by management. Directors, who may be inadequately informed of the banking business and the changes occurring in the financial market environment, are expected to act in a manner that preserves public confidence in their banks and ultimately in the entire banking system.

Bank regulators and supervisors have the challenge of establishing the framework that permits risk taking without endangering the safety and soundness of the banks operating in their jurisdictions. The main emphasis of their regulatory and supervisory programmes would be on the prudential aspects of financial monitoring, such as assessing the quality of the banks' assets, and the adequacy of their accounting and other records and control systems. In cases where deposit insurance exists, bank supervisors would have the additional challenge of providing a substitute for the market discipline removed by such insurance.

This book is intended as a reference guide for those interested in ensuring the existence of banks that are capable of meeting the challenges of developing financial markets effectively and successfully. It, therefore, focuses on bank directors and bank management; on bank regulators and supervisors; and on policy makers in governments, central banks, and regulatory and supervisory agencies. The book will also be useful for graduate and undergraduate students with courses in emerging financial markets, money and banking, and economic development.

I have relied on work done by others on the subject of bank management and supervision in developed and developing financial markets, and have acknowledged their contribution throughout the book. Fernando Capablanca of Banco Exterior de los Andes y de Espana, and Alcides Avila of Holland & Knight have provided me with some of the references used in this book. Much of my comments and observations, however, have been influenced by my own experiences as a bank regulator and supervisor in the state of Florida, as a member of senior management of a bank that operated in a repressed financial market, and as consultant with a group of financial companies operating in a developing financial market.

I am indebted to the Board of Directors of Eagle Merchant Bank of Jamaica for the opportunity to consult with this bank and with the other financial institutions included in the Eagle Merchant Bank of Jamaica group of companies. The directors have allowed me to share in the proceedings of their various boards and to obtain a practical knowledge of their handling of the complex issues of board supervision of the management and operations of banks in the developing financial markets of Jamaica.

Trevor Ffrench, of the Miami representative office of Eagle Merchant Bank of Jamaica, and Arthur Bell, of Geyco International, have provided me with professional advice when requested. Kyree Pina, of First Equity Corporation, has prepared the diagrams, revised the text, and helped me to unravel the intricacies of working with computers. I am indeed indebted to her for the assistance she has provided, and the competence and dedication she has demonstrated throughout this project.

Finally, I would like to express my deep and sincere appreciation for the encouragement and understanding provided by my wife, Wendy, and my daughters, Jessica and Jacqueline, during the weekends and holidays that I have devoted to this book instead of to them.

WILBERT O. BASCOM

1 Introduction

Financial markets which are at different stages of liberalization, reform, or deregulation are considered developing financial markets. More specifically, these are markets that are in the process of deregulating interest and exchange rates, reducing or eliminating directed and subsidized credit, abolishing commercial banks' credit ceilings, and removing market entry barriers to financial intermediaries.

Developing financial markets are found in different regions of the world and in countries with different national income levels. They are in countries, with high-middle- and low-income levels, in Africa, Asia, Europe, the Middle East, Latin America, and the Caribbean. In these countries, financial markets are at different stages of liberalization depending on the duration of the financial reform process and the success or failure in implementing the liberalization programme.

However, these markets have certain common characteristics. Particularly in the early stages of reform, the markets tend to experience high and volatile real interest and exchange rates; and high levels of non-performing assets in a financial system dominated by commercial banks. In addition, most developing financial markets have recognized the need for strong prudential regulation and supervision of commercial banks' and other financial institutions' activities. Generally, the need for such regulation and supervision, and their effective implementation, are recognized only later in the reform process. That is, after the markets have experienced a series of crises in part due to management indiscretions as reflected in high levels of non-performing assets.

Financial liberalization has important effects on bank management and supervision. Among these effects are the growth in commercial banks' balance sheets; the channelling of banking resources into riskier and more unfamiliar activities with consequent increases in loan losses; rising competition between banks and non-bank financial intermediaries for deposits and high grade assets; and increased bank insolvencies. Bank management may not have the technical competence to control these effects; and the system of bank supervision may be incapable of monitoring and evaluating the management's responses to them. Thus, particularly at the initiation of financial liberalization, the need for competent bank management must be emphasized; and effective regulation and supervision must be implemented.

1

This chapter provides a feel for the totality of the issues of bank management and supervision in developing financial markets. It highlights a set of principles for competent bank management and discusses these principles in the context of already liberalized, and developing financial markets. It argues that non-compliance with these principles can result in banking crises. This chapter also reviews the requirements for effective bank regulation and supervision, and outlines the plan of the book.

1.1   COMPETENT MANAGEMENT

Before financial liberalization, banking markets were cartelized and bank regulation and supervision tended to restrict competition between financial intermediaries. Banks, therefore, enjoyed excess profits, obtained mainly from their customers with limited choices between financial services providers and products.

In the repressed financial markets, an important determinant of the market value of commercial banks' capital was the discounted value of the excess future profits banks themselves were expected to earn. Competition for the excess profits, however, increased with financial liberalization. This competition was reflected in prime borrowers accessing lower-cost alternatives to bank credit, and savers acquiring higher-yielding alternatives to bank deposits. The higher funding costs and higher loan losses associated with a lower average quality of borrowers combined to reduce excess profits and to induce management to take unaccustomed risks in order to maintain their banks' pre-liberalization profits.

Apart from the competition arising from financial liberalization, bank management in developing financial markets is faced with another reform-related challenge rooted in the price system and the system of enterprise subsidies common in developing economies. This challenge is how to manage efficiently in the absence of correct price signals that price and enterprise reform should provide. The liberalization programme might have failed to address financial, enterprise, and price reforms in any systematic or appropriately sequenced manner. Bank management is assisted if financial reform is accompanied by changes in the prevailing price system distorted by various subsidy and other price support programmes. Such price reform would enable banks to lend on the basis of correct price signals.

Enterprise reform that emphasizes improving credit worthiness and profitability enables firms to become increasingly responsive to market signals. Price and enterprise reform would, therefore, assist in strengthening credit risk management in developing financial markets. In other words, the improved price signals and business responses to these signals would facilitate management selection of borrowers. They will also assist in the valuation of the collateral held against credit extension, the identification of actual and potential problem assets, and the implementation of adequate asset loss reserves and asset charge-off policies.

Enterprise and price reforms may be delayed because the government's economic and social objectives may require the preservation of price subsidies and directed credit under certain circumstances. The experiences of some Asian countries indicate that directed credit programmes with strict performance standards could be consistent with competent bank management. These countries' directed credit programmes were designed to achieve their government's policy objectives while stipulating strict performance criteria. In Japan, for example, bank managers have employed rigorous credit evaluations to select among applicants falling within government sectoral targets. In Korea, the government's monitoring of large borrowers was based on such market-oriented criteria as export and profitability performance standards. Borrowers that failed to meet these criteria were sometimes driven into bankruptcy.[1] In such situations, management will be strengthened if the reform policies include clearly defined objectives that are linked to the performance of the banks and their borrowers, as well as clearly defined measures that bank regulators and supervisors must implement if these objectives are not met.

The success of directed credit programmes in developing financial markets would, therefore, be influenced by the existence of strong performance-based standards, and the effective imposition of these standards on borrowers. The importance of directed credit programmes would decline or become more compatible with the objective of optimizing banks' profitability when: (1) the practice of applying strict performance criteria to lending is implemented; (2) borrowers' creditworthiness is objectively evaluated; (3) assets being funded are competitively priced, and (4) supporting collateral is not over-valued.

The increased risks inherent in developing financial markets underlie the importance of at least five principles for competent bank management that are relevant whether or not directed credit programmes are in place. These principles are: (1) avoid an undue concentration of credit to any single borrower or activity; (2) ensure that the collateral for credit is not exposed to the same shocks that weaken the borrower; (3) expand cautiously into unfamiliar activities; (4) control the bank's asset-liability mismatches; and (5) know the counterparties in any transaction.[2]

Non-compliance with the principle of avoiding undue credit concentration, by the failure to specify single borrower limits, has been a major reason for banking crises in several developing financial markets. Of course, this non-compliance cannot be explained by the lack of awareness of the purpose of such limits or the failure of bank regulators and supervisors to specify and implement credit concentration limits on banks. It is well known that single borrower limits are intended to prevent excessive bank credit to an individual borrower or a group of borrowers, and to safeguard the bank's depositors by spreading the risk among a relatively large number of borrowers engaged in different activities.

In some countries, credit concentration regulations prescribing single borrower limits have been in place since the 1920s and 1930s.[3] However, in spite of the regulations, these countries have experienced costly bank failures attributed mainly to large credit concentrations to related parties. Undue concentration avoidance regulations, and the ability of bank supervisors to enforce compliance with them are necessary to minimize banks' risk exposures and the potential for bank failures in developing financial markets.

Regulations on single borrower limits have differentiated between secured and unsecured borrowers as well as allowed for exceptions to these limits. In Chile, borrowing in excess of 5 per cent of capital and reserves must be adequately secured; in Peru, the limit is 10 per cent, unless approved by the central bank based on a report of the superintendency of banks, then it can increase to 20 per cent; in Ecuador, the limit of 15 per cent can be increased to 25 per cent if appropriate collateral is provided; in Colombia, there are several credit categories that are exempted from lending limits (for example, lending to official institutions, and lending based on resources obtained through central bank discount and rediscount facilities). Although the exceptions to these limits imply that, under certain conditions, credit concentrations are permitted, such exceptions should be strictly monitored and controlled by management. At the minimum, such monitoring and control will require adequate credit policy and guidelines on single borrower limits; approval, internal control and review procedures, and management's ability to implement these policy, guidelines, and procedures.[4]

The second principle of competent bank management addresses the relationship between credit, collateral, and economic shocks. This relationship may be explained by the impact of asset price inflation and deflation on the amount of credit risk banks are willing to take, the ability of borrowers to meet their obligations, and the bank's ability to collect problem credits through collateral sales. Increased risks taken by banks during periods of asset price inflation, can often turn into losses during periods of asset price deflation caused, for example, by an unexpected sectoral shock, or an extended period of slow economic activity. Particularly in a situation of asset price deflation, credit portfolios, considered adequately collateralized will be adversely affected, in view of the fact that the economic factors that explain the asset price deflation may also affect the borrower's ability to repay. The experiences of liberalized financial markets in developed countries with asset price inflation and the reaction of the monetary and regulatory authorities to the problems of excess debt accumulation and risk taking are instructive in many ways for bank management in developing financial markets.

The 1980s have witnessed pronounced asset price inflation in Japan, the United Kingdom, Australia, and New Zealand. It was less pronounced in the United States. Bank credit extended during this period was mainly collateralized by the assets acquired through such credit. The 1980s have also witnessed the intervention of the monetary authorities when they considered the need for an adjustment in the process of debt accumulation and asset price inflation as critical; and the corrective measures by regulatory and supervisory agencies when they recognized that the systems in place were ineffective in dealing with the impact of debt accumulation and asset price changes on inadequately capitalized banks.

The inflationary pressures in these countries' asset markets have been explained by such factors as: (1) the excess credit channelled to specific groups of institutions and individuals after financial liberalization; (2) the consequences of financial liberalization, namely, the intense competition among financial intermediaries, the waves of financial innovations, and the high-risk lending in new areas of business; and (3) the role of expectations in asset price determination.[5]

Among the specific groups of borrowers were corporations and individuals that accumulated assets such as real estate, corporate equities, art, and commodities in global markets. In the United States, ongoing financial innovations and tax reform measures provided investment opportunities and incentives that were particularly significant for the corporate sector and high income earners.[6] The expansion in bank credit financed mergers and acquisitions, leverage buy-outs, commercial and residential real estate. In Japan, the construction of apartments and condominiums and the upgrading of real estate purchases stimulated by tax incentives, were financed by bank credit. Moreover, in the late 1980s spending in Japan shifted increasingly toward luxury items, business investment, and durable goods financed by bank credit.[7] In the United Kingdom, as debt accumulation in the 1980s reflected a backlog of unsatisfied demand released after financial liberalization, the increase in borrowing tended to be more broad based than in the United States and Japan.

The increased risk taking and upward pressures on asset markets were not only fuelled by the deregulation of lending practices, but, as in the case of the United States, were promoted by the failure to reform the country's deposit insurance system. As banks increased their lending collateralized by the very assets they financed and employed government insured deposits to fund their lending activities, they exposed themselves to deflation in asset prices. In fact, in the 1980s a large number of financial institutions (savings and loans, and commercial banks) experienced severe financial distress in the form of high non-performing assets and erosion of their franchise values.[8]

With asset price inflation in process, expectations of future price increases and capital gains became an important factor in explaining the rise in demand for assets and for credit to fund their acquisition. Past asset price inflation influenced expectations of future asset price changes, and lending rates in the highly competitive markets lagged the increase in asset prices. Thus, the real cost of borrowing for asset acquisitions tended to be negative and fuelled further asset price inflation.

For bank management in developing financial markets, these experiences indicate that: (1) the increased risks taken by banks after financial liberalization can turn into losses after a shift in economic conditions; (2) even loans considered adequately collateralized during the period of asset price inflation could be adversely affected, as the same shock that reduced the borrowers' repayment ability would simultaneously reduce the value of the collateral held; and finally, (3) in cases where credit risks are inadequately protected by increases in banks' operating profits or capital base, the problem of non-performing assets and losses associated with asset price deflation could result in substantial distress in the banking system.

In developing countries, bank credit normally is collateralized by the borrowers' real property. As financial markets are liberalized and as new borrowers emerge with little of no real property as part of their assets, the relative position of collateral based lending declines. Competent bank management in these markets requires that loan repayments be structured on the basis of anticipated cash flows from the transactions or enterprises being financed. These cash flows must be adequate to repay the loan. Where repayment is based only on the collateral held, an added element of risk is built into the credit process. This risk can be minimized by limiting the credit exposure to a realistic valuation of the collateral.

The third principle of competent bank management cautions about the rate of credit or other expansion into unfamiliar activities. Banks in developing financial markets have responded to financial liberalization by expanding in unaccustomed activities in their bid to maintain profitability or to prevent a loss in market share. In these markets, banks' tolerance for risk, increases with the intensity of the competition from non-bank financial intermediaries. In the 1980s, banks in developing financial markets experienced serious asset quality deterioration resulting from their credit expansion into unfamiliar activities. In the financial markets of Latin America, the non-performing loan ratio increased dramatically from 6 per cent in 1981 to 11 per cent in 1983. This percentage continued increasing and reached 14 per cent in 1987.[9]

Management may want, at some stage in the financial liberalization process, to venture into new areas of risk taking. However, in doing so, competent management may be reminded of the tale of the gambling Chinese merchants who recklessly overextended themselves during the construction of the Great Wall. First they lost the money in their pockets, then the merchandize in their carts, and finally the clothes on their backs. They were frozen to death in the bleak north by the cold winds of the Gobi.[10] For the sake of their own survival and the safety and soundness of the banks they manage, management must establish loss limits for these high-risk activities and stick to them. The limits, should be based on the rate of growth of the banks' deposits and capital resources, as well as on the capital constraints imposed by bank regulators and supervisors.

Management may be able to conform their own appetite for risk to their banks' capacity for risk taking by employing a number of risk controlling techniques. In the area of short term lending, for example, management may: (1) ration available credit lines to the more creditworthy customers; (2) price the credit facility in line with preconceived repayment risks; (3) obtain guarantees and collateral or other appropriate credit enhancements; and (4) share the risk for larger transactions through the process of loan sales.

For medium-term financing, management may reduce credit risk by: (1) using a secured payment stream requiring cover from a reputable guarantor; (2) eliminating the loans from the bank's balance sheet by converting them into securities and placing them with private investors; and (3) instituting asset-backed lending that requires the borrower to extract from its balance sheet, liquid and marketable assets that serve as credit enhancement to the lender. In the case of long-term lending, the collateralization, escrow accounts, co-financing and guarantees, and credit securitization techniques may all be used in managing risks.[11]

The fourth principle of competent bank management deals generally with liquidity and its related maturity-gap management. The management of gaps or mismatches between a bank's asset-liability maturities helps to demonstrate the bank's capacity to meet all obligations as they fall due. In fact, a bank's capacity to meet the obligations of its customers may be enhanced by a set of techniques that may be used separately or in some appropriate combination. These include: (1) holding a stock of cash and immediately liquid assets; (2) implementing asset matching policies to ensure that a proportion of potential cash outflows from maturing liabilities and other commitments is covered by cash available from maturing assets; and (3) purchasing funds in the interbank market to finance cash outflows in the form of deposit withdrawals or new lending. Management may decide to use cash inflows from maturing assets to meet potential cash outflows, thus avoiding or limiting recourse to the market for liquidity.

A principal objective of maturity-gap management in developing financial markets is to ensure the adequacy of bank liquidity while exploiting the profit opportunities offered by interest rate volatility and maturity mismatches. At all times, however, management should be satisfied that maturity gaps are appropriate to the circumstances of the bank including the scale and nature of its operations.

Finally, the fifth principle of competent bank management refers to the importance of knowing the counterparties in any transactions so as to minimize default or credit risk. This principle is relevant in developing financial markets where banks are actively diversifying into off-balance sheet and other fee earning activities to prevent downsizing, and to hedge against risks. As bank borrowers switch from bank credit, to borrowing directly from the securities market through the issuance of short and medium term notes or commercial paper, bank management may provide underwriting services to the issuers. While bank management may minimize risk by underwriting the notes issued by the most creditworthy enterprises, it is possible that, in an effort to increase income, the issues of unfamiliar counterparties may also be underwritten by some banks.

Unlike direct lending by the banks, the credit risk associated with note issuance is normally not sustained by the bank alone but is shared between the note holders and the underwriters. This unbundling of risk should not encourage management to be less cautions about evaluating the counterparty to the transaction. It is possible that the bank, acting as an underwriter to the issue, may face the prospect of having to take up the notes of an issuer in whom the investors have lost confidence. To minimize the risk associated with fee-earning borrowing enhancement activities, bank management must carefully evaluate the counterparties involved.

As interest and exchange rate risks increase with financial markets liberalization, instruments are developed to hedge these risks. No doubt, these hedging instruments can be valuable if used properly (for example, for hedging rather than for speculative purposes) and if the parties involved are credible and have the ability to perform in a manner specified by the underlying agreement. However, management must be aware that the use of hedging instruments creates exposure to counterparties that is often not properly evaluated and controlled. Competent management, through careful evaluation, would ensure that counterparties have the ability to offset payments and receipts arising from different hedging instruments. Together with the ability to perform, management must also ensure that offsetting by counterparties can legally be enforced. Hedging instruments can create an exposure to counterparties because of improper documentation that may result in litigation and enforcement problems.

Two banks may enter into a forward rate agreement to protect themselves against future changes in interest rates – one bank against a future rise, the other against a future fall in interest rates. Without any commitment to lend or borrow the principal amount, the two banks or counterparties agree to an interest rate for a certain period in the future. At maturity, the banks are expected to settle by paying or receiving only the difference between the interest rate agreed earlier and the current interest rate. The benefit of this hedging arrangement is that it covers the banks' rate exposure without expanding their balance sheet to the advantage of their capital ratios and return on assets. This benefit should, however, be set against the expected cost of default by the counterparties involved. Knowledge of the counterparty in any hedging arrangement is an indispensable component in the evaluation of this cost.

The expected cost of default by a counterparty may be formulated as follows:

$$E(C) \; = \; p \times E(V) \qquad\qquad (1.1)$$

where:

$E(C)$ = expected cost of default
p = the probability of the counterparty defaulting, and
$E(V)$ = the expected replacement value of the contract at the time of default

The size of p is mainly a function of management's knowledge of the counterparty's ability to perform as prescribed by the underlying agreement or contract. Together with a careful evaluation of the counterparty, management may minimize the size of p by requiring collateral or margins when appropriate. Management may also diversify the bank's off-balance sheet and hedging activities across individuals and types of counterparties.

These five principles of competent bank management aim at providing guidelines for the management and control of unaccustomed risks in developing financial markets. With financial liberalization, bank management, in becoming more active risk-takers, may increase their return on assets and capital and may participate in the creation of new products for unbundling and controlling risks. However, the experiences of developed, and some developing financial markets have shown that management, with the objectives of defending their relative competitive position, and maintaining earnings and the value of their franchise, may make unwise business decisions, resulting in defaults and losses on a variety of off- and on-balance sheet activities.

1.2   BANK SUPERVISION

Financial market liberalization could have serious implications for the effectiveness of traditional bank regulatory and supervisory systems. Such systems, appropriate for repressed financial markets, would be inappropriate for developing financial markets with their high price volatility and intense competition. Supervisors have acknowledged that banks in repressed financial markets were highly profitable and risk averse in the sense that they demonstrated little incentive to risk their capital by exploring into unaccustomed areas.

With financial reform, developing financial markets grew less segmented, financial intermediaries replicated each others' profit centres, and risk taking became widespread resulting in high levels of non-performing assets. In cases where increased risk taking was not adequately compensated by an increase in operating income or protected by an adequate capital base, the losses associated with such risks resulted in serious banking crises. It was not until the effects of such crises overspilled into other sectors of the national economies and banks had to be rescued by governments, was the need for a change in the regulatory and supervisory systems fully appreciated.

Supervisors must, therefore, recognize the forces that influence the performance results and condition of banks in developing financial markets and determine whether these are likely to be temporary or permanent. Asset price inflation and its impact on banks' performance and condition, for example, may be a temporary factor and is not likely to give rise to a need for basic changes in the bank supervisory system and practices. But where the financial system is changing in response to more durable forces, such as the adverse consequences of deregulation, the regulatory and supervisory changes would have to be more fundamental. Such changes would have to focus on a regulatory and supervisory system designed to minimize the risks banks assume, and to ensure the safety and soundness of individual banks as well as the system as a whole.

In fact, the aim of bank regulation and supervision is to prevent systemic financial instability and improve bank efficiency. The system of regulation and supervision within which banks are expected to operate must therefore be designed to instill a new discipline consistent with the risk characteristics (for example, market or price risk, credit risk, liquidity risk, and settlement risk) of developing financial markets. The establishment of exposure limits and capital adequacy guidelines, ensuring greater transparency, proper valuation of assets and timely recognition of losses are examples of the components of a regulatory and supervisory system relevant for liberalized financial markets.

The effectiveness of bank supervision in developing financial markets would depend on at least three factors. These are: (1) the existence of laws and regulations that clearly define the supervisory functions and responsibilities, and give the supervisors sufficient authority to enforce compliance with these laws and regulations; (2) the presence of a unified and autonomous bank supervisory system; (3) the establishment of a system of reliable and timely evaluation of banks' overall condition, operations and risk management practices.

Banking laws and regulations in developing financial markets would no doubt have the general objectives of reducing market distortions, encouraging greater competition between financial institutions, and integrating the domestic financial system more closely with the global financial system. However, a more specific objective of banking laws and regulations is to determine whether banks are operating in a safe and sound manner and to empower bank supervisors to take appropriate action if they are not. These laws and regulations must therefore give bank supervisors the authority to request management to provide information deemed necessary for effective supervision; they must also indicate the general and specific corrective measures that the supervisors could impose on bank management. Such measures may include: (1) the imposition of fines and/or removal of management, including the board of directors; (2) the issuance of administrative orders requiring management to cease and desist from taking actions that endanger the institution; (3) the limitation on special financial operations for which the technical competence of management and internal controls are inadequate; and (4) the establishment of capital adequacy standards with respect to the risk characteristics of the bank's assets and activities. The laws and regulations must also enable the supervision of banking activities on a consolidated basis.

While these laws and regulations may be established, bank supervision may still be ineffective if political and other constraints are imposed on their enforcement. Thus, a political commitment to the autonomy of bank supervisory process would complement the effective implementation of banking laws and regulations. This commitment could be demonstrated by an adequate availability of resources for the bank supervisory function and a careful location of the supervisory function in the governmental structure.

Resources are required to hire, train and retain competent personnel, develop an effective and autonomous prudential supervisory system, and acquire appropriate technology. Surely, the bank supervisory skills utilized in repressed markets would be inadequate for developing financial markets with their new products and increased risks. Given the complexities of banking activities that may result from financial liberalization, bank supervisors would be required to develop uniform procedures and methodologies and to incorporate these in a refocused and comprehensive supervisory system. With the emphasis being shifted from determining compliance with economic regulations, as in the repressed financial markets, to one of determining the existence of safe and sound banking operations, particularly in the area of risk management, accounting and other records and control systems, bank supervisors in developing financial markets would need to create an off-site system for analysis and early warning of potential problems.

The location of the bank supervisory function within the government may affect supervisory autonomy and effectiveness. To achieve the desired autonomy and effectiveness, it may be necessary for bank supervision to be separated from, for example, the country's Ministry of Finance, or its central bank. In cases where bank supervision is a function of one of these entities, the supervisory objectives may be muddled or diluted with the other objectives of that entity. However, such a separation must be combined with a legal system that explicitly provides for supervisory autonomy, and with the competence of the supervisors themselves to act independently and effectively. Unfortunately, in many developing financial markets, few bank supervisors are autonomous.[12]

It has been argued that sound monetary policy requires the bank supervisory function be located in the central bank. This argument, however, has not been supported by the experience of the Bundesbank in Germany and other central banks in the Organization for Economic Development countries that have no regulatory or supervisory authority. While the Bank of England has such authority, many feel it is undesirable because of the potential for conflict between its supervisory and monetary functions. An example of such a conflict is when monetary policy requires a credit expansion but supervisory responsibility mandates credit restrictions considered risky.

Supporters of having the central bank in charge of supervision argue that supervision and central banking are linked and since the central bank is the lender of last resort it makes sense for it to be in responsible for assessing the operating conditions and management of banks that access this borrowing facility. Evidence from Latin American countries has shown that, with few exceptions, the countries (for example, Argentina, Bolivia, and Uruguay) that experienced more domestic banking crises were those in which banking supervision was the responsibility of the central bank.

In some liberalized financial markets, the bank supervisory function is shared between several entities. This is especially the case in the United States with at least three bank supervisory agencies (for example, the Federal Deposit Insurance Corporation, the Board of Governors of the Federal Reserve System and the Office of the Comptroller of the Currency) each having a piece of the country's federal bank supervisory system while at the same time having overlapping responsibilities. The high costs, in terms of duplication and delays, of this sharing arrangement, support a strong argument for a unified and autonomous supervisory system in developing financial markets.

In establishing a system for evaluating a bank's overall condition, the bank supervisor may emphasize such individual components as the bank's capital adequacy, assets quality, management performance, earnings and liquidity and based on the evaluation of these components, assess the bank's current overall condition. In evaluating the future condition of the bank, the supervisor may focus on management's plans and projections and on its ability to achieve them.

Even in repressed financial markets banks are exposed to risks. This is more so, however, in developing financial markets with their intense competition and price volatility. In the latter markets, the problem of risk management is compounded by the inability of management to identify and measure untraditional risks, or by the failure of management to have in place a reliable risk management system. No doubt, such a system would require: (1) a comprehensive risk assessment approach; (2) a detailed structure of limits, guidelines and other parameters for traditional and new risks; and (3) reliable risk management reporting and control systems.

Bank supervisors in developing financial markets may want to assist in promoting risk management competence and systems in each bank. Such assistance may take the form of creating training opportunities for bank and supervisory agency staff, and providing recommendations for corrective measures, based on supervisory examination findings. Once the risk management competence and systems are developed to a reasonable degree, the supervisor's evaluation may focus on at least six issues. These are: (1) the extent to which the bank is competent to manage the risks inherent in its activities, specifically its ability to identify, measure and control these risks; (2) the soundness of the assumptions implicit in the bank's risk management systems; (3) the consistency of the bank's risk policies, guidelines, and limits with its activities, overall financial condition and management's experience level; (4) the ability of the management information system to control the bank's risk exposure and monitor its compliance with established limits; (5) management's ability to recognize and accommodate new risks; and finally (6) the competence of management to identify, quantify, and control any current risks considered imprudent.

By assessing these issues, bank supervisors would be able to determine the extent to which the bank's risk management system and practices are adequate to control the risk exposure associated with its traditional and new activities. Should the supervisors determine that risk management is deficient, they would suggest a set of corrective measures to protect the safety and soundness of the bank's operations. These measures may require management to limit the size of the bank's exposure, decrease the probability of default or minimize the probable effect of a default; engage in arrangements to hedge existing or potential risks or curtail any activity if the risk of such activity is determined to be too high for the expected return.

1.3   PLAN OF THE BOOK

This book examines the challenges for bank management and supervision in developing financial markets. Excluding this introductory, and a concluding chapter, the book is divided into eleven principal chapters, eight dealing mainly with bank management issues and three with regulatory and supervisory ones.

Chapter 2 focuses on some of the constraints on bank management in developing financial markets and the role of planning in overcoming them. Chapter 3 discusses the nature of interest rate competition between banks and non-bank financial institutions within the domestic and external financial markets, and suggested a set of management responses to this competition. Chapter 4 provides a set of descriptive information on banks' foreign currency trading activities, identifies the types of risks inherent in them, and reviews the approaches for limiting these risks. Chapter 5 reviews the impact of overdraft financing on liquidity management and argues that management should consider replacing overdraft financing with term-loan financing of business working capital and capital expenditures. It also argues that the sale or securitization of term loans, and the requirement to hold compensating balance can assist liquidity management and expand business loan volume. Chapter 6 identifies challenges in the credit function, and discuses a set of issues relating to the management of credit risk. Chapter 7 deals with the complex challenge of loan and deposit pricing, and demonstrates a loan-pricing system that recognizes capital to asset ratios, desired return on equity, and the marginal cost of funds. Chapter 8 addresses the management of asset-liability risk from the point of view of information, policies and assessment of this risk. Chapter 9 concludes the chapters on bank management challenges. It reviews the challenges of effective human resource planning and utilization, identifies a set of objectives to be emphasized by management, and describes measures that may be implemented to achieve these objectives.

A selection of bank regulatory and supervisory challenges is addressed in Chapters 10, 11 and 12. Chapter 10 recognizes the need for effective bank regulation and supervision in situations of transition from a planned to a market economy, and from a repressed to a liberalized financial market, and argues that both situations are concerned with the regulation and supervision of unaccustomed risk. Chapter 11 deals with the regulatory and supervisory issues of capital adequacy, providing in the process, some prospective on the quantitative and qualitative factors for evaluating such adequacy. It recognizes the close relationship between maintaining adequate capital and prompt corrective action for capital impaired banks. Finally, Chapter 12 addresses issues relating to the establishment and maintenance of adequate accounting and other records, and internal control systems, and focuses on the connection between these systems and banks' asset quality condition.

Chapter 13 concludes the book by highlighting most of the issues covered and presenting these issues in the context of their influence on the bank's board of directors. It shows the difference between banks and other corporations and emphasizes the responsibilities of bank directors.

2 Strategic Management

Developing financial markets are more competitive and complex than the repressed markets they replaced. Commercial banks in repressed financial markets fund their activities mainly with deposits that invariably carry fixed nominal, and negative real interest rates. They use these funds to finance government directed credits or a selection of traditional activities at lending rates that tend to be higher than the inflation rate.[1] Banks in repressed financial markets, therefore, have been among the most profitable in the world. With financial liberalization, banks are faced with increasing competition as other intermediaries replicate their profit centres and introduce new and more attractive products and services. As the competition intensifies, banks have tended to increase their tolerance for risk as reflected by a lower quality of borrowers, and an expansion in unfamiliar activities.

In many cases, management's decision to expand the dimensions of their bank's risk tolerance has been the result of an unplanned reaction to the competitive pressures and a desire to prevent the potential contraction in their bank's market share. As operating results deteriorate and as bank supervisors tighten the capital adequacy, asset quality and other prudential requirements, some banks recognize the need to redefine their objectives, and develop effective competitive strategies for achieving them.

The importance of strategic management cannot be overemphasized. Such management attempts to understand why some banks develop and thrive while others stagnate or become insolvent. It addresses the problems and opportunities that management faces as well as the long-term prospects of the organization itself. The very nature of the decisions that must be made emphasizes the relevance of strategic management and its principal components – strategic planning and implementation – for banks in developing financial markets. These decisions, for example, tend to be unusual with no precedent in the developing financial markets to follow; they commit substantial resources and demand a great deal of commitment; and they establish the stage for other decisions and future action in the organization.[2]

This chapter recognizes that, in some developing financial markets banks are required not only to be operationally efficient but also to be involved in improving the financial discipline of the enterprises to which they lend. The demands on bank management, combined with the unstable and often unpredictable economic environment in which the banks operate, create constraints on bank management and emphasize the critical importance of strategic planning for banks in these markets. The chapter, therefore, has five main objectives. These are: (1) to highlight some of the constraints on bank management in developing financial markets and the role of planning in overcoming them; (2) to distinguish between the platforms and levers in the planning process and to review these as important planning components of a comprehensive plan; (3) to identify the various sources of a bank's competitive strength, and strategies for its continuing viability; (4) to review banking markets and marketing plans; and finally, (5) to focus on the roles of various management levels in the planning process and the phases of strategic management.

2.1 CONSTRAINTS AND PLANNING

Banks in developing financial markets face many constraints. These include: (1) the absence of a risk management system that clearly identifies, measures and monitors the banks' risk exposures; (2) shortages of technically competent staff; (3) an unstable macroeconomic environment; and (4) limited access to domestic and foreign capital resources. Box 2.1 highlights some of these constraints, and comments on the role of planning in minimizing their impact on a bank's competitive ability. No doubt these constraints will have different effects on each bank depending on the differences in the banks' management, geographic coverage, and existing and anticipated products and services.

Capacity limitations and temporal factors as constraints on achieving a bank's mission and strategic objectives must not be overlooked. Management's ambition and passion constitute a poor basis for setting realistic mission and objectives. They will normally lead to an overestimation of the bank's competitive ability and failure to achieve the targetted outcomes. The bank's mission and objectives must be in line with its capacity to achieve them over a realistic period of time. Management must therefore include temporal factors into the projected course of action. At least such inclusion will require management to distinguish between objectives that can be achieved within the plan period and those that cannot.

In dealing with the time constraint, management may consider dividing the long-term objectives into realizable short-term programmes and ensuring that the contributions of each programme towards the long-term

Box 2.1   Constraints and planning

- *Market characteristics*: financial liberalization has changed the manner in which banks operate, for example, from a homogeneous cartel to autonomous and fiercely competitive units. The market for banking services tends to be fragmented, for example, banks for households, state enterprises, domestic private sector businesses, and multinational corporation subsidiaries. Planning for survival and profitability becomes a critical necessity in this competitive and fragmented environment.
- *Insolvency*: bank insolvency caused by a high level of non-performing assets in the wake of financial liberalization induces financial restructuring. Planning will assist in determining the appropriate restructuring measures.
- *Resource limitations relative to responsibilities*: banks are sometimes required to continue credit allocation to preferred sectors and firms; provide technical assistance and venture capital to new and restructured enterprises, and combine development agency and commercial bank functions. Planning identifies the resources and strategies required to perform such responsibilities while maintaining competitive strength.
- *Diversification*: some markets offer limited risk diversification opportunities because of the narrow range of lending opportunities. Planning addresses a mix of new products, services, and geographical areas and assists in identifying the risk of asset or activity concentration.
- *Weaknesses*: a set of general and specific weaknesses may limit a bank's strategic options. These include asset portfolio weaknesses; shortages of skilled staff; unstable macroeconomic conditions; deficient enterprise reform and enterprise management and control systems; lack of appropriate technology; market intervention by government through taxation and regulatory policies; and radical changes in customer base. Planning assists in identifying these weaknesses and their impact on a bank's viability, while defining appropriate strategic options and tactics for survival.

objectives are synchronized. If, for example, a long-term objective is to have the dominant share of the market's deposits, the programme increments may first target core deposits, then the mid-sized certificates of deposits (CDs) and eventually the more volatile price sensitive large CDs. Simultaneously, products and services required by the various segments of depositors may be provided – electronic funds transfers, and mortgage loans for core depositors, portfolio diversification and investment advisory services for CD customers.

Furthermore, it must be emphasized that the effectiveness of the programme approach will depend on the implementation procedures or tactics employed by management. Management might consider subdividing each programme into tactical segments with recognizable beginnings and endings. The decision might be to begin the core deposit programme on a specific date from the adaption of the plan and end this programme one year after that date. To complement the core deposit programme, improvements in existing services or new services demanded by core depositors should be implemented at a specified time. At predetermined intervals the programme should be reviewed, imbalances addressed, and complexities and misunderstandings resolved. However, management may want to ensure that the review intervals are not so long as to lose the momentum between programmes. The competition must be given no respite until the long-term objectives have been achieved.

2.2 PLATFORMS AND LEVERS

The effectiveness of planning depends on, among other things, management's ability to distinguish the platform for operational success from the levers for achieving such success. Platforms relate to the broad and strategic; levers are pointed and tactical.[3] Bank management in developing financial markets may spend a great deal of energy building a platform to replicate their competitors' profit centres, to acquire their competitors, or to venture into new products and services. However, failure to distinguish between the platform and the levers of the plan can result in overlooking the specific action required to bring about a profitable outcome.

This failure may be illustrated by the case of China. In that country, certain banks have included in their planning their mission and market objectives but have failed to specify and quantify the human resources, services, products, and technology required to achieve them.[4] On the contrary, management may focus on levers to achieve competitive advantage without first establishing a suitable platform. Both planning situations, strategic planning without a tactical plan, and tactical planning without a strategic plan, can place the bank at a disadvantage relative to its competitors.

Once the distinction has been made, management will need to consider the honing of strategies and tactics to achieve the plan's general and specific objectives. In this honing process, management may be required to: (1) modify the bank's strategic objectives to its available resources; (2) define the targets that directly relate to achieving the bank's strategic objectives; (3) allow for alternative tactical targets, rank their priorities while recognizing that at times it may be necessary to reorder them as the environment changes; (4) exploit the bank's sources of strength, then fortify its areas of weakness still focusing on the ultimate objectives; and (5) avoid pursuing a strategic objective or applying certain tactics that previously have failed to enhance the bank's competitive position – this reduces the bank's ability to achieve more realizable objectives.

It may be useful to illustrate the applicability of some of these requirements to the strategic management of banks in developing financial markets. Management, after careful consideration, decides that to maintain market share it will be necessary for the bank to expand its deposit base by acquiring another bank. This objective may be achieved if the acquiring bank's available capital and human resources are adequate enough to support the acquisition campaign, to fund the acquisition, and to manage effectively the expanded facilities resulting from the acquisition itself. If the bank's resources are currently inadequate, it may consider expanding them prior to launching the campaign or downsizing the acquisition target.

Whatever steps it decides to take, management must clearly identify its acquisition target. In doing so, management may decide on a bank that has a large deposit base, but is deficient in operations, staffing and technology support. Such a bank will contrast with the acquiring bank that aims at expanding its deposit and has an efficient operating system, competent staff, and appropriate technology support. The aim of management of the acquiring bank will, therefore, be to find a target that is of the wrong size but for opposite reasons.[5] As the acquiring bank wanted to expand its deposit base to maintain its market share, it will have to find an acquisition target with too large a deposit base relative to its operational capacity. Furthermore, management will have to determine whether the product lines and services between the acquiring bank and the targetted bank are compatible. Compatibility will minimize any operational inconvenience to the depositors after the consolidation of the two banks is effected.

With Bank A being the identified acquisition target, and in compliance with the country's acquisition laws, management may decide to purchase, quickly and imperceptibly, a certain proportion of Bank A's outstanding stocks at a price that will enable the acquiring bank to resell at a profit in the event that the acquisition fails. Such a purchase will require the retention of reliable firms or individuals to purchase these stocks and to resell them to the acquiring bank at the appropriate time. Alternatively, management may require these firms or individuals to acquire the stocks on behalf of the acquiring bank.

If through these purchases, the acquiring bank obtains, say 20 per cent of Bank A's outstanding stocks, it will need only 31 per cent for majority ownership of Bank A. With 20 per cent ownership, it will be positioned for an effective offensive on Bank A. On the other hand, the results of an open offensive without prior ownership of some of Bank A's stock will be dubious and the acquisition campaign, if successful, will be more costly. If in attempting to acquire an open purchase of 51 per cent of the outstanding stocks, the acquiring bank discovers that Bank A has an effective defense strategy, it will have to call off its acquisition campaign or revise its offensive strategy.

The success of any product or territorial offensive will, therefore, depend on the existence of a clear understanding of the requirements appropriate for achieving the strategic objective. This understanding will be facilitated by the existence of at least three types of plan – strategic, tactical, budget and financial – that are individually and carefully designed and coordinated to achieve the targeted objectives.

A well designed strategic plan may perform many roles. For example, it may: (1) state clearly the bank's mission and objectives; (2) specify the bank's target markets while acknowledging the competitive forces at work; (3) provide guidance on the methods appropriate for profitable exploitation of these markets; and (4) identify the human and technological resources, as well as the products and services required to achieve the bank's objectives. A plan with these characteristics would provide a standard against which management could monitor and control the bank's performance.

The tactical plan specifies the measures for implementing the strategic plan and translates the agreed strategy into operational results. In this regard, it identifies the anticipated outcomes of each department and division, or functional area of the bank, and the task of each individual responsible for accomplishing these results. It also evaluates and quantifies, on an on-going basis, the impact of the strategic initiatives on the bank's overall financial condition and operating results. It is not unusual for banks in developing financial markets to create planning functions with such broad strategic objectives as improving profitability through expansion into new product and service areas. While the development of broad strategies is necessary, it is normally not sufficient to achieve any planning objectives. Operational specifics, as indicated in the tactical plan, therefore become an integral part of the planning function.

2.3   FINANCIAL PLANNING AND BUDGETING

Budgeting and financial planning are important examples of the operational specifics of any strategic plan. Although for theoretical purposes budgeting and financial planning can be considered separate components, these are so closely related that they could be combined into one planning function. However, financial planning may be considered a more complex process than budgeting. Financial planning establishes the bank's financial parameters and stipulates the assumptions on which these parameters are based. Of course, information derived from the financial plan would be used in the budget process. Examples of such information are: (1) the adequacy of existing banking and computer facilities; (2) decisions to rent or buy fixed assets; (3) the number and quality of individuals required to perform the bank's current and future activities; (4) expected productivity levels; and (5) salaries and benefits that would retain and attract technically competent personnel. Financial planning starts with an attempt to establish the bank's profit goals in terms of actual and projected financial performance indicators of earnings and profitability, loans, liquidity and capitalization.

The variety of indicators in Box 2.2 supports the view that monitoring a bank's competitive strength requires an array of measures. No single index should be used for this purpose. Capital may be adequate but liquidity may not be, because of maturity mismatching and other management problems;

Box 2.2   Selected performance indicators

- *Capital adequacy*: includes equity capital, reserves and retained earnings to average total assets; and equity investment to net worth.
- *Liquidity*: includes liquid assets to deposits; and loans to deposits.
- *Funding*: includes demand deposits to total liabilities; and total deposits to total liabilities.
- *Asset quality*: includes loan loss reserve to total loans; loan loss reserves to non- performing loans; and non-performing loans to total loans.
- *Earnings*: include net interest margin; net interest margin after provisions; return on average assets; return on capital; operating expenses to average total assets; non-interest expenses to average total assets; total other income to total assets; and provisions to total assets.
- *Growth*: includes growth in average total assets; loans outstanding; deposits of various types particularly core deposits; off-balance sheet activities; interest and non-interest expenses; fees and commissions; and net profit after taxes.

growth may be strong but earnings may not be, because of asset quality problems; funding may exceed the bank's ability to lend, because of the state of the economy and the existence of over-leveraged firms. No single indicator would adequately attest to the bank's viability.

For banks in developing financial markets, a critical financial planning variable is the adequacy of the bank's capital. A bank with inadequate capital, as measured, for example, by the regulatory capital ratios may have to limit the growth of its assets and may, if it can, increase earnings only from its fee-income off-balance sheet activities. If capital is considered inadequate, the financial plan could suggest the most appropriate methods for raising it. The plan could also specify the growth options available to the bank, given the capital constraint. In some cases, a bank may have to develop a financial plan that incorporates debt financing for raising capital. Debt financing, of course, would have bank performance implications that are different to those associated with equity financing. At least the debt has to be serviced and eventually repaid; equity capital receives dividends based on performance and policies while remaining permanent funding of well-managed and profitable banks.

It may be emphasized that financial planning directs management's attention to improving earnings and profitability relative to assets and capital, and focuses on liquidity and asset quality as being key indicators of the bank's viability under competitive and volatile market conditions. Furthermore, financial planning helps to communicate management's expectations to bank personnel. As the eventual financial outcome will depend mainly on personnel performance, a well communicated financial plan can provide a catalyst for improving such performance and strengthening the bank's competitive position.

The budget details the financial resources required to achieve the bank's mission and strategic objectives, and quantifies the financial results that management can expect under certain assumptions. The budget goals as indicated in the projected balance sheet and income statement provide an overview of the bank's expected performance. Variances from these goals serve as a basis for operational control and performance evaluation and provide important information on a functional basis for managing costs, as well as monitoring budget performance. In other words, deviations from expected goals give early warnings that the actual and the planned results may be at variance within the performance monitoring intervals specified by management.[6] Timely information on budget variances for the bank as a whole and for its individual functional areas will enable management to

Box 2.3   Budget and financial planning components

- *Balance sheet*: balance sheet information will indicate the balance sheet components and their percentage share, for each year of the plan period. The broad asset categories that may be projected, depending on the instruments available in the developing financial markets are cash, interbank balances, government securities, loans less loan loss provisions, accrued interest receivable, equity investment, other assets, fixed assets, and total assets. The broad liability categories that may be projected are deposits, interbank borrowing, bills payable, other liabilities, provision for taxation, and total liabilities. To obtain the bank's projected total capital and liabilities, capital as a liability component must also be projected. This projection may include equity capital; reserves; and retained earnings.
- *Income statement*: this statement may reflect earnings and profitability in terms of levels; will include total operating income comprising net interest income, net interest income after provisions, commission and fees; total operating expenses including personnel and other expenses; net profit after tax derived from operating profit before tax, and taxes payable; total reserve fund obtained by deducting form net profit after tax, dividends, and appropriations.
- *Forecast assumptions*: these assumptions may include specific percentage growth rate assumptions for each asset and liability component in the bank's balance sheet for the plan period; interest statement assumptions such as interest on each interest earning asset, interest rate on each interest bearing liability, yield on interest earning assets, cost on interest bearing liabilities and net interest spread; growth rates of commission and fees, other income, operating expenses such as personnel and other expenses; tax rate; dividend payout and appropriation ratios.

implement appropriate measures for maintaining or rebuilding the bank's profitability and viability.

Box 2.3 indicates the type of information about the bank and its functional areas that may be derived from the budget and financial planning process and available for strategic management decisions. The specific items in each asset-liability category would depend on the financial reform measures already implemented, the deposit and lending instruments available in the markets, the bank's current product and services and the innovations management intends to implement over the plan period.

2.4   SOURCES OF COMPETITIVE STRENGTH

An important objective of strategic management is to identify the various sources of a bank's competitive strength, determine the threats to these sources, and decide on the measures appropriate for coping with them and maintaining the bank's competitive advantage. Box 2.4 identifies some of these sources. Of particular importance for banks in developing financial markets are such sources as capital adequacy, the availability and competence of human resources, and asset quality.[7]

The competitive advantage of a bank operating in developing financial markets may be explained by the adequacy of its capital relative to the size and risk of its assets. The primary purpose of a bank's capital is to

Box 2.4   Sources of a bank's competitive strength

- *Capital adequacy*: adequate capital lowers the probability of bank failures; reduces the incentive to take excessive risks; increases long term competitiveness; cushions equity owners and debt holders from losses; and provides resources for offensive or defensive competitive strategies. However, a regulatory increase in capital requirements beyond a certain point may cause banks to increase their risks in order to achieve a desired rate of return.
- *Asset quality*: asset quality indicates the level of asset losses the bank's capital will have to bear; and the threat to the bank's viability resulting from credit and transfer risk classifications, credit concentrations, and non-performing and renegotiated credits. The higher the asset quality, the greater the bank's competitive strength.
- *Human resources*: human resources determine the bank's ability to meet the increasing demand for and complexity of banking regulations in competitive markets; to succeed in competitive markets through improved productivity; to respond to the growing geographical and technological sophistication of competitive markets; and to identify and exploit market opportunities. The greater the ability of management to recruit and retain the most competent staff and to motivate their peak potential and enthusiasm as a team, the greater is the bank's competitive strength.
- *Information*: information is a source of strength under certain conditions. For example, information and data must be considered corporate resources and be managed as such; a bank's information system is an investment, not an expense, and the return on this investment can be maximized with optimum utilization of the information; technological changes, for example, from a manual to an automated information system, must be implemented gradually and effectively; and management must be competent in the use of information for risk monitoring and control, credit activities, and product development.
- *Financial innovation*: financial innovation is a source of strength if it offers a broader and more flexible range of instruments for borrowing and saving, and for hedging interest, exchange rate, and other risks; aids banks and their customers to cope with stresses associated with the greater market volatility; and by their very complexity and use, does not result in additional risks to banks and their customers.
- *Technology*: technology is a source of strength if it facilitates the bank's internal, and financial controls, and its performance monitoring, measurement, and reporting systems; it improves bank customer services through greater functional capability and lower transactions costs; and it enhances decision making, and operating results.

cushion both its equity owners and its debt holders from unexpected losses. The more capital a bank has, the more it can withstand these losses without becoming insolvent. Adequate capital, therefore, decreases the likelihood of failure by giving bank management time to find solutions to competitive and other problems. Since capital helps to ensure a bank's long-term viability by lowering the probability of its failure, it helps the bank to develop and maintain long-term customer relationships and to retain the most competent management, support personnel, and technology.

Successful and profitable bank operations require retaining the most competent staff. As financial markets grow deeper, wider and more complex with liberalization and market integration, banks in these markets will need competent staff to identify and exploit the competitive opportunities the markets offer; to process and use the information they generate; and to adapt from the global markets, the products, services, and technology that strengthen the banks' competitive position. Obtaining the required level of competence would demand the allocation of substantial amount of resources for training and recruitment.

Banks in repressed financial markets have tended to be very labour-intensive, their wages and bonuses often represented their main operating costs, and followed or exceeded the general trend in the rest of the economy. Surely, these tendencies could be explained by the banks' ability to meet these costs because of the potential to earn higher than normal profits. With financial market liberalization, creating competitive pressure on profitability, the retraining or retaining of existing high cost – low productivity personnel becomes an important management consideration.

The quality of a bank's assets can weaken or strengthen its competitive ability. In some developing financial markets, banks have experienced serious financial distress because of poor asset quality, linked in part to problems of definition, accounting and regulatory treatment of non-performing assets. A survey of Latin American banking markets has shown that asset quality of banks operating in these markets varied significantly across countries because of at least four reasons: (1) differences in accounting and prudential regulations have prevented a unified definition of non-performing loans; (2) regulations varied as to when and under what conditions loans must be written off; (3) in some financial markets, unlike others, the tax incentives for maintaining good asset quality were significant; and (4) economic and political conditions were divergent so that the measures taken to resolve non-performing loan problems varied between markets.[8]

In an environment where there are opportunities for wide discretion with regard to the definition and treatment of non-performing loans, management must aim at ensuring that targets are established with respect to asset classifications, and non-accruals relative to loans and other earning assets outstanding. Assets classified as loss, for example, must be adequately provisioned or written off. Interest accruals on such assets merely misrepresent the bank's earnings and mislead its stock holders, management and the competition. But this misrepresentation will be only a short-term phenomenon. Eventually, failure to acknowledge the bank asset quality condition and take the necessary corrective measures will weaken the bank's competitive strength and result in financial distress. Strategic management must, therefore, ensure that the bank's performance is based, at all times, on sound assets.

2.5 BANKING MARKETS

Management may identify two distinct product markets, a consumer oriented or retail banking market offering banking products and services, including savings and time deposits, transactions accounts, and consumer and residential mortgage loans to individual customers; and a business oriented or wholesale banking market offering banking products and services, such as demand deposits and commercial, including inventory, accounts receivable, and term loans to businesses in the manufacturing, distribution, agricultural and mining sectors. Management may also identify the major bank and non-bank players in these markets to determine the nature of the competition and the relevance of acquisition, merger, or consolidation as a competitive strategy.

The products and services may be marketed in a limited geographic area, such as the community or in a broader area such as the region or the nation. If the bank's core business is in retail banking then its primary service area may be the immediate community; and its competitors will be those banks in that community supplying retail banking products and services. However, if the bank's core business is wholesale banking with large firms, then the bank's primary service area will tend to be regional or national.

In some developing countries, with their small population size, low actual and potential per capita income, and geographic market concentration, the distinction between community, national, and regional markets may not be as important as the distinction between product markets. In other developing countries, with large population size, low actual but high potential per capita income, and wide geographic market spread, the distinction between product and geographical markets can be important for market positioning decisions. In other words, strategic management will have to make decisions on whether the bank will operate in the retail or wholesale banking market or both, and whether it will be a community, regional or national bank.

In evaluating the likely impact of market expansion, strategic management may try to determine the reaction of incumbent banks, consumers of financial services, and bank regulators to a potential entrant into that market. If the entrant will enhance competition and provide products and services at lower transactions costs, bank supervisors, and consumers may encourage entry while incumbent banks may not, as such entry may erode their market power. On the other hand, if the market is perceived to be well served by existing banks, any new entrant may be discouraged by bank supervisors unless such entrant has identified a potential market niche that it can exploit profitably. However, a bank may still be able to enter a well served market, if it has the resources to acquire the market leader or some other incumbent bank. Developing a marketing strategy will, therefore, require specific information on profitable marketing opportunities for the bank, and an analysis of the responses of competitor banks to any new market positioning proposed by the bank.

Determining whether a bank has been appropriately positioned will require answers to a number of questions. Will the bank be in the retail or wholesale banking market? Can the bank serve some elements of the wholesale market while primarily being a retail bank? Can it expand its existing geographic area, and its products and services to include new ones such as mortgage lending, agricultural credit, trade financing, and risk hedging contracts?

Box 2.5 summarizes the market factors that will influence the strategic decisions made by management in developing financial markets. Such decisions may have to be modified to reflect changes in product and service prices. To minimize these modifications, management may assume a set of price scenarios and the adjustments in interest rates, fees and commissions to fit these scenarios. Should management decide to increase the bank's share of small savers' deposits, under a particular interest rate scenario, but the actual rate scenario has changed say by 5 per cent, the marketing strategy will have to be revised accordingly. For example, the cost of obtaining an additional $10 million in 5 per cent savings accounts may justify a certain amount of promotional expenses, given a prime lending rate of 7.5 per cent. However, if the prime lending rate increases to 8 per

Box 2.5   Marketing strategy factors

- *Strategic objectives*: determine the key positioning issues. These issues include: what kind of bank it is currently, and what kind of bank it will be? What markets will the bank serve (for example, retail, wholesale or a combination)? What products and services does the bank want to offer?
- *Market analysis*: determine the important characteristics of the market. This determination may be based on the following questions. Who are the bank's customers and prospects (name, type, size)? Who makes the decision to buy banking services (for example, male, female, financial vice president, or president)? What is the location of the bank's customers? How price sensitive is the target customer group? What are the group's banking characteristics (for example, average deposit size, average loan size, seasonal credit requirements)? What is the attitude of the target market towards the bank?
- *Market share*: determine the bank's current market share to evaluate market share changes resulting from the strategic plan implementation. Identify a measure that reflects marketing effectiveness. Examples of these measures are the share of demand deposit, savings or time deposits under a certain value; and the share of deposit accounts by size range.
- *Competitive factors*: identify the competitive factors in a targetted market, including the bank and non-bank competitors (for example, credit unions, finance and insurance companies). Such identification may require a determination of the strengths and weaknesses of all competitors in terms of pricing policies, locational convenience, reputation, staff quality, customer base, promotional techniques, and product and service quality; and an analysis that enables the bank to capitalize on its strengths, eliminate its critical weaknesses, and prevent resource wastage on products or services with little or no likelihood of competitive success.
- *External environmental factors*: determine the external environment that has a bearing on the strategic management decisions. These factors may include the economic environment; anticipated technological changes; the sociological environment; and regulatory and supervisory positions.

---

cent, a different strategy, and different promotional expenses may be justified.

It is also important to make certain assumptions about the technological, sociological, regulatory and supervisory environment. They all affect the decision process and the results obtained. The following situations illustrate the impact of these factors on strategic management decisions. A bank may not achieve its strategic objective of increasing its services to customers by installing banking machines in a number of off-site locations. This failure may be explained by the fact that its customers may perceive bank machines or any unaccustomed bank technology as being unfriendly and something to avoid; or they may prefer the direct contact with tellers and customer service personnel to the use of these machines. The mobilization of rural savings may be achieved more effectively by providing banking services to the traditional rural savings institutions and credit unions than directly to the rural savers themselves. As a result of legislative and regulatory changes, direct branches may become the preferred vehicle for geographic expansion and product and service delivery or acquisition of existing entities.

Many successful banks in developing financial markets have tended to have narrowly focused strategies, such as concentrating on wholesale corporate banking and high value-added services.[9] Similarly, other successful banks have served a diversified market and strived to be low cost providers of services. In determining whether to pursue a narrowly focused or a diversified strategy, management may want to know what is the least diversification the bank requires to achieve its mission and objectives and continue to be profitable. Concurrently, management may also want to know what is the most diversification the bank can manage and the degree of product and service complexity its operational systems and personnel can bear. Surely, the optimum will be between the two extremes. The closer the diversification is to the minimum, the easier it will be for the bank to manage effectively. The burden of proof may always be on those advocating increased diversification rather than those supporting product and service concentration.[10]

This, however, may not be a burden after all, as developing financial markets evolve and technology, with its tremendous information processing capacity, creates an environment for banks to become all-purpose financial service firms. The origin of these firms may be based on a reconceptualization of the financial industry's product and geographic boundaries broad enough to encompass the range of activities undertaken by banks and other financial institutions in competition with each other.[11] Thus, market freedom or the removal of product and entry restrictions on all financial services firms, combined with the transfer of technology, will encourage banks and other financial institutions to replicate the activities of each other and to develop by merger, acquisition or other arrangements, a wider range of financial products and services.

While the strategic marketing objectives may be broad and general the tactical objectives must be specific and focused. These tactical objectives may be established in a variety of ways, including the establishment of volume expansion, say in total commercial loans outstanding, or in total deposits; or be expressed as increases in percentage market share, if such data are available. No doubt, there are refinements that can be made to the bank's tactical marketing objectives.

In setting a deposit volume objective, for instance, the plan may require that the average deposit account be increased by a certain dollar amount. The purpose of this increase may be to ensure that the volume objective is achieved primarily by changes in the average balances on existing accounts rather than by an increase in the number of accounts with small balances. A loan volume objective may require increasing the amount of loans outstanding and the interest spread over a projected cost of funds. It may also specify the loan loss ratio that must not be exceeded over a specified period. These refinements may aim at achieving consistency between the bank's marketing and its overall strategic objectives.

At least profitability, market share, volume, and economies of scale must be addressed. Strategic management decisions that have the sole purpose of generating volume and increasing market share, without consideration for profitability, will adversely affect the bank's long-term competitive strength. The objective of increasing volume and market share may be pursued if its attainment will contribute to increased profitability within a specified period of time. It must be noted, however, that an increase in volume and market share can lower the unit cost of transactions and consequently make an existing product or service more profitable, thus improving the bank's overall performance. Exploiting economies of scale is, therefore, an important element in the bank's strategic marketing decisions.

2.6   THE PLANNING PROCESS

Strategic management may require the establishment and continuing review of the bank's planning process. In reviewing the planning process for banks operating in developing financial markets, two areas may be emphasized. The first relates to the planning roles at different management levels. The bank is assumed to have a board of directors, a chief executive officer, senior managers, middle managers and supervisory managers. Top management, comprising the board and senior managers is responsible for establishing the bank's mission and objectives; middle management is responsible for the performance of departments; and supervisory management, for the performance of divisions within the departments. Essentially, management is interactive but responsibilities, at various management levels, must be clearly assigned.

Planning is a major responsibility for the bank's chief executive officer and its other managers. One of their responsibilities is to state as clearly as possible, the bank's mission. The mission statement must not be mere generalities. Instead, it must specify the bank's nature and purpose, and provide guidance to management as it introduces new products and services, and enters new geographic areas. Moreover, the statement should be placed in the context of the relevant regulatory and supervisory policies and practices that would affect the bank's operations and performance results, and the measures that must be taken to cope with any regulatory and supervisory limitations. The mission statement must be approved by the board before its formal communication to the staff by the bank's chief executive officer.

Although managers at all levels allocate some of their time to planning, the relative proportion of time spent in planning activities will vary at different levels of the organization. The bank's top management will spend a greater proportion of its time engaged in planning than middle-level and supervisory-level management. Moreover, top management is likely to devote more of its planning activities to longer-term strategic planning, while middle-management will tend to focus on narrower tactical plans for their departments. Supervisory management are more likely to be engaged in developing specific programmes to meet their divisions' goals.

The bank's chief executive officer is the key individual in initiating the planning process. Without this initiative, a top-down leadership type of planning process will not be possible. Some banks may have a bottom-up planning process that pyramids to the top management level. However, this type of planning may reflect only the sum of departmental plans instead of a strategic plan for the bank as a whole. A strict bottom-up planning approach may be educational and informational in character, but it may not result in a significant directional change, as may be required for banks operating in developing financial markets.

The chief executive officer is also responsible for: (1) delegating some of the planning tasks and establishing a system of decision making; and (2) confirming and reinforcing the reasons for planning and the results expected during the plan period. Managers are unlikely to dedicate themselves to the process until they see clear evidence that the chief executive officer intends to use planning as a means of addressing the competitive and other challenges facing the bank. Each management level must be prepared for planning through a carefully designed training programme. After their training, they should be given adequate time to perform the planning tasks assigned to them.

Constant monitoring of performance results against plan expectations, and management's ability to reformulate strategies as conditions change, cannot be overemphasized. For example, regular meetings on certain critical areas of the plan, such as the bank's budget performance, and its asset liability condition must be held in order to oversee the bank's position and make any necessary adjustments. Regular monitoring meetings are also useful for comparison of unit performance (division, department or functional area, for example, loan or deposit growth) with the plan goals for each unit.

Finally, the overall mission and objectives of the bank should be reviewed on an annual or semi-annual basis. An objective of this review is to recognize that management's position might have changed from what prevailed at the origin of the plan; and that the plan itself may no longer be an effective driving force in the bank if this position change is not recognized and accommodated.

The second area of emphasis in the planning process relates to the different phases of planning. The bank's planning process may be divided into phases dealing separately with: (1) compiling and evaluating of information; (2) establishing the bank's priorities and programmes; (3) documenting and implementing the plan; and (4) reviewing the targetted and actual performance. An elaboration of these phases is contained in Box 2.6. Successful planning will require the bank to have a planning mechanism that designs, coordinates and monitors the development of the plan. For a large bank, a separate planning department may be justified. For smaller banks, the planning function may be located in the office of the chief executive officer. In any event the planning process must be kept simple, as over ambitious planning systems tend to become a strategic management burden rather than an effective tool.[12]

2.7 SUMMARY

This chapter has identified the constraints faced by banks in developing financial markets and has argued that strategic management decisions must focus on minimizing the impact of these constraints on a bank's competitive ability. Planning is considered a critical element of strategic management decision. However, the effectiveness of planning would depend on management's ability to distinguish between strategic planning and tactical planning. Once this distinction has been made, management would need to consider the honing of strategies and tactics to achieve the

Box 2.6   The planning process

- *Information*: this phase compiles and analyzes information that enables management of the bank's prospects and its ability to compete. It also identifies the short-term and long-term profit opportunities and risks for the bank. The relevant information compiled and analyzed covers economic, including interest rates and exchange rates, political, social, and regulatory factors; actual and prospective growth areas for the bank; and actual and prospective competition for the bank; the strength of the bank relative to its peers in the market.
- *Decision*: this phase covers decisions on strategies, action plan and budgets; and the translation of the bank's objectives into department and division plans. The department and division plans must contain information for making decisions. Such information may include the business outlook, present operational status, division objectives consistent with the bank's overall objectives, strategies and support requirements, and implementation plan.
- *Documentation*: this phase entails documenting the bank's mission, objectives, strategies, and tactics, the department and division implementation plans, the capital and operating budgets, financial statements and expected performance results.
- *Review*: this phase includes the plan review which involves management agreement with the plan documents; and board approval of the plan; and performance reviews at certain intervals, for example, quarterly and annually, and by the different levels of management.

plan's general and specific objectives. Requirements for honing the two have been provided and illustrated. The chapter has also emphasized that an important objective of planning was to identify the sources of a bank's competitive strength, ascertain the threats to each source and determine the strategies and tactics that would contribute to the maintenance of the bank's competitive ability.

In coping with the competitive environment, management might decide that the bank should restrict its operational scope to the retail banking market or the wholesale banking market. The bank might even develop a niche in either of these markets and become more specialized in the products and services it offered its customers. However, the advent of technology and the intensity of the competition between banks and other financial services firms would cause a replication of products and services between these firms. Market freedom would create opportunities for banks to specialize or diversify in product markets, depending on their mission and objectives and the competence of the management and other personnel. The chapter has therefore highlighted a set of planning factors that would influence a bank's marketing decisions. Finally, the chapter has specified the phases in the planning process and the role of the board and management in each phase. It has also argued against overambitious plans, with a perfunctory mission statement, and unspecified or unattainable objectives.

3 Interest Rate Competition, Structure and Forecasting

An important objective of asset-liability management is to minimize the exposure of a bank's net operating cash flow, and its equity, to changes in interest rates. Achieving this objective would be facilitated if bank management in developing financial markets clearly understands the nature of interest rate competition and the relationship between yields, prices and maturities of investment securities. In addition, the achievement of this objective is facilitated if management has the ability to forecast interest rate changes, and appropriately adjust the bank's portfolios to these changes.

Unlike the case of repressed financial markets, bank management in developing financial markets may have little or no control over the changes in market interest rates. Such changes arise from a number of interconnected factors – exchange rate changes, capital flows, inflationary expectations, and monetary policies. However, while the management of a particular bank may not be able to control the changes in market interest rates, it may implement certain measures to minimize the negative impact of these changes on the bank's financial condition and operating results.

This chapter discusses the nature of interest rate competition between banks and non-bank financial institutions within the domestic and external financial markets, and suggests a set of management responses to such competition. It defines the external market as the eurocurrency market where domestic financial institutions may have branches or subsidiaries, and where large domestic savers and borrowers are actively involved. It illustrates the complex nature of interest rate changes on a bank's average rate of return and emphasizes the importance of a system that informs management of these changes in a timely manner. The chapter specifies the relationship between yields, prices and maturities, and reviews yield curves and their implications for bank management in developing financial markets. It argues that it may not be possible to construct reliable yield curves for the domestic market. However, to the extent that domestic financial institutions may be issuing debt and investing in external markets, yield curve behaviour in these markets will have important implications for banks' asset-liability management. Finally, the chapter discusses the various approaches to interest rate forecasting and argues that in the context of developing financial markets, such forecasting may be limited to very short-term interest rate changes.

3.1   INTEREST RATE COMPETITION

In liberalized financial markets, the monetary policy actions of the central bank have important implications for market interest rates. Moreover, as market entry restrictions are reduced or abolished, and financial institutions compete on the basis of prices, no single commercial bank can effectively enforce administrative rates as was possible in repressed financial markets. In fact, banks in developing financial markets face two major forms of competition: (1) competition within the domestic financial market, and (2) competition between the domestic and external financial markets. Bank management in developing financial markets must understand the implications of these forms of competition for asset-liability management and for pricing of bank products and services.

The efficient market hypothesis states that competition within and between financial markets tends to equalize expected rates of return on similar financial assets (for example, loans, securities, and deposits) and effective interest rate differentials persist only if these assets possess different risk attributes, or if impediments prevent arbitrage between the markets. In this regard, banks with deposit insurance may be able to pay deposit interest rates that are lower than such rates offered by non-bank financial institutions with no deposit insurance. Similarly, capital controls in developing financial markets may enable domestic banks to pay lower interest rates on deposits than rates offered by banks in external markets.

Banks tend to have higher operating costs than their non-bank competitors. The higher operating costs are mainly the results of reserve requirements, normally inapplicable to non-banks, and deposit insurance fees. Of these costs, by far the most important are the reserve requirements on deposits. The effect of reserve requirements is to remove some of these deposits from being available for investments or lending by the banks. For example, if a bank receives $1,000 deposits and the reserve requirement is 5 per cent, the effective funds available for lending amount to only 95 per cent. But the bank must pay an interest rate of say 5.5 per cent on the full $1,000. The effective cost of funds to the bank is therefore 5.79 per cent derived from equation (3.1).

$$EC = \frac{i}{1 - RR} \qquad (3.1)$$

where:

EC = effective cost of reservable deposits
i = interest rate
RR = reserve requirement

Thus, the additional cost of reserve requirements is 29 basis points (for example, 5.79 per cent − 5.50 per cent), and this is the extra amount a non-bank financial institution may have to pay to achieve the same cost of funds. Thus, with no reserve requirements, non-bank financial institutions may offer: (1) higher deposit rates; or (2) divide their cost savings between depositors and borrowers by offering them higher deposit rates and lower loan rates than their bank competitors can offer.

Bank management in developing financial markets may be faced with a dilemma. This dilemma is to increase deposit and loan volumes, and maintain market share while pricing their products and services to reflect the reduced risk of insured deposits and the effective cost of funds. To maintain volume and market share, however, management may be inclined to match the higher deposit interest offered, and establish loan interest rates at levels lower than those charged by their non-bank competitors. Obviously, such measures will compress interest margins and reduce net operating cash flows. Bank management will have to recognize the cost differences associated with reserve requirements, and insurance fees between a bank and its non-bank competitor, and respond to these differences by, among other things, increasing staff productivity and reducing loan loss provisions through improved asset quality and effective internal control systems.

Management should also be mindful of the competition between their banks operating in the domestic financial market, and banks and non-bank financial institutions operating in external markets. Bank customers interested in depositing or borrowing in the external markets will most likely be: (1) large depositors wanting higher interest rates on their uninsured deposits and perhaps secrecy of their banking transactions; and (2) large borrowers wanting foreign currency loans and credit lines at rates lower and more stable than those available in the domestic market.

The risk differences between the developing financial markets and the external markets may explain the interest rate differences between these markets. Banking transactions in domestic markets may be subject to less risk that such transactions in external markets as capital controls are removed and the safety and soundness of banks in the domestic markets are improved. On the other hand, depositors and borrowers from the domestic markets conducting banking business in external markets may perceive higher risk in the latter markets with the weakening of bank secrecy laws, and the unwillingness of central banks to function as lender of last resort to banks that are not directly supervised by them or banks operating in external jurisdictions.

The existence of a more competitive and reserve requirement-free banking environment in the euromarket may in part explain the ability of banks in this market to offer more attractive interest rates than banks in domestic markets. Such an offer may also reflect a management response to what may be perceived as euromarket risk, by large depositors and borrowers. This risk may be linked to the fact that a euromarket transaction may be subject to the laws of more than one jurisdiction. For example, if a Colombian depositor holds a US dollar claim on a eurobank located in the Cayman Islands, the depositors may be deprived of his or her funds by an action of the Cayman, Colombian, or US regulatory authorities. Similarly a Colombian borrower may perceive a eurodollar loan commitment from a Cayman bank as being less reliable than a freely convertible currency loan from a domestic bank. This perception may be based on the risk that the commitment may not materialize due to regulatory and supervisory measures implemented by one or more of these authorities. After all, euromarket transactions may be subject to a greater degree of sovereign risk (for example, the ability of the authorities to interfere with the successful completion of a deposit, investment or lending transaction) than domestic market transactions.[1]

Banks in developing financial markets may be able to compete effectively with banks in external markets only if the former banks establish offices or subsidiaries in the external markets and if there are no controls on international capital flows. However, in order to attract business in these markets, given the sovereign risk, interest rates on external deposits not subject to reserve requirements, must be higher and rates on external loans must be lower than such rates in the developing financial market. Moreover, both the eurobank, if it is a wholly owned subsidiary, and its domestic bank owner must be well managed and adequately capitalized.

In addition, the parent bank's ability and readiness to support its euromarket subsidiary must be transparent and explicit in order to maintain confidence. The risk of a loss of confidence in the bank and its external subsidiary may be small, yet what counts is the market's perception, and empirical evidence shows that the risk premium (for example, the premium over equivalent domestic rates), that eurobanks must pay on deposits, amounts to anywhere from 20 to 100 basis points.

Increased interest rate competition between banks and non-banks in the domestic market, and the increase in such competition between domestic and external market participants, tend to accentuate the interdependence of interest rate and other changes in the two markets. As large depositors and borrowers have a choice of financial institution and investment instruments in the domestic and external markets, interest rate changes in the larger external market will induce similar changes in the domestic markets, given the absence of capital controls.

3.2   INTEREST RATE AVERAGING

In repressed financial markets, with their capital controls and other restrictions on competition, a depositor may hold a constant amount of deposits at a fixed-rate for a year, or a borrower may have a fixed rate mortgage for five to ten years. In these markets, financial instruments or transactions tend to be standardized in principal, interest rates, and maturities. In developing financial markets, financial instruments may have several combinations of principal, rates and terms. Bank management may be faced with situations of: (1) constant principal but varying rates and terms, or varying principal, rates, and terms; and (2) multiple investments with different maturity dates and interest, but made at the same time. One of the problems facing bank management, unaccustomed to this comparatively complex financial market environment, is to determine the average interest rate on the bank's asset and liability transactions with different maturities. Nevertheless, such averages provide important information for asset-liability management.[2]

The following are examples of how to obtain interest rate averages under changing conditions. Assume that a bank has invested in the market an amount of $100,000 for a period of 90 days. The investment yielded 8 per cent for 30 days, 10 per cent for 45 days and 12 per cent for 15 days. At each maturity date the interest is withdrawn. The investment principal is therefore constant, but the interest rates and maturities change. The average return on this investment will be 9.6 per cent based on equation (3.2).

$$i_a = \frac{\sum i_j \, n_j}{\sum n_j} \times 100 \qquad (3.2)$$

where:

i_a = average interest rate or average rate of return
i_j = interest rate for the specified term or time
n_j = number of days in the specified term or time

Again, assume that over a period of 90 days, management invested at day one $100,000 at 8 per cent for 30 days, $120,000 at 10 per cent for 45 days and $140,000 at 12 per cent for 15 days. Since the principal varies during the term of the investment, the average rate of return, i_a, is determined from equation (3.3), where i_j and n_j are as specified in equation (3.2). Based on equation (3.3) the average rate of return in this example of varying principal, rates and terms is 9.5 per cent.

$$i_a = \frac{N \sum P_j \, i_j n_j}{\sum P_j \, \sum n_j} \times 100 \tag{3.3}$$

where:

N = the number of investment terms (3)
P_j = the principal for each specified interest period

Finally, assume that one day, the bank invested $100,000 at 8 per cent for 30 days, $150,000 at 12 per cent for 90 days, and $200,000 at 15 per cent for 180 days. When multiple investments with different maturities

$$i_a = \frac{\sum P_j \, i_j}{\sum P_j} \times 100 \tag{3.4}$$

are made at the same time, the average interest rate to the earliest maturity date may be determined by equation (3.4), where i_a, P_j, and i_j are as stated in equations (3.2) and (3.3). Based on equation (3.4) the average interest rate on this investment portfolio for the first 30 days is 12.4 per cent.

The above illustrations make the point that in developing financial markets, there are several combinations of investments with varying maturities and interest rates, and with different principal and interest reinvestment or roll-over. In order to evaluate the bank's performance on an ongoing basis, management must be able to have timely and reliable information on the bank's average costs of funds and return on assets. No doubt, management may adopt the appropriate technology that provides the required averages and other information in a timely manner.

A prime consideration in asset-liability management is setting the targetted rate of return for invested capital so that a bank's stockholders will be sufficiently rewarded for their investment. The goal might be an average of 10 per cent or 20 per cent depending on the projected economic and financial condition, including interest rate outlook. Another target may be the projected return on average assets, which must be consistent with the targeted return on capital. The return on average assets may be set at say .90 per cent, 1.00 per cent, 1.10 per cent or higher, and include the combined return on loans, investments, and other assets after interest and non-interest expenses are covered. Thus, more than ever, effective bank management is a function of reliable and timely information that reflects whether or not the bank is achieving its financial targets given the interest rate changes in domestic and external markets.

With fixed interest rates, limited availability of long-term securities and activity concentration in the domestic markets, management in repressed financial markets tended to show little or no concern about changes in yields, prices or maturities of their investments. This situation changes as financial markets are liberalized, market interest rates and securities' prices become volatile, and the choice of investment securities with different maturities expands. In such an environment, effective bank management will require a clear understanding of the relationship between yields, prices and maturities of securities.

In addition to determining the average interest rate on the bank's assets and liabilities, bank management in developing financial markets must be assured of their understanding of certain basic performance indicators of their securities portfolio. Among these indicators are, nominal yield, current yield, yield maturity, yield to call, and the relationships between yield and price, and between short-term and long-term yields (yield curves). Most of these indicators had little relevance to bank management in repressed financial markets where interest rates were fixed and securities were mainly short term or were held to maturity.

The prices and yields of securities move in opposite directions. As bond prices increase, yields go down (and vice versa). If a bond is trading at a discount, the current yield increases, if it is traded at a premium, the current yield decreases. As a rule of thumb, when comparing two premium or two discount bonds, the bond with the interest rate that is farther away from the current market rates will be more volatile in price.

3.3 YIELD CURVES AND SPREADS

Because of the relationship between the market prices of securities and their market yields, and between the price of securities and their maturities, information about the expected yields of securities, and yield spreads between securities, can be important for the management of a bank's investment securities portfolio. The term structure of interest rates depicts the relationship between yield-to-maturity on securities of a particular risk class, and years-to-maturity of these securities. This relationship is normally referred to as a yield curve. Isolation of the relationship between yields and maturity requires that all other factors affecting yield (for example, risk of default, liquidity, and cost of acquisition) be held constant. Thus, yield curves are drawn only for securities that are identical except for maturity (for example fixed income government securities).

Yield curves can provide management with information on growth, inflation and interest rate expectations. The information is reliable if the curves are constructed in the context of a securities market that is well developed in terms of volume and maturities. Interest rates on US Treasury securities are commonly accepted as being reflective of the general level of interest rates in the US economy. This acceptance is due to three main reasons: (1) there are more Treasury securities outstanding than any other securities in the world; (2) the Treasury issues securities of every maturity spectrum on a regular basis; and (3) these securities have practically no credit risk. At any given point in time, there are factors that cause interest rate differences among the Treasury securities themselves and between the Treasury and non-Treasury securities.

The securities markets in most developing countries are not sufficiently developed in terms of volume and maturities to enable the construction of reliable yield curves. Investors tend to hold short-term CDs, and 90-day Treasury bills as their principal investment instruments. In some countries there may be long-term US dollar denominated bonds originating from the conversion of foreign debt into bonds.[3] No doubt, reliable yield curves on domestic securities will be available as developing countries' financial markets expand in volume and maturities. Meanwhile, as domestic and foreign financial markets integrate, yield curves on foreign securities may provide a reliable guide on the future course of interest rates.

With financial market integration, a growing number of private sector issuers from developing financial markets have been tapping the external bond market. These issuers include developers of infrastructure projects, state-owned enterprises, private construction companies and large commercial banks in Asia and Latin America. The timing of their bond issues has been influenced by expected interest rates, as reflected in the shape of the yield curve. With an expected increase in interest rates in the late 1994 and early 1995, most bond issuers from developing countries delayed their entry into the external market. In late 1994, bond issues were shelved for placement at an appropriate time in 1995.[4] Yield curve analysis is therefore important for bank and non-bank management in developing financial markets. At least, it provides information that influences the timing of bond issues in foreign financial markets.

Varying factors produce yield curves that have one of three basic shapes as indicated in Figure 3.1. A flat curve means that yields on short-term, intermediate-, and long-term maturities are almost the same, suggesting that the supply of, and demand for, loanable funds are roughly in balance throughout the market. An upward-sloping curve indicates that yields are higher on longer maturities and suggests that the demand for short-term funds relative to supply is greater than it is for long-term funds. Finally, a downward-sloping curve shows that yields are higher on shorter maturities, indicating the demand for longer-term funds relative to the supply is greater than that for short-term funds. Term structure or yield curve hypotheses are concerned with explaining why the yield curve has a particu-

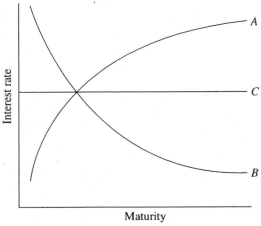

Figure 3.1   Yield curves

lar shape over a certain period of time. The three most cited hypotheses are the liquidity preference, market segmentation, and expectations hypotheses.

The liquidity hypothesis states that investors place a premium on liquidity, the ability to convert an asset into cash quickly without loss. Since shorter maturities are somewhat more liquid than longer ones, shorter maturities will command higher prices and therefore lower yields than longer maturities. No doubt, each investor can buy either long-term securities and hold them, or buy short-term securities and continually reinvest in such securities at each maturity, over a period similar to the maturity of a long-term security.

However, there is little evidence that liquidity-seeking investors dominate the fixed-income securities markets. In fact, these investors might actually prefer paying a premium for an assured long-term rate rather than confront the uncertainty of what rate they will receive on funds reinvested each time the short-term securities mature. Although the liquidity hypothesis explains an upward-sloping yield curve, it fails to do so for a flat or downward-sloping one.

The market segmentation hypothesis asserts that there are separate markets for short-term and long-term fixed income securities, and that demand and supply in each market determine yields on short and long maturities. Because the market is segmented, any pattern of yields can result depending upon the demand for, and supply of, short-term funds relative to the demand for, and supply of, long-term securities. Thus, the market segmentation hypothesis attempts to explain why yield curves come in a variety of shapes. But the hypothesis denies that capital funds may be mobile among different maturities. In other words, it states that portfolio managers will hold only short-term or long-term maturities and that governments and firms will not vary the maturities of their debt issues. Available evidence, argues against this position. Although perfect substitutability among various maturities does not normally exist, portfolio managers do alter the maturity composition of their portfolios, and governments and firms do vary maturities when issuing new debt obligations, as they respond to changing differentials between short-term and long-term yields.

The expectation hypothesis holds that investors' expectations about future short-term rates determine the relationship between short-term and long-term yields. If investors expect short-term rates to increase, the yield curve will slope upward; if they anticipate falling short-term rates, the curve will slope downward; and if they believe that these rates will remain the same, the curve will be flat.

Assume that an investor plans to invest funds for 2 years and has a choice between a 1-year and a 2-year Treasury security, each yielding 8 per cent. If short-term rates are expected to increase to say 10 per cent, investors will buy a 1-year security. Then 1 year hence when the security matures, the investor reinvests the funds at 10 per cent raising the average annual rate of return above what will have been received on the 2-year security. A relatively greater demand for short-term securities will tend to push up their prices, reduce their yields, and induce an upward-sloping yield curve. The opposite occurs if falling short-term rates are expected. The investor will acquire the 2-year security, prices of longer maturities will increase, their yields decline, and a downward-sloping yield curve will result. Finally, if short-term rates are expected to remain unchanged, investors will be indifferent as to a choice between the two securities, and demand will be about even throughout the market resulting in a flat yield curve.

The expectations hypothesis can explain different yield curve shapes. However, it differs in a fundamental way form the market segmentation hypothesis in its assumptions that all maturities are perfect substitutes and that no market segmentation exists. However, some investors, such as banks tend to favour shorter maturities while others, such as life insurance companies tend to favour longer maturities. Empirical studies suggest that the expectations hypothesis explains the shape of the yield curve more adequately than the liquidity and market segmentation hypotheses.[5]

The shape of the yield curve has been a good leading indicator of economic activity. This attribute is associated with the fact that investors normally demand higher yields on longer-term securities to compensate for the greater risk – the liquidity hypothesis. The required premium, however, tends to vary according to the investors' expectations of growth, inflation and interest rates. For example, the US yield curve sloped steeply upwards in 1992–3, reflecting the market's expectations that future growth, inflation, and short-term interest rates would increase. Investors, therefore, demanded a larger premium on long-term securities. When the central bank increases short-term rates in order to reduce growth and inflationary expectations, the gap between short-term and long-term bond yields narrows. While yields on short-term bonds are pulled up by rising short-term interest rates, those on long-term bonds fall as inflationary expectations ease. If the central bank continues to tighten monetary policy, short-term rates eventually will rise above long-term rates and the yield curve will become inverted. Because investors expect weaker growth in the future, and hence lower interest rates, they will tend to accept lower rates on long-term securities.[6]

Monetary policy, as in part indicated by the shape of the yield curve, can be used to improve the condition of problem banks in developing financial markets as it was used, in the 1980s, to assist weakened banks in the US. If the yield curve is steeply positive and the central bank lends to problem banks at low short-term rates, the banks can then buy higher yielding government bonds and improve their interest margins. By promoting a positive yield curve the central bank encourages the commercial banks to sell their short-term securities at a high price, to buy long-term securities at a low price and to increase their net operating cash flows. With an inverted yield curve, short-term rates are higher than long-term rates, and the prices of short-term bonds are lower then those of long-term bonds. Banks will therefore have the incentive to sell their long-term bonds, buy short-term ones and improve their liquidity and operating cash flows. Thus, a monetary policy that encourages increased earnings through liquidity transformation can strengthen the financial condition of problem and other commercial banks.

Yield curve analysis can assist bank management in developing financial markets as it does in developed financial markets. In order to achieve a targetted rate of return on investment, management will have to determine where the bank's funds will be placed in the maturity spectrum – will these funds be invested and reinvested in short-term securities, or in longer-term securities? While short-term securities usually return less income than long-term securities, the spread between short-term and long-term securities tends to narrow at the late stages in the business cycle, and the yield curve may even invert. Decisions as to maturity structure of a bank's securities portfolio, and investment tactics for achieving income goals and minimizing investment risk clearly will be influenced by interest rate expectations. In determining what investment approach is appropriate for achieving certain income and risk minimizing goals, management will need to forecast whether interest rates will rise or fall.

While the relationship between bond yield and maturity is of great interest to bank management, and investors generally, the relationship between yield and other bond characteristics, such as quality, call features and tax status is also of interest to them. The latter relationships are referred to as yield spreads. For example, the yield on unrated or low-rated bonds will be higher than those on high-rated bonds. Lower quality results in higher risk and yield.

Given the yield curve, management may increase return on investment by acquiring non-investment grade securities with yields and risk higher than those of investment grade securities. In developed financial markets, investors require a premium for below investment grade bonds, and bank regulators and supervisors in these markets discourage the holding of such bonds by limiting their relative share in banks' portfolio and requiring the maintenance on credit risk information of their issuers. In an effort to increase their net interest margins, some financial institutions, in the 1980s, invested large amounts in non-investment grade securities, resulting in significant losses when the issuers failed to meet their obligations and the market for these bonds collapsed.[7] If a recession is expected, a lower rated bond will be riskier than the same bond at a time when the economy is growing.

Yield spreads are determined not only by investors' but also by issuers' preferences. A large issue of Treasury bonds by the government may cause the narrowing of spreads between yields on corporate bonds and those on Treasury bonds. The corporate bond yield will tend to be higher than the Treasury bond yield because of credit risk differences between these bonds. However, the yield spread may be narrower than usual because the large increase in Treasury bonds will cause their yields to rise.

Change in expectations also explains changes in the yield relationships among bonds of equal quality but with different call provisions. Thus, if interest rates are expected to fall, callable bonds will become relatively less attractive to investors than bonds with non-refunding features. Other things being equal, therefore, yields on callable bonds will be higher in relation to yields on non-refundable bonds than will be the case if interest rates are expected to rise.

Similarly, assume two bonds of equal quality and maturity, and similar call provisions, but with different coupons (for example, a 10 per cent coupon high-grade callable bond, selling at par, compared to a 5 per cent coupon high-grade callable bond selling at a deep discount). The bond most likely to be called if interest rates fall sharply is the 10 per cent coupon bond. Therefore, if rates are expected to fall, the high coupon bond is less attractive relative to the low coupon, deep discount bond, than it will be if rates are not expected to fall. Accordingly, the yield spread between the two issues depends mainly on the market's expectations regarding future interest rate levels.

3.4   INTEREST RATE FORECASTING

When market interest rates are volatile, deposit and lending rates tend to be adjustable. Adjustable deposit and loan rates are typically pegged to the interest rate of a particular government security or an index of securities, and the periodic resetting of these rates will depend on the behaviour of a predetermined benchmark rate. Adjustable-rate mortgages as well as commercial loans are normally repriced in this manner. Variable-rate corporate debt issues as well as variable-rate CDs will also reprice periodically, with rates fixed in relationship to some market index (for example, the London Interbank Offer Rate (LIBOR), Treasury Bill rate, prime lending rate, inter-bank lendine rate, etc.)

Because of the likely proliferation of variable-rate instruments in developing financial markets with their intense competition, and interest rate volatility, there will be a heightened concern about the level and changes of market interest rates. Decisions affected by interest rates depend not only on current but also on the likely future levels of interest rates. Moreover, as the constituency concerned with interest rates grows, whether because of new variable-rate instruments or because of the growing size of public and corporate debt outstanding, the concern over the likely future interest rate level will also grow.

Bank management may therefore find it necessary to use forecasted interest rates for repositioning the bank's balance sheet. In a volatile interest rate environment, management will have to determine the cyclical pattern of interest rates and reposition the bank's balance sheet for the next phase of the interest cycle before the current phase ends. This is because transactions take time to plan and execute. Thus, a bank that positions its balance sheet to maximize earnings at either the top or the bottom of the rate cycle will necessarily fail to maximize earnings over the entire cycle.

Interest rate forecasts may be derived from market yield curves, published economic forecasts, and internal forecasting techniques. Yield curves may not be available for domestic securities, and if they are, the maturities may be short-term and unreliable. Bank management may, therefore, have to rely mainly on an internal system for forecasting domestic interest rates.

In establishing the bank's internal forecasting system, management must be aware that interest rate forecasting may take the form of a specified or formally quantified model (for example, the scientific approach) or may simply be unspecified or informal hunches and guesses (for example, the judgmental approach). Frequently, the belief that recent experience will be repeated is considered as useful as any formal forecasts. However, because of the high probability of significant swings in actual and expected inflation and interest rates, recent inflation and interest rate changes may at times, be unreliable in predicting future interest rates.

In fact, a distinction may be made between conditional and unconditional forecasts. In an unconditional forecast, values for all the explanatory variables in the forecasting equation are known with certainty. An *ex post* forecast is, of course, an unconditional forecast, but an *ex ante* forecast may also be unconditional. Suppose for example, that interest rate (i_t) is linearly related to money supply (M) and prices (P) but with lags of 3 and 4 months respectively. This relationship may be specified as follows:

$$i_t = \alpha_0 + \alpha_1 M_1(t-3) + \alpha_2 P_2(t-4) \tag{3.5}$$

If equation (3.5) is estimated, it could be used to produce unconditional forecasts for i_t, 1, 2, and 3 months in the future. For example, to produce a 3-month forecast of i_t, the current value of M_1 and the last month's value of P_2 both of which are known, will be used. In a conditional forecast, values for one or more explanatory variables are not known with certainty, so that guesses for them must be used to produce the forecast of the dependent variable. If the intention is to use equation (3.5) to forecast i_t 4 months into the future, it will be necessary to forecast $M_1(t)$ 1 month into the future making the forecast conditioned upon the forecast value of $M_1(t)$. If the right hand side of the forecasting equation contained no lags as indicated in equation (3.6) then every *ex ante* forecast generated by the equation would be a conditional forecast.

$$i_t = \alpha_0 + \alpha_1 M_1(t) + \alpha_2 P_2(t) \tag{3.6}$$

Interest rate forecasting in developing financial markets would tend to be conditional mainly because current values of most of the explanatory variables will not be known with certainty or may contain errors and thus be subject to frequent revisions.[8]

In addition to the distinction between conditional and unconditional forecasting, interest rate forecasts may be separated into two types. These are: (1) those which do not rely upon economic theory and instead extrapolate the past values of the interest rates, by simple or sophisticated means; and (2) those which seek causal relationships among economic variables as posited by economic theory and are expressed empirically by a single or multiple regression model or by indices of time series for selected indicators such as the level or changes in disposable income, changes in money supply, and changes in price levels.

Advocates of the extrapolative approach may argue that causal relationships affecting interest rates in developing financial markets are too complicated to discern, possibly unknowable particularly for markets that have recently been liberalized, or are too costly to pursue. In general, these advocates have stated that the traditional extrapolative method of time series forecasting has produced biased results. Time series models, however, can be useful in short-term interest rate forecasting when causal factors that might offset the historical pattern are ineffective. Such factors may be a sudden change in monetary policy and exchange rate policies, inflation and interest rates, and in capital flows.[9] In cases when such factors are effective, as may be the situation in developing financial markets, the judgmental approach may complement and modify the results of the time series model. Interest rate forecasting, at best, is a combination of analytical techniques, experience, and sound judgement.

Single-equation models and least square estimation of these models may be adequate for management's short-term interest rate forecasting needs.[10] Management, unaccustomed to using econometric models for forecasting or any other purposes, must be aware that the validity of such models rests on proper identification of the major variables that reliably explain the changes in interest rates. Tests of statistical significance (for example, the null hypothesis, goodness of fit and particularly for serial correlation) may identify some sources of forecasting error. Such errors must be corrected or reduced to improve the forecasting results.

Changes in disposable income, money supply and price levels explain changes in interest rates. These variables, particularly the money supply and price variables, may have some lagged effect on interest rates. In forecasting short-term interest, management may specify a single-equation model and estimate this model using monthly time-series data running from January of the initial year to January of the final year of observation. The variables may be:

i_{tb} = interest rate on 3-month Treasury bills (dependent variable)
Y = aggregate disposable income
M = aggregate money supply (currency and demand deposits),
P = consumer price index

The model with i_{tb} as the dependent variable may be specified to accommodate lags in the independent variables of income, money supply, and price variables as indicated in Box 3.1.

Box 3.1   Selected independent variables for short-term interest rate
forecasting

$$Y_t$$

$$\Delta Y_t$$

$$\Delta M_t + \Delta M_{t-1} + \Delta M_{t-2}$$

$$\frac{\Delta P_t}{P_t}$$

$$\frac{\Delta P_t}{P_t} + \frac{\Delta P_{t-1}}{P_{t-1}}$$

$$\frac{\Delta P_t}{P_t} + \frac{\Delta P_{t-1}}{P_{t-1}} + \frac{\Delta P_{t-2}}{P_{t-2}}$$

Disposable income is expected to have a strong positive effect on interest rates, increases in disposable income imply increases in the demand for liquid assets. The change in disposable income may be added to the model to include the time involved as interest rates adjust to changes in disposable income. The model may also include a moving-sum of money supply changes, perhaps a simple sum of money supply changes over a 3-month period. It is expected that, other things being equal, increases in the average of past changes in the money supply will lead to lower interest rates. Finally, a variable should be entered to account for the effect of the rate of change of prices. It is expected that an increase in the rate of price change will lead to an increase in interest rate. The inflation variable may be changed from a 1-month rate of change to a 2-month moving-sum rate of change. As in the case of the money supply, it is suspected that inflation affects interest rates with a lag.

The estimation of even a single-equation short-term interest rate forecasting model, with disposable income, money supply and prices as explanatory variables may not be easily estimated, because of data availability problems. While most developing countries, with a central bank or monetary authority will have published money supply data, many may not have current or monthly aggregate income, or price level data. They, however, may have data which may be used as proxies for income and prices. For example, changes in export value may be closely correlated with changes in aggregate income, and changes in exchange rates with changes in domestic price levels.

Estimating models for interest rate forecasting in developing financial markets can be a complex and demanding process due mainly to data reliability problems.[11] Information derived from such models would no doubt be supplemented by judgmental forecasts based on the monitoring of money supply, exchange rate, and perhaps selected price changes.

It has been reported that some countries are suspected of fiddling their economic figures deliberately.[12] Included in such figures are trends in inflation rates, industrial production, income and investment – data that would facilitate the estimating of interest rate forecasting and other models. Part of the problem, is that in many of these countries the mechanisms for gathering official statistics until recently were not developed. The problem is most acute in Eastern Europe with their previously command economies where statisticians were required to monitor central plans and production targets. Consequently, most of the data collected were about volumes, not costs or prices as would be required for interest rate forecasting. Improving the availability and reliability of official data on money supply, foreign exchange reserves, inflation rates and other interest rate forecasting indicators would, undoubtedly, improve the effectiveness of bank management in developing financial markets.

3.5 SUMMARY

This chapter has attempted to focus on the interest rate environment with a view of encompassing the complex elements of this environment and extracting some of their implications for bank management in developing financial markets. The chapter has argued that the element of competition between banks and non-bank financial institutions in domestic and external financial markets has restricted the freedom of banks to price their products and services. Moreover, to the extent that banks in developing financial markets are subject to reserve requirements, they are at a competitive disadvantage relative to their non-bank competitors not subject to such requirements. An implication of competition is that bank management would have to recognize the cost differences associated with reserve requirements and other bank specific costs and respond to these differences by reducing non-interest expenses and increasing staff productivity. The chapter has addressed such elements as interest rate averages, and the relationships between yield curves and spreads. It has argued that all these relationships provide important information for effective asset-liability management.

4 Managing Foreign Currency Risks

Banks in developing financial markets would no doubt have assets, liabilities, capital, and off-balance sheet positions in foreign currencies. Such positions would result from their activities in providing banking services to the government and government agencies in the public sector, and to their domestic and foreign customers in the private sector. Some banks may even have foreign exchange positions associated with their speculative activities in foreign currencies or with their attempt to make markets in particular currencies. While these positions can enhance the bank's cash flows from foreign currency trading, they can also expose the bank to unaccustomed risks that must be minimized through effective management, and control systems.

This chapter provides a set of descriptive information on the foreign currency trading activities of commercial banks, identifies the types of foreign currency transaction and the risks inherent in them, and reviews the approaches for limiting these risks. It analyzes the dollarization phenomenon that occurs particularly in the early stages of financial reform and identifies the foreign currency risk management implications of this phenomenon. Furthermore, it discusses the responsibilities of management, and the need for formal policies and limits on foreign currency positions. Finally, the chapter examines techniques for forecasting exchange rates.

4.1 TYPES OF FOREIGN CURRENCY TRANSACTION

The foreign currency markets of developing countries, like the markets of developed countries, are dominated by spot transactions. Spot transactions are those transactions that require immediate (that is two business days from the transactions date to the settlement date) delivery of the related currencies. Spot transactions are normally linked to international payments for goods, and to investment and financial transfers. Quoted spot rates serve as reference rates for other foreign currency transactions. As developing financial markets evolve and bank customers demand an increasing range of foreign currency services, some banks may respond by offering their customers forward and swap contracts.

Spot transactions are associated with customers' demand for, and supply of, foreign currencies. If excessive selling activities cause the price of a foreign currency to fall below its normal level, and the currency is viewed as being temporarily underpriced, the bank may consider buying the currency when the price falls to a certain level and selling it again when the price rises. If, in fact, the price increases, the bank would have assisted in stabilizing the market, while making a profit. With given overhead expenses, and a large volume of daily spot transactions, banks can make substantial profits form the correct prediction of very small movements, and turning points of the spot exchange rate. But they can also make significant losses if their predictions are wrong.

The following example illustrates the completion of a spot transaction between two banks. At J$33.00 for US$1.00, Bank A agreed to buy J$10.0 million worth of US dollars from Bank B. Both banks are operating in the same developing financial market, but Bank B has US dollar balances in its US correspondent bank account and wants to buy Jamaican dollar (J$) by using some of these balances. Two working days from the transaction date, Bank A will play J$10 million to Bank B and receive US$303,030 from Bank B. In a developing financial market, where banks deal directly with each other and not through independent brokers and dealers, Bank A might call Bank B and request a quote for US dollars. Bank B in turn would respond with the rate and between themselves, a deal would be completed. Normally, however, brokers and dealers are involved, and quotes would be sought from several banks with US dollar deposits to sell.[1]

A forward exchange transaction is one for which the exchange rate is established for delivery of the currencies at a date beyond the spot date. A transaction that occurred on 30 June for delivery on 31 August is a forward one. The forward rate is obtained by a combination of: (1) the current spot rate; and (2) the difference between the interest rates in countries of the transaction currencies. Table 4.1 illustrates the determination of the J$/US forward exchange rate. It should be noted that the difference between the spot and forward exchange rate is 2.2 per cent which is equal to the difference in the interest rates for 3-month J$ CD and US$ CD.[2] It should also be noted that the forward rate of the Jamaican dollar is 2.2 per cent below the spot rate.

Interest rate parity states that the forward exchange rate will tend to be greater than its spot value, in percentage term, by as much as the domestic interest rates are lower than the foreign interest rates, or tend to be lower than its spot value by as much as the domestic interest rates are higher than the foreign interest rates. Thus, in establishing the forward exchange

Table 4.1   Forward exchange rate determination

- Current Jamaican/US dollar spot exchange rate = J$33.00/US$1.00
- Forward rate to be calculated: 3 months (90 days from spot)
- Assume Jamaican dollar 3-month CD interest rate = 15 per cent per annum
- Assume US dollar 3-month CD interest rate = 6 per cent per annum
- Available investment amount J$1.0 million
- Investor's alternatives:
  - Invest in 3-month J$ 15 per cent CD – earn interest of J$36 986.30
  - Principal and interest = J$1 036 986.30 (A)
  - Convert J$1.0 million to US$30 303.03 at the current spot rate
  - Invest US$30 303.03 in 3-month US$ 6 per cent CD – earn interest of US$448.32
  - Principal and interest US$30 751.35 (B)
- Divide (A) by (B) and obtain the forward rate = J$33.7216/US$1.00

---

rate for the domestic currency, management should: (1) determine the appropriate interest rate differential; (2) adjust the spot exchange rate upward or downward by this differential (that is upward if the relevant interest rate in the domestic currency market is lower than the rate in the foreign currency market, and downward if the interest rate in the domestic currency market is higher than the rate in the foreign currency market); and (3) further adjust the rate derived from (2) for risk premium, and charges to cover transactions costs.

In the developed financial markets, the pricing of forward contract is not a complicated process. Arbitrage prevents a forward rate that differs from the rate suggested by interest rate parity, where the difference between the spot and forward exchange rates equals the difference between the domestic and foreign interest rates. In developing financial markets, however, the equality of these differences may not occur because market participants may not want to exploit the arbitrage opportunities arising from the inequality. In other words, small changes in interest and exchange rates may not induce any switching between domestic and foreign deposits.

Forward exchange rate determination is based on certain assumptions about the spot and forward rates, financial market access, and currency convertibility. Among these assumptions are: (1) the presence of an active spot and forward exchange market for the currencies involved; (2) the availability of comparable financial instruments in both currencies; and (3) the existence of free currency convertibility for both trade and capital transactions.

The importance of the forward exchange market is that it enables transactions to be conducted at agreed future exchange rates. Management must therefore determine the most effective means of conducting such transactions without exposing the bank to the risk of an adverse exchange rate movement at the time of delivery of the foreign currency. At least two such means may be considered: (1) matching the transactions; and (2) conducting deposit transactions to ensure the availability of the related currencies on settlement date.

Matching transactions presumes the existence of a coincidence of buyers and sellers of the currencies. For example, one customer may want to sell in 3 months a certain amount of Jamaican dollars for US dollars, and another customer may want to sell in the same period an equivalent amount of US dollars for Jamaican dollars. Should this coincidence occur, and there is a high probability that it would occur if the bank is actively involved in trading these currencies, then the only concern facing management would be the credit risk of the customers. If the customers do not default, the bank will be exposed to no risk, and may even make a profit by quoting slightly different rates for the two transactions.

In the absence of a coincidence of customers' foreign currency needs, the bank may be able to cover its forward transactions through a foreign currency deposit process. Assume a customer wants to sell Jamaican dollars for US dollars in 3 months' time. On quoting the customer a firm rate, the bank agrees to provide the customer US dollars in 3 months in return for Jamaican dollars. The bank can take a Jamaican dollar deposit for 3 months, use the deposit to buy US dollar at the spot rate, and then place the US dollar on deposit for 3 months. The proceeds received on the maturity of the US dollar deposit will be exchanged for the Jamaican dollar deposit in 3 months' time.

Forward contracts are available in many developing financial markets although not for all maturities and all currencies. They are commonly used to manage exposures. However, firms also frequently choose to leave their foreign exchange exposures unmanaged when conditions are viewed as stable or the cost of a forward contract is perceived to be excessive.[3] Bank management in developing financial markets may have a profit opportunity to exploit by offering forward market contracts to their customers, pricing these contracts to reflect interest rate differential, transactions costs and default risk, and promoting the use of these contracts among their corporate customers.

Swaps may be another foreign exchange service banks in developing financial markets may provide their customers. Surely, forward contracts are ideal for hedging single and short-term foreign currency transactions. However, as developing and developed financial markets become increasingly integrated, firms in developing financial markets have shown an interest in medium-term foreign currency project financing and in instruments for hedging the foreign exchange risk connected with such financing. Swaps serve as one of these instruments.

A swap is a transaction in which both a spot transaction and a forward transaction are agreed upon simultaneously. Should the spot part of the transaction represent a purchase of a foreign currency, the forward part would represent a sale of the foreign currency. Conversely, should the spot part represent a sale, the forward part would represent a purchase of the foreign currency. A customer holding US dollar balances may want to sell these balances spot for yen balances while simultaneously arranging for a forward contract to repurchase US dollars for yen. Thus, the parties to this arrangement are swapping the currencies for a fixed period using the spot and the forward rates for the two contracts.

In most developing financial markets, forward markets for local currencies seldom extend to more than 6 months although there may be a substantial demand for long-term forward contracts. Moreover, existing markets with 6-month maturity are often illiquid. The absence of long-maturity forward markets is, therefore, a major reason why swap markets in developing countries currencies are scarce. In some countries, India and Chile, for instance, swap markets exist. Some Indian manufacturing companies have accessed low cost US dollar financing that resulted in considerable currency exposure, given that their revenues were mainly in rupees. At the same time some Indian financial institutions, with ready access to rupee financing, wanted US dollar financing for their international operations, but could not access the low cost US dollar financing of some of the Indian manufacturing companies. In the circumstances, a swap of US dollars and rupees provided an ideal solution and a rupee/US dollar swap market was developed. Chile has also developed a peso/US dollar market under circumstances similar to those of India.

With inactive long-term forward markets in India, no Indian financial institution was able to sell its customer a rupee/US dollar swap without the ability to cover the resulting currency exposure. By teaming up offsetting transactions, however, the financial institutions minimized their exposures. Although the offsetting element in a swap arrangement should be emphasized, this emphasis should not imply that all forward exposures are always covered. Sometimes, banks do take open swap positions and, within established limits, accept exposure to foreign currency risks. In developed countries, the pairing of offsetting exposures is made easier by a wholesale market of different currency deposits available for swap activities.

Swaps are, therefore, rooted in deposits. Many deposit transactions are undertaken to produce swaps. Assume a corporate customer has requested its bank to purchase US$1.0 million for delivery in 6 months. The bank calculates the forward price and enters into the transaction with the customer. Now the bank is faced with the task of covering its position, that is purchasing US$1.0 million for delivery in 6 months. The bank may purchase the US dollar for spot delivery. However, the bank does not want this amount for spot and will not have the domestic currency from the customer until the 6-month delivery.

As the bank does not have the domestic currency to pay for the US dollars on spot delivery, a swap will have to be arranged to offset the bank's commitment to deliver US$1.0 million 6 months later. To do so, the bank finds another customer with a US$1.0 million that the customer wants to exchange at the spot rate and to deposit the domestic currency equivalent in a 6-month CD with the bank. The bank, in turn, makes a deposit of US$1.0 million with its US correspondent bank. Six months later, the US dollar deposit is applied to settle the forward contract, the corporate customers make the equivalent domestic currency payment to the bank, and the bank applies this domestic currency payment to the maturing CD. The deposit and forward exchange markets are therefore interdependent.

4.2   OPEN FOREIGN CURRENCY POSITIONS

Traditionally, commercial banks have made international payments for their private and public sector customers. Such payments will continue and expand as financial markets are reformed, and the volume of international transactions grows. The role of commercial banks in the international payments system has been facilitated by the banks' account relationship with a worldwide network of correspondent banks and, in some cases, with their direct offices in international financial centres. Banks are engaged in international payments or in the exchange of currencies not only for their customers' benefit but also for their own benefit of increasing their operating cash flows.

A bank's foreign exchange trading activities expose it to exchange rate risk. This is the risk of loss resulting from exchange rate changes. Trading losses from foreign exchange activities are determined by revaluing the banks' foreign currency positions in domestic currency terms. Usually, a bank maintains its financial statements, including its foreign currency assets, liabilities, and off-balance sheet items, in domestic currency. In accounting for its foreign currency positions, the bank revalues these positions using current exchange rates to obtain the positions' domestic currency value. Exchange rate changes since the previous revaluation would, therefore, be reflected in changes in the domestic currency value of the bank's foreign currency position.[4]

When a bank has an open position in a foreign currency, its assets and liabilities in that currency are not equal. With such a position, revaluation will create a gain or loss depending on the direction of the exchange rate change and on whether the open position in the foreign currency is a net long or net short one. A net long position exists when the bank is holding net assets in the foreign currency, and a net short position occurs when the bank owes more in that foreign currency than it holds, or is in a net liability position in that currency. The revaluing of the bank's foreign currency position will produce a gain to the bank if the value of the foreign currency in terms of the domestic currency increases, and a loss if this value decreases while the bank has a net long position. Conversely, the revaluing will show a loss if the foreign currency increases, and a gain if the foreign currency decreases relative to the domestic currency, while the bank has a net short position.

Box 4.1 attempts to summarize the valuation or revaluation procedures for determining the results of a bank's foreign exchange trading activities for any selected accounting period (for example, monthly, quarterly, and annually). The procedure for adjusting spot transactions is simple when compared to that for forward ones. As indicated in Box 4.1, the income results from a revaluation of the bank's forward transactions can be distorted by the use of an inappropriate exchange rate to revaluate a forward gap position.

Box 4.1   Valuation or revaluation procedures

- *Spot transactions*: adjust the domestic currency value of the bank's foreign currency balances that reflect all transactions concluded during the accounting period. Apply the spot rate to the net balance and adjust the existing domestic currency value as required.
- *Forward transactions*: if for every forward contract to buy there is an offsetting contract to sell, apply either the existing spot rate or the forward rate. If there are gaps the use of the spot rate will distort profitability. This use of the spot rate will not reflect what the gain or loss would be if the gap position is closed out as of the valuation date. To determine the gain or loss accurately the actual market rates that would prevail for the forward contracts should be used. This will produce an unrealized gain or loss.

Under repressed financial market conditions bank management was, for the most part, unmindful of their foreign exchange positions, because the domestic currency was fixed relative to the foreign currency and changes in the exchange rate could have been anticipated. In fact, the fixed exchange rate system was characterized by relatively large, discrete and infrequent changes. Consequently, bank management, if concerned about a potential devaluation, focused attention on balance of payments, and foreign exchange reserves data. A sustained payments imbalance along with substantial shifts in foreign exchange reserves would increase the probability that the central bank could no longer support the pegged rate.

The magnitude of the exchange rate change, or the amount required to restore payments balance, and stop the depletion of the foreign exchange reserves, could be estimated from a purchasing power parity model. However, while bank management was able to determine the need for adjustment in the exchange rate, and to estimate the size of the adjustment, they could not determine the time the adjustment would occur because the ultimate decision to change the peg was a political one. Meanwhile, management might maximize the bank's operating cash flow by creating a net long position in the foreign currency expected to appreciate in terms of the domestic currency. Under a floating exchange rate, or any other exchange rate arrangement where the exchange rate is subject to frequent and sometimes unpredictable changes, management of foreign exchange positions needed to be more aggressive than it was under a fixed exchange rate arrangement.[5]

In minimizing the risk inherent in its foreign exchange trading activities, the bank should operate within certain established guidelines. These guidelines, no doubt, will vary from bank to bank but, at least, they should address each bank's overnight and intraday positions, and its gap limits. The process of establishing foreign currency exposure limits (for example, limits on credit, overall, settlement, and unsettled contract risks) should be integrated with the bank's overall credit approval mechanism to ensure the maximum effectiveness in monitoring and controlling the bank's long or short positions with any borrower, counterparty, or country. In general, the responsibility for managing the bank's foreign exchange trading activities, and ensuring compliance with established exposure limits must be clearly defined.

The overnight position is the total long or short foreign currency position that the bank has been authorized to hold. If a bank has an overnight limit of J$10 million, its net purchases and sales of foreign currencies at the end of the day should not exceed J$10 million long or short. Within this overall limit, there may be sub-limits for individual currencies, thus enabling management to control, on a daily basis, the bank's exposure in any one currency as well as its overall exposure.[6]

The intraday position is one that can be held at any time of the trading day. To accommodate the bank customers' demand, for, and supply of, foreign currencies, the intraday position limit may be larger than its overnight position limit. Maintaining an overall intraday position in a multicurrency trading operation can be a complex process. As such, it might be useful to establish separate intraday limits for each currency.

The gap limit refers to the timing of the bank's foreign currency transactions. If, for example, a bank purchases US dollars for spot value and sells an equivalent amount of US dollars for some forward date, the overall position is matched or squared, but the timing of delivery is unmatched. The bank, therefore, has an exposure associated with the timing difference. This difference allows for profit and loss opportunities associated with the difference in interest rates between the two currencies. By instituting gap limits in terms of currencies and contract maturities, management will indicate the extent of exposure the bank is willing to accept.

In establishing position limits, management might consider the extent to which the bank's capital, assets, or earnings should be exposed to foreign currency risk. Net open position limits may, therefore, be expressed as a percentage of the bank's capital, its assets, or its earnings. However, even before the limits are established, management may want to estimate the loss that could be incurred and sustained, should the exchange rate move against a set of assumed open positions. Such an estimate may be based on assumptions about the size of potential adverse exchange rate changes, and the size and nature of the open positions.

The assumptions about the exchange rate changes are very important in setting position limits that would minimize the bank's exposure. Management must be satisfied that the assumed adverse change in the exchange rate relates to a worst case scenario. For banks, with open positions, and operating in countries with stable money supply and national income growth, and where the domestic currency is freely convertible, the assumed exchange rate changes may be gradual and may reflect past exchange rate changes. However, for banks in countries where the exchange rate is subject to government intervention, the assumed changes in the exchange rate may be rapid and sizeable. In such a situation, management may want to set position limits based on the assumption that the government will not intervene to support the exchange rate.

Once the exchange rate assumptions are made, the loss will be estimated by revaluing the bank's open positions at the assumed exchange rates. The size of the estimated loss will provide the basis for setting the open position limits. The initial goal of management is to prevent the losses from substantially diminishing the bank's earnings. Ultimately, management will be concerned with protecting the bank's capital and assets from such losses.

Most banks in developing financial markets do not conduct multiple foreign currency trading or trading between the domestic currency and several foreign currencies. Generally, the net open position reflects foreign currency liabilities funding domestic currency assets.[7] In situations where the bank is trading in more than one foreign currency, the net open position limits may be established for all the currencies as if they are a single foreign currency. The reason for grouping the foreign currencies is that the risk arising from a position involving one hard currency against another (for example, pound sterling liabilities funding US dollar assets) will tend to be much lower, because of lower exchange rate volatility, and assured convertibility, than the risk involving the domestic currency of a developing country and foreign currencies. Management must recognize, however, that this practice of managing foreign currency risk by treating a group of foreign currencies as a single currency does not capture the risk from cross positions in the foreign currencies.

4.3   DOLLARIZATION

With the removal of domestic financial market and exchange restrictions, individuals and firms in developing countries with high and variable inflation rates tend to abandon the domestic currency as a store of value and to turn to foreign currency as a refuge for their financial savings.[8]

This process has occurred in many Latin American countries (for example, Argentina, Bolivia, Mexico, Peru, and Uruguay), with a history of high inflation rates. In these countries, a large proportion of financial assets was kept in the form of interest bearing foreign currency deposits, usually US dollars. However, the attractiveness of a stable foreign currency as a vehicle to protect the real value of financial assets has not been confined to Latin American countries. During the 1980s rising inflation led to widespread dollarization in such European countries as Poland and the former Yugoslavia.

Dollarization is often a manifestation of underlying fiscal and monetary disequilibria represented by chronic fiscal deficits and accommodating monetary and exchange rate policies. Of course, removing such disequilibria is not the responsibility of bank management but that of the fiscal and monetary authorities. However, management response to dollarization must reflect a clear understanding of its underlying causes. For example, continued fiscal and monetary disequilibria will impact inflation, interest rate expectations, and portfolio allocation between foreign and domestic assets.

The experience of Latin America suggests that combating dollarization with artificial measures such as using indexed financial instruments, paying interest rates on highly liquid assets that are used as money, or forcing conversion of foreign assets into domestic assets magnifies the eventual inflationary explosion. A portfolio switch in favour of domestic currency denominated assets should be encourage if it is induced by the existence of sound fiscal and monetary policies. While the switching to domestic currency assets may increase domestic currency deposits, bank management may still have to respond to the fact that some dollarization is a normal outcome of portfolio diversification by individuals and firms that are managing the risk inherent in their wealth portfolio.

This response may take the form of encouraging their customers to conduct their foreign currency transactions (for example, the foreign currency deposit activities) with the banks' foreign offices or subsidiaries, and by carefully managing the risks associated with any related gaps in their foreign currency positions. Some US offices of banks from developing financial markets have been successful in controlling their foreign exchange exposures while recycling the funds they capture, to the domestic financial markets. They have been able to do so by extending US dollar denominated trade credits to their clients, or by providing other types of US dollar denominated loans to borrowers with predictable US dollar cash flows.

There is, however, the high probability that in capturing the foreign currency deposits of their domestic clients, banks may have foreign liabilities in excess of their foreign currency assets, or vice versa, while the domestic currency exchange rate is volatile. The preferred position to hold is a long position (where foreign currency assets exceed foreign currency liabilities) in the appreciating currency or a short position (where foreign currency liabilities exceed foreign currency assets) in the depreciating currency. If, for example, a bank has a direct office in a foreign country where it books the foreign currency deposits it receives from its clients and it uses these deposits to make loans denominated in the domestic currency it could experience a substantial translation loss should the domestic currency depreciate, and a substantial profit should the domestic currency appreciate relative to the foreign currency.

Assume a Jamaican bank has J$20 million in cash and J$20 million in capital. It also has, at its Cayman Islands' branch, deposits amounting to U$100 million, and uses all of these deposits to fund its Jamaican dollar denominated loans at fixed interest rates. The Jamaica dollar depreciates by 20 per cent from J$33.00 to J$39.60 per US dollar. In Jamaica dollars, the bank's US dollar liabilities will increase to the full extent of the depreciation while its other Jamaica dollar assets and liabilities will remain unchanged. The translation loss resulting from the currency exposure and the 20 per cent depreciation would move its capital from a positive J$20 million to a negative J$46 million, a reduction of J$66 million. The management of the net foreign exchange position of the bank's foreign offices can explain the success or failure of the bank itself. Table 4.2 illustrates the changes.

Furthermore, assume that the dollarization process provides the major source of US dollar deposits for the bank at an attractive cost, and that the interest rate paid on these deposits is tied to a US Treasury security index (that is, interest moves in step with changes in the index). The bank on-lends the funds on a fixed rate basis in Jamaican dollars. Unless management changes the interest rate and currency basis of the US dollar deposits, the bank is assuming financial risk to the extent that its assets and liabilities are mismatched. To minimize the interest rate and currency risks, and to ensure the availability of US dollar assets to meet the bank's US dollar deposit obligations, management may obtain a swap that enables the bank to convert the fixed interest Jamaican dollar loans to a floating rate US dollar loan. The availability of a wide range of assets and liabilities in terms of currencies, fixed and variable interest rates and terms would also facilitate the swap process in developing financial markets.

Table 4.2   Pre- and post-depreciation changes in assets and liabilities
(J$ million)

Pre-depreciation		Post-depreciation	
Assets		*Assets*	
Cash	20	Cash	20
Loans	330	Loans	330
Liabilities		*Liabilities*	
Deposits	330	Deposits	396
Capital	20	*Capital*	−46

4.4 TRADING PROFITS AND RISKS

Commercial banks derive their foreign exchange profits from two major sources: (1) from customers' foreign currency transactions; and (2) from taking positions. In purchasing from or selling foreign currency to a customer, a bank will add a small margin to the currency's market price. As competition between banks intensifies and bank customers, particularly the larger companies, seek to obtain the best price for their foreign currency transactions, banks will quote rates that are closer or even better than market rates to retain their existing customers or attract new ones. A competitive rate that is better than the market rate is one somewhere between the bid and offer rates of the foreign currency. The system of fixed bid and offer rates common in repressed financial markets is therefore replaced by one of competitive pricing in developing financial markets, where the opportunity simply to mark-up the price of a currency for profit maximization purposes is removed. Banks will, therefore, have to exploit other methods for making profits in foreign currency trading.

Position taking is one of these methods. The taking of foreign currency positions assumes the ability of the bank to judge the likely movements and measure the fluctuations in market rates. If, for example, the bank anticipates that the price of the US dollar in terms of the domestic currency will increase during the day, and estimates that demand for US dollars by its corporate and other large customers for that day, it may build an inventory of US dollars early in the day before the anticipated price increase. With this inventory, the bank positions itself to sell US dollars more competitively than the current market price and make a profit. However, it may record losses, if the anticipated price rise does not materialize or if the price at sale is lower than the initial purchase price of the currency.

Taking positions, based on an anticipated price changes and estimated demand for or supply of foreign currencies, is no doubt speculative trading. The issue for management is whether such trading should be encouraged and if so how should it be controlled. No doubt, in taking speculative positions, the bank becomes a market maker by being willing to quote buying and selling prices even though it has no particular transactions to settle on behalf of its customers. These positions, therefore contribute to the market's liquidity and depth, while assisting non-speculators to transact their foreign currency business. As a speculative position taking can increase the profitability and the trading risk of the bank, and improve the efficiency of the domestic foreign exchange market, management should ensure that the traders taking positions are technically competent to do so, and are operating in strict compliance with the bank's policies and guidelines and established risk limits.

Together with the risk of exchange rate changes, foreign currency trading activities expose the bank to overall risk, as well as settlement risk. Overall risk is concerned with the effects, on the bank's operating cash flow and capital accounts, and of customers' or counterparties' non-performance on their foreign currency contracts. Settlement risk is concerned with the probability of non-delivery of the currencies in the transaction.

The overall risk may be illustrated by the case of a bank entering into a set of forward contracts with one of its corporate customers that eventually goes into bankruptcy. Assume that the total number of such contracts booked by the bank for this customer is 20, and the value of each contract is J$500,000, giving a total of J$10 million in contracts. Furthermore, assume that the contracts were negotiated in February and March, and matured in December of the same year. Based on the bank's policy, all forward contracts must be matched with other counterparties. If the bank buys a certain amount of US dollars from the customer, it will be required to enter into an offsetting contract with another bank or another customer to sell this amount, thus equalizing or squaring its position. For instance, the bank may buy, from its corporate customer, the US dollar equivalent of J$500,000 now and agree to sell this amount to the customer 3 months later. In turn, the bank may sell the US dollar equivalent of J$500,000 to another bank on the condition that it will repurchase an equal amount 3 months later. The bank is faced with the risk that the two counterparties, the corporate customer and the other bank, may not be able to perform 3 months later, for one reason or another.

Assume that prior to December, say in August of that year, the corporate customer becomes bankrupt and is eventually liquidated. The company will be unable to meet its obligations for any outstanding forward contracts, and the bank will have to replace these with other contracts. In this replacement process, the bank is exposed to exchange rate risk. The exchange rate may be better than the original rate with the corporate customer, it may be unchanged, or it may be worse.[9] Because of the high probability that the original contracts will be replaced by other contracts if the foreign exchange market is liquid and active, the overall risk is not so much the full amount of the contract as it is the difference between the original, and the replacement contract rates of exchange. An important responsibility of management, therefore, is to estimate the exchange rate changes that may occur over any given period of time. Assume that between January 1996 and January 1997, the Jamaican dollar depreciated by 50 per cent against the US dollar. However, from June 1996 to December 1996, this depreciation was only 15 per cent. With such volatility it would be difficult, if not impossible, to determine with any certainty, the potential changes in exchange rates. Nonetheless, the difficulty of any such determination would not justify the absence of clear guidelines and limits on the overall risk acceptable to management. Banks tend to define their overall foreign currency risk as a proportion, between 10 per cent and 30 per cent, of the contract amount.[10]

Settlement risk is the other type of risk that must be monitored. This risk is linked to the delivery of the foreign currency at a specified time, or maturity date. Settlement risk may be illustrated by two examples: the first relates to a corporate customer that buys a foreign currency amount from the bank and thus owes the bank the domestic currency equivalent; and the second relates to a corporate customer that sells a foreign currency amount to the bank, and in turn receives the domestic currency equivalent. As time zone differences add to settlement risk, assume that the domestic and foreign currency markets are in different time zones – the foreign currency market is about 8 hours ahead of the domestic currency market. Assume also that the two currencies being traded are Jamaican dollars and pound sterling.

In the case of a corporate customer buying pound sterling from the bank, the amount purchased will be delivered to the customer account at a bank in the UK or be paid as instructed by the customer. Because the UK market is about 8 hours earlier than the Jamaica market, the Jamaican bank's instruction to pay in pound sterling must be sent about a day prior to the settlement day. On the settlement day, the pound sterling amount will be transferred from the Jamaican bank's account with the UK bank to the customer's account at the same bank or at some other bank account in the UK. About 8 hours later in the settlement day, the Jamaican bank will charge the customer's account the Jamaican dollar equivalent of the pound sterling already credited to the customer account or paid on behalf of the customer. Suppose within that 8 hour interval and prior to the charging of the corporate customer account, this customer declared bankruptcy, and consequently the bank cannot collect the Jamaican dollar equivalent of the sterling amount paid to the customer earlier in the business day. The bank will therefore lose the entire amount on this contract.

The second case is where the company sold foreign currency to the bank for domestic currency. Using the pound sterling and Jamaican dollar as examples, the customer will arrange for the pound sterling to be delivered to the bank's UK account at the beginning of the business day in Jamaica, and the bank, in turn, will credit the customer's account with the

Jamaican dollar equivalent. The bank's policy may stipulate that the foreign currency payment to its account must be confirmed prior to crediting the domestic currency equivalent to the customer's account. In practice, however, this policy might not always be observed because of transactions volume, accounting and operational procedures, and time zone differences. Moreover, the UK correspondent bank may not confirm delivery of the sterling amount until the next business day. In the event that the pound sterling amount was not credited as was expected, and the Jamaican dollar equivalent was already paid to the customer, the bank may not be able to recover especially if the customer declared bankruptcy in the interim.

To minimize settlement risk, bank management in developing financial markets will have to define, in a clear and specific manner, the bank trading relationship with its corporate and other large customers. Such a definition will address: (1) the overall exposure or the foreign currency line to the customer; (2) the daily settlement limit, or the amount of foreign currency transactions that the bank will settle for the customer on a daily basis; and (3) the total exposure for unsettled contracts taking into account the overall exposure, the settlement limit, and a foreign exchange risk factor. For example, a bank may establish for one of its corporate customers an overall limit of J$5.0 million, a daily limit of J$1.5 million, and a limit for unsettled contracts of J$700,000 given a risk factor of 20 per cent.[11]

Implied in the overall and settlement risks is credit risk or the probability that a corporate customer will fail to perform according to the terms and conditions of the contract, either because of bankruptcy or any other reason, thus causing the bank to suffer financial loss. In order to limit the bank's credit risk, management should ensure that the limits established for settlement and overall risks represent sub-limits of the bank's total credit limit to the customer. Moreover, credit risk can be reduced by requiring collateral for the customer's total credit line. There are also interest rate and liquidity risks that are associated with banks' foreign currency trading activities.

Although a bank may have a policy of avoiding open positions, it may still be exposed to interest rate risk as a result of its foreign currency trading activities. Interest rate risk arises from interest rate volatility, and the repricing mismatch of assets and liabilities. Given this volatility, interest rate risk can be minimized if the bank's foreign currency assets and liabilities are repriced simultaneously. A bank that hedges all of its transactions completely may be able to avoid interest rate risk.

Foreign currency positions can also expose a bank to liquidity risk. This risk may result from cash flow imbalances because of the failure of a

counterparty to deliver a specified amount of currency at the time stipulated in the contract, or the failure of the bank to hedge its foreign
currency obligations. The failure to acquire foreign currency in spite of a
possible high domestic currency liquidity of the counterparty may be explained by the government's imposition of foreign exchange controls, or
by its modifications of existing currency convertibility restrictions. At a
minimum, these restrictions may cause performance delays by the counterparties in the country where the controls or restrictions are imposed. In the
extreme, the country may lose access to sufficient foreign exchange, and
the counterparties, bank customers and the banks themselves, may be
unable to fulfil the requirements of their foreign currency contracts for extended periods. Exchange controls and convertibility restrictions will limit
the availability of foreign currency for liquidity purposes. To minimize
the liquidity risk, management may have to restrict the bank's trading
activities, and reduce or eliminate any open foreign currency positions.

4.5 FORECASTING EXCHANGE RATES

Exchange rate forecasting becomes an important management tool for
banks that take foreign currency positions. Such forecasting in developed
financial markets has focused mainly on the quarterly or yearly exchange
rate changes and has experienced some success. However, attempts to
forecast daily or weekly exchange rate changes have not been successful.
The difficulty in forecasting the shorter-term exchange rate changes may,
in part, be explained by the fact that some of the variables used in the forecasting models (for example, money supply, and national income) may
not be available on a daily basis, while other variables (for example, expected inflation and interest rates, or expected growth in money supply)
cannot be observed directly.

Apart from the data availability and data observation problems, the
difficulty in forecasting short-term exchange rates may be due to more
arcane reasons. For example, an economic theory that states that the spot
rate is a function of a set of variables cannot be used to forecast the spot
rate unless the variables themselves can first be forecasted. Thus, the need
to forecast the explanatory variables, before the dependent variable can be
forecasted may only compound the difficulty. Moreover, a major consideration of some forecasting models is that exchange rate changes result from
unanticipated economic and political events, or news. However, as it may
be impossible, to predict news, forecasting results may be an unreliable
guide for taking profitable foreign currency positions.

Nevertheless, in developing financial markets with volatile exchange rates, improved exchange rate forecasts, if available, may facilitate informed position taking and minimize risks. Several approaches have been used to determine the timing and size of an exchange rate change. One of these is the political approach often used in countries where exchange rates are managed by the central bank and other government entities. This approach is based on the premise that if enough is known about the monetary and fiscal policy positions of the senior officials of these entities, especially the finance minister and central bank governor, forecasting exchange rate changes would be greatly facilitated.[12] However, despite the importance of political variables in explaining short-term exchange rate changes, dependence on these variables alone may not assure reliable forecasting results.

Senior government officials may not be straightforward in stating their intentions about future exchange rates, and even if they are straightforward, market forces, or changes in the fundamental economic variables that explain exchange rate changes may vitiate their stated intentions. A country with a fixed exchange rate system, or a country that guarantees convertibility at a fixed rate or within specified exchange rate bands, may face inescapable devaluation if its foreign exchange reserves are declining without hope of being rebuilt, or if inflationary expectations are high in part because of excessive money supply expansion. In addition, short-term capital movements, with their destabilizing effect on domestic money supply and price levels, can induce exchange rate changes, in spite of the commitment by the government or central bank to maintain the exchange rate at a fixed level or within specified bands.

The efficient market approach is another technique for exchange rate forecasting. This approach is based on the assumption that all anticipated political events and economic information (for example information on money supply, national income, expected inflation and interest rates, capital flows, and current account balance), is discounted in the current spot and forward exchange rates. Therefore, if the foreign exchange market is considered inefficient, under a floating or a managed exchange rate system, some corrective response, such as increased speculation, distribution of accurate market information, or central bank intervention, would ensue.

In an efficient foreign exchange market, management tends to follow passive hedging strategies, such as avoiding speculative activities, and hedging their spot and forward transactions. In an inefficient foreign exchange market, however, management with improved or better information tends to implement active strategies, such as taking speculative positions to exploit profitable market opportunities. The efficient market approach assumes that the discounting of all relevant information has been so complete that, apart from forward exchange rate, no other exchange rate forecast is necessary. Thus, under the efficient market approach, the forward rate is considered an accurate reflection of information about the political and economic variables that explain exchange rate changes, and an unbiased and excellent predictor of the future spot rate.[13]

Empirical tests have been conducted to determine the relationship between current forward rates and the future spot rates. Results of early tests have indicated that the foreign exchange markets in developed countries are efficient and that forward rates are reliable predictors of future spot rates. Recent studies, however, have challenged this view and have suggested that other methods for forecasting future spot rates have outperformed the forward rates.[14] For example, a model that incorporates relevant news as an explanatory variable may outperform the forward rate as a predictor of future spot rate.[15]

A third approach to exchange rate forecasting is the technical one. This approach focuses on the direction of shorter-term exchange rate movements and aims at providing information that facilitates decisions on position taking in particular currencies. These directional forecasts are based on statistical analyses of recent exchange rate changes, and judgement based on available and anticipated information. The technical approach, like other approaches to exchange rate forecasting, is grounded on solid economic theories that attempt to explain the relationship between the fundamental variables and exchange rates. The three most cited theories for exchange rate forecasting are the purchasing power parity theory, monetary theory, and portfolio balance theory.

The purchasing power parity theory (PPP) is one of the most intuitive bases for modelling exchange rate behaviour. It postulates that exchange rates are set to equalize the real purchasing power of currencies, and that the bilateral exchange rate reflects the differential in inflation rate between countries. In other words, if prices in country A rise at a rate faster than that of country B, the exchange rate of country A's currency will fall in terms of country B's currency, and if prices in country A rise at a slower rate than country B, the exchange rate of country A's currency will increase in terms of country B's currency. The PPP theory may be specified as follows:

$$r = \frac{P}{P_f} \qquad (4.1)$$

where:

r =   the exchange rate of domestic currency relative to the foreign currency (say J$/US$)

P =   the domestic price index

P_f =   the foreign price index

The basic relationship depicted in equation (4.1), or refined variants of it, has received mixed empirical support. Its testing is complicated by the fact that each country has several price indices, each one often moving in a different direction making the choice of an index for PPP testing quite arbitrary. Nonetheless, the theory serves somewhat to predict the movement of exchange rates over long time periods and large price movements. Some studies have in fact established a long-run correlation between relative rates of inflation and currency depreciation or devaluation. Countries with higher inflation have experienced depreciating currencies, and those with lower inflation, have found their currencies rising in value. For the short-run, however, PPP has a poor track record. Price ratios indicated in equation (4.1) have failed to follow short-term exchange rate movements closely.[16] The monetary theory of exchange rate determination has combined the PPP equation (4.1) with the money supply equations (4.2) and (4.3) to forecast exchange rates based on the money supply or money demand, and gross national product of the home and foreign countries.

$$M = k\ P\ Y \qquad (4.2)$$

where:

M =   home country money supply

k =   a constant (or a behavioural ratio)

Y =   real gross national product

and

$$M_f = k_f\ P_f\ Y_f \qquad (4.3)$$

where the subscript for each variable indicates the foreign country's money supply or money demand, constant or behavioural ratio, and real gross national product.

The quantity theory of money demand postulates that in any country the money supply is equal to the demand for money, which is directly proportional to the value of the gross national product, and that price levels are determined by money supply. PPP postulates that nominal exchange rates reflect relative prices. Thus, equation (4.4) combines equations (4.1), (4.2) and (4.3) to establish a relationship between nominal exchange rate, relative prices and money supply. On the basis of equation (4.4) the country with a greater money supply expansion, and slower real income is likely to have a depreciating currency; while the country with a slower money supply expansion and faster real income growth will have an appreciating currency. Equation (4.4) has some forecasting value when monetary disturbances dominate national income and other domestic economic aggregates. It may also be used in forecasting short-term exchange rate changes if relative national income and other data are available.

$$ r = \frac{P}{P_f} = \frac{M}{M_f} \frac{k_f}{k} \frac{Y_f}{Y} \tag{4.4} $$

The portfolio balance theory is an extension of the monetary theory of exchange rate determination, in the sense that the demand for a currency is to acquire a set of financial assets for an investor's portfolio. The portfolio balance theory, therefore, postulates that the demand for currencies is derived largely from demand for financial assets in domestic and foreign currencies. If a country has a current account surplus and holds the wealth accumulated from this surplus in US dollar assets, this action will help to maintain or increase the US dollar price depending on the size of the surplus. On the other hand, wealth accumulation combined with prudent risk management will suggest portfolio diversification with resulting shifts in demand for domestic and foreign currencies.

An advantage of the portfolio balance theory is its emphasis on flow changes in wealth associated with the theory's ability to establish a link between wealth accumulation, portfolio diversification, and the current account balance. But it has certain disadvantages that may explain its failure to forecast exchange rate changes in any successful manner. These disadvantages are mainly the difficulty in obtaining reliable information on actual or expected asset portfolios distribution by currencies, and the complexity of specifying a demand function for assets denominated in any one currency. However, the portfolio balance approach influences the spectrum of financial assets included in M, and M_f of equation (4.4). In other words, a wide range of domestic and foreign currency flows influences exchange rate changes.

4.6   SUMMARY

This chapter has argued that as developing financial markets evolved, management would have to provide more foreign currency services for its corporate and other customers. Banks would have to provide their customers not only spot, but also forward and swap transactions. It described these transactions and illustrated how the forward exchange rate could be determined by a combination of the current spot rate and interest rate differentials. The fundamental roles of financial market access, and currency convertibility, in facilitating foreign currency transactions at market rates were emphasized. In addition, the chapter has recognized that a bank's foreign currency trading activities, particularly if they result in open positions, would expose it to a variety of risks. These risks must be clearly understood and carefully managed, at least by monitoring compliance with established limits on credit, settlement, liquidity, and other risks. The dollarization phenomenon that enabled banks from developing financial markets to capture large amounts of US dollar deposits might encourage open positions that could result in positive or negative cash flows for the bank, depending on nature of the positions and the direction of any unanticipated exchange rate changes.

Finally, the chapter discussed the problems of forecasting exchange rates, and has suggested that current exchange rate forecasting techniques tended to produce long-term exchange rate forecasts that could not be effectively utilized by banks for their day-to-day or week-to-week management of their positions. However, on the assumption that foreign exchange markets are efficient, bank management could rely on current forward rates to predict future spot rates. If the markets are not efficient, and some banks have better information than others, there could be profit opportunities for the banks with the better information. No doubt, given a satisfactory level of technical competence in the bank's foreign currency trading department, such opportunities should be exploited within the established risk limits.

5 Term Financing and Compensating Balances

Banks in developing financial markets are faced with two conflicting requirements. The first is to serve as an important source of funds for firms wanting to expand or modernize; the second is to accommodate the capital funding needs of these firms through a method other than overdraft financing. In repressed financial markets, banks extended overdraft facilities to their business customers. These facilities were used to finance inventories, plant and equipment expansion or modernization, funding business losses, and for other unspecified purposes. While limits and review periods were established, these limits tended to be increased, and reviews were mainly to justify limit expansion. Business borrowers were seldom required to repay overdrafts or to demonstrate to management the assets being funded by the credit facility.

With increased interest rate volatility and deposit mobility that accompany financial market deregulation, controlling maturity and interest rate sensitivity gaps becomes an important element of liquidity and profitability management. Overdraft financing, with its tendency for unlimited maturity, increases the difficulty in managing maturity gaps and in adjusting asset portfolios to benefit from interest rate changes. At the same time, commercial banks will continue to be an important source of capital funds for businesses until securities markets develop to replace this funding source. Meanwhile, management will be expected to provide medium- and long-term funding for businesses while efficiently managing their maturity and interest rate sensitivity gaps.

This chapter argues that, through term-loans, banks in developing financial markets will continue to be the main providers of funds for business capital expenditures. However, because term-loans may be funded by short-term deposits and other liabilities, bank management will have to devise ways of minimizing the liquidity and interest rate risks associated with the resulting maturity gaps. Such devices may include compensating balances for term-loans extended under credit lines, loan sales with or without recourse, and credit securitization. The chapter, therefore, focuses on these devices and strongly suggests the need to review and abolish the practice of overdraft financing, standardize and improve credit documentation, and strengthen credit risk evaluation and loan pricing methods.

77

5.1   NATURE OF CAPITAL FUNDS

A bank loan has many dimensions including purpose, maturity, collateral, method of repayment, and type of borrowing. Banks providing capital funds for businesses may do so through term-loans identified by two of these dimensions, purpose and maturity. There are various types of term-loan for business purposes, as indicated in Box 5.1. The traditional overdraft facility common in many developing financial markets is not defined as a term-loan because more often than not it has no clear purpose or maturity. Overdraft financing may be replaced by intermediate term-loans that are repaid from the borrower's earnings or by interim credits repaid from the proceeds of new bond or stock issues.

The many firms with no access to the long-term securities market, will find bank credit the only practicable source of capital expenditure financing. Even for the few firms with access to this market, borrowing from banks may be a quicker, cheaper, and more convenient method of raising long-term funds, particularly through loans with maturities of 5 to 10 years, than the public offering of bonds or the floating of equities in the securities market.[1] Moreover, bank loans may be tailored to the needs of the individual borrower through direct negotiations with the lending bank,

Box 5.1   Term-loan categories

- *Ordinary term-loans*: these are business loans with an original maturity of more than 1 year and repayable in a lump sum or in periodic installments. Such loans typically are based on a formal loan agreement containing the terms and conditions of credit extension as well as various provisions regarding the loan administration and financial conduct of the debtor.
- *Bank credit extended under revolving credit agreement*: such loans may be classified as short-term business loans, because the notes evidencing the debt are of short-term maturity (for example days). The loan agreement, however, permits the borrower to renew the note at maturity for the next 90-day period, and so on, with the credits remaining on the books for periods as long as 2 years or more. Since the borrower enjoys a long-term use of credit, such loans might also be classified as term-loans.
- *Continuously renewed short-term loans*: many short-term loans are in effect term-loans because they are more or less routinely renewed whenever they come to maturity.
- *Business loans secured by real estate*: business firms often borrow from banks on a pledge of business property. A significant portion of such loans is of long-term maturity and the proceeds are typically used to finance capital expenditures or additions to permanent working capital.

thus giving the borrower more flexibility in determining repayment schedules, and frequently permitting more efficient use of the loan proceeds.[2]

Since long-term bank loans will be used to finance capital expenditures and will be repaid from the borrowers' internal cash flows (for example, current earnings or depreciation allowances) they are analogous to long-term credits extended by life insurance companies, pension funds, and other financial institutions and by individual investors in the bond, stock, and mortgage markets. However, the original maturity of new publicly offered corporate bonds may be considerably longer than the average maturities of a bank's term-loans.

Consequently, banks will be provided each year with a flow of repayments that is larger than the flow received by non-bank holders of corporate bonds, equities, and mortgages. The funds to be repaid to and relent by banks will reflect only shifts of existing funds from one business borrower to another. However, these shifts will represent a redirection of resources, from firms that are no longer in need of them to firms seeking to finance their capital expenditures through external financing. By shifting existing credits among various businesses, banks that move away from providing overdraft with no repayment term to term-loan financing will contribute a great deal of flexibility to the financing of capital formation.

Banks may offer a second type of capital funding assistance to firms by providing interim credits for financing the initial stages of new plant construction and other projects. The need for interim credit to fund capital projects may arise only gradually as work proceeds. Some firms, therefore, may be reluctant to borrow the full amount in the securities market at the outset. They may prefer interim financing in the form of a formalized revolving credit agreement or a short-term line of credit, with such facility being available for use for a specified period of time.[3] These arrangements that enable firms to borrow only the amount needed at each stage of the project, economizes on borrowing costs. At or near the time of completion of the project, and when exact long-term credit needs are finally known, the borrower will repay the interim bank debt from the proceeds of a new bank loan carrying a longer maturity or in countries with active securities markets, from the proceeds of sales of new securities in such markets.

Strategies for minimizing credit risks, and concerns about the cost and adequacy of capital of banks, particularly if the loan portfolio is funded by debt issues, are among the important management issues related to term-loan financing. Risk in lending comes from least two sources: (1) the borrower may not repay; and (2) the interest on funding sources (for example, deposits or debt) may not match the terms and pricing of the loans, thus exposing the bank to interest rate and repayment risk. Strict loan policies and procedures will have to be established, and compliance with them must be ensured. In addition, loan sales or credit securitization may be used to manage interest rate risk.[4]

Banks may attempt to minimize credit risk in two principal ways: (1) initially, through a review process before granting the loan, and (2) subsequently, through continuous credit monitoring and servicing. They may absorb the credit risk by holding the loan in their portfolios and ensuring that the ratios of capital to assets are equal or greater than their expected charge-offs on their asset (including term-loan) portfolios. In other words, banks will insulate their depositors and other creditors that fund their loan portfolios by supporting their obligations with adequate capital and competent management. In fact, competitive market conditions require banks to have an adequate level of capital that is subordinated to the claims of depositors and other creditors.

Because of this subordination, and the combination of risk and uncertainty associated with term and other lending, equity capital could be considerably more costly than deposit or debt funding. For banks to receive a reasonably low rate of interest on their bond issues, they will have to support their capital market borrowing with adequate equity capital. However, if the banks in developing financial markets are well managed and their liabilities are insured by the government or other reputable entity, they may be able to tap the capital markets with less equity than uninsured or unsatisfactorily managed financial entities.

Furthermore, capital markets will insist on adequate capital because beyond the expected credit risk there are certain risk factors that enhance the risk of lending by banks in developing financial markets. In return for the additional risk and uncertainty associated with these factors indicated in Box 5.2, capital markets will expect greater protection in the form of higher bank equity capitalization, higher yields on their funds, or both.

5.2   ALTERNATIVE CREDIT SOURCES

For business borrowers, at least two major types of funding arrangements may be available in some developing financial markets. These are capital markets instruments (for example, shares, bonds, and debentures) and commercial bank financing (for example, term-loans). Because of tax reasons, expenses associated with securities offerings, and the prevalence of family-owned and family-operated businesses, the market for new equity issues may be inactive in some developing financial markets.

Box 5.2   Loan portfolio risk enhancing factors

- *Expected loss rates*: each bank may concentrate the credit risk in its portfolio (for example, by region, industry, demographic strata and so on). Such concentration may render the concept of 'expected' loss rates inadequate. Expected loss rates are a reasonable measure of total risk for diversified portfolios, but the undiversified asset portfolios of banks in developing financial markets make the risk of catastrophic loss highly probable (for example, unanticipated events affecting the tourist, agricultural, and export sectors).
- *Lending discretion*: the bank can use its deposits and borrowings from the securities markets to finance its existing loan portfolios and to extend future loans with greater risk. This future credit extension capability further heightens creditors' level of uncertainty.
- *Non-credit risks*: banks in developing financial markets face a number of non-credit risks. Prominent among them are interest rate and prepayment risks, which may overweight credit risk under volatile interest rate and competitive market conditions.

Moreover, because of a long tradition of bank financing, and the relative efficiency and competitiveness of some banks, the banking market may be more attractive alternative to bond and equity markets in some countries. It is not surprising, therefore, that long-term bank loans, and especially loans against real estate and other fixed assets, continue to be used extensively for financing the capital needs of business in many developing countries.

In many Central and East European countries (CEECs), for example, securities markets are very small. It is quite normal for countries in their early stage of economic transformation, as has been the case of the CEECs, to have underdeveloped securities markets. The development of markets for government and corporate bonds, and other financial assets takes time. It involves setting up new institutions and trading arrangements. In addition, potential capital market participants such as households, institutional investors, and banks are inexperienced or have other reasons for not being able to build-up substantial financial portfolios. The development of equity markets is closely led by the pace of privatization. In the wake of the large scale privatization, investment funds and securities markets will begin to play a more important role.

In some countries, the long-term bond market is an important source of funds for the corporate sector that raised more by debt than by equity issues. However, some bond markets may experience a decline in corporate issues despite the need for external financing by firms because of: (1) the high levels and volatility of interest rates, and (2) the weight of the government's borrowing requirements. To the extent that governments dominate the bond markets, and interest rates are high and volatile, corporate borrowers will continue to access commercial banks for capital funding.

The role of banks in supplying capital funds to firms will be affected by the overall demand and supply for such funds. An important factor that affects this demand is an increase in the firms' internal cash flows (for example, retained earnings and depreciation allowances) relative to their capital expenditures. The effects of an increase in internal cash flows may be: (1) a reduction in business demand for bond market credit; (2) an unchanged demand for equity funds, and (3) an increased demand for intermediate bank credit.

There may be good reasons to believe that an increase in internal cash flows may result in a rise in the demand for bank credit. For instance, some firms, expecting an increased flow of cash from internal sources, may want to repay borrowings in a shorter period than that normally specified for a publicly offered bond, thus making bank term-loans a feasible alternative. Experience in developed financial markets has indicated that shifts between the banks and the bond market by borrowers are a feature of business cycles that affect variations in firms' internal cash flows.[5] Bank lending and bond financing tend to have an inverse cyclical relationship. Banks' extension of intermediate-term-loans tends to increase in the early part of business expansion, and thereafter to decline through mid-recessions. Bond financing generally tends to peak around recessions and to trough during business expansions.

It should be noted, however, that the inverse cyclical movements of bank lending and bond financing over a business cycle may be modified by factors that are unrelated to any stage of the cycle. In those developing financial markets that are at an advanced stage of evolution (for example, with active and competitive banking and securities markets) there may be several institutional and cyclical factors that induce firms to borrow less in one credit market and to borrow more in another during a given stage of a business cycle. For example, borrowers' preference for bank credit to bond market credit in the first phase of a business expansion may be explained by the relative ease of obtaining bank credit. At that time, it may be simpler to borrow from banks than to go through the relatively time-consuming procedures required by some bond markets. In addition, firms that are embarking on new capital expenditures, may want interim bank credits, to be repaid at the completion of the project from the proceeds of new bond issues.

During recessions, the long-term borrowing undertaken by firms may occur mainly in the bond market. By that time many firms might have completed their new capital projects and accessed the long-term bond market to refinance their interim bank indebtedness. In addition, during recessions the cost of bond market borrowing will tend to decline, and borrowers may want to refund a portion of their outstanding high-coupon bond debt with low-rate issues. Still, other borrowers may substitute bond credit for stock market financing during recessions, because stock prices tend to be depressed during such periods.

Management may realize that the timing of loan refundings in the bond market will be related to the level of interest rates in that market, and to firms' expectations of future interest rate changes. If these firms expect bond rates to increase in the near future, they may be inclined to borrow in the bond market before the increase occurs. Changes in the relative costs of bank and bond market borrowing may also explain the timing of bank loan refunding. When relative costs move in favour of bond financing, firms that want to refinance their interim bank debt will have an incentive to do so through bond financing. Conversely, if the cost of bond market credit becomes relatively high, business borrowers will have a reason to defer their loan refundings until a more favourable situation arises.

Even as the bond market matures and firms access that market for capital funds, banks in developing financial markets will continue to be an important source of capital finance. In fact banks will act as a buffer for the capital market, absorbing a significant proportion of the initial pressures for capital funds by medium-sized and large firms. They will, therefore, contribute to: (1) the relative stability of the market for business capital expenditure financing within a business cycle; and (2) more efficient financial planning by borrowers and ultimate lenders of long-term funds.

Possibly, even more importantly, banks may be significant lenders to firms with no access to the bond market and with insufficient internal cash flows to finance new plant expansion, or their more permanent working-capital needs. Banks may also lend to firms with internal cash flows that facilitate their contracting for capital expenditure financing of shorter maturity than are typical in the bond market. Particularly for those borrowers with no access to the bond market, the possibility of borrowing from the banks may be the decisive factor in the success of their capital expansion plans.

Management must adopt a structured approach to capital expenditure financing so as to cope with the risk inherent in developing financial markets. This approach emphasizes, among other things, term-loan financing, compliance with strict underwriting standards, credit policies and procedures, and informed and transparent loan pricing practices. Indeed, the structured approach reflects a changing function of banks in these markets. In addition to supplying short-term funds to businesses, a traditional commercial banking function, banks in these markets will be providing substantial amounts of medium-term funds, thus emerging as an important intermediary in the savings-investment process. However, these term-loans will have to be structured in a manner to allow for well defined exposure amounts, and repayment terms.

Indeed, the need for clearly defined lending dimensions (for example, purpose and maturity) is closely related to the need for careful management of the bank's liquidity condition, and earnings performance. This type of management may in part be achieved through the mechanisms of direct loan sales, and credit securitization. The overdraft method of lending does not permit adequate scope for utilizing such mechanisms. The service of providing capital funds for businesses will generate capital formation and facilitate the evolutionary adaptation of commercial banks and evolving securities market to the financial needs of savers and investors. The traditional overdraft service provided by banks in repressed financial markets and persisted in the liberalized ones will have to be reexamined, modified or replaced.

5.3   BALANCE REQUIREMENTS AND EFFECTS

Bank management may expect business customers to hold minimum average balances as a condition for extending term-loans made under a credit line arrangement. As banks become increasingly involved in financing capital projects, the practice of requiring such balances may become more widespread. Compensating balance requirements are usually expressed as a percentage of the line of credit or term-loan extended. The specific percentage may vary from bank to bank, and from borrower to borrower. In most cases, however, the volume of deposits is defined in terms of average balances held over a period of time, so that required balances may also serve to meet customer working balance needs.

Balance requirements may be raised or remain unchanged when the line is activated. Actual balances in such cases may indeed be at their lowest level when the credit line is used fully, the small balances at such times being offset by higher balances during periods when the line is being used less intensively or not at all. If loans are made to borrowers that are not required to maintain compensating balances against a credit line, or did not have a line before, balance requirement may become effective at the time of the loan approval. However, the lending bank may not require compensating balances if the borrower has been maintaining balances, or promises to do so in the future. These considerations underscore the fact that compensating balance requirements may be based on an informal understanding in which exact percentages are not specified. If the customer voluntarily holds balances in excess of what the bank requires, the subject of compensating balance is not likely to arise.

Of course, management's ability to impose compensation balance requirements on its borrowers will depend on the availability of alternative funding sources and the condition for accessing such sources. As competition for prime borrowers intensifies, the bank's ability to impose such requirements will decline. Meanwhile, the imposition of compensating balance requirements may take to the form of persuasion, higher interest rates, reduction in credit lines, or even outright cancellation of borrowing privileges, depending upon the persistence of the deficiency, the customer's current and potential value to the bank, and the credit market condition.[6] Under increasingly competitive conditions, large and prime borrowers may be more inclined to pay a market determined fee for all bank services than to maintain compensating balances. The issue for management then becomes one of efficient pricing of banking services provided to these borrowers.

Compensating balances may moderate fluctuations in deposit balances and improve liquidity management. Moreover, such balances may minimize credit risk to the extent that they may be used to offset part of the loss on a non-performing credit. Apart from liquidity issues, management may be interested in compensating balance requirements because of their influence on lending capacity, and earnings growth.

For an individual bank, compensating balance requirements can increase both deposits and loans, and thereby expand interest earnings. Table 5.1 illustrates that these requirements, however, can reduce the volume of withdrawable resources available to borrowers because part of the bank's funds is tied up in required reserves held against the borrowers' compensating balances. The illustration is based on the following assumptions: (1) a bank obtains a deposit of $1,050,000 from the public and is required to hold 20 per cent of this amount or $210,000 in required reserves; (2) the remaining $840,000 can be made available as loans to borrowing firms that immediately withdraw these funds to make payments. If the bank requires compensating balances of 20 per cent of the loan, given a 20 per cent reserve requirement, it can extend credit amounting to $1,000,000. The required reserves will be increased to $250,000, $40,000 more than the reserve needed in the absence of a compensating balance requirement. With a compensating balance, loan volume, liquidity reserves, and earnings potential will expand.

Table 5.1   Bank's balance sheet with and without compensating balances

	No compensating balances required ($000)		
Assets		*Liabilities*	
Required reserves	210	Initial deposits	1 050
Credit	840		
Total	1 050	Total	1 050
	Compensating balance required ($000)		
Assets		*Liabilities*	
Required reserves	250	Initial deposits	1 050
Credit	1 000	Compensating balance	200
Total	1 250	Total	1 250

Although an individual bank can increase its deposits through compensating balance requirements, the ability of the banking system as a whole to create deposits is limited by changes in the minimum required ratios, and actual reserves maintained. The higher the required reserves, the lower the systems's ability to create deposits through lending. However, to the extent that compensating balance requirements reduce day-to-day deposit volatility, they may increase the willingness of some banks to increase their lending capacity more fully than otherwise, thus increasing their deposits. Aside from these influences, compensation balance requirements will have no effect on the banking system's total deposits.

A bank that increases its own deposits by requiring compensating balances reduces deposits of other banks by the same amount. This is obviously the case where the borrower obtains the compensating balances by withdrawing funds deposited in other banks. It is also the case where the compensating balance is obtained directly from the lending bank as part of the loan, as illustrated in Table 5.1. In this illustration, the $200,000 compensating balance absorbs $40 of reserves that otherwise would have been available to support $200,000 of deposits by credit expansion elsewhere in the banking system.

5.4   BALANCE REQUIREMENTS AND THE CUSTOMER

Informal and flexible arrangements may be common where there is a continuing relationship between the bank and its customer. Compensating balances and credit lines may be merely one aspect of such a relationship.

The bank may be performing various services for the customer, in addition to extending credit, and in turn the customer may be promoting the bank to other firms. If such relationships are mutually beneficial, the exact nature of the customer's obligation to comply with the balance requirements may not be explicitly stated. In fact, the borrower may view compensating balances as the price to be paid for the bank's loan or credit commitment. At the same time, the balances may also serve to compensate the bank for other services. The cost to the borrower will depend on whether the balances needed exceed those the customer would voluntarily hold to carry on the business even in the absence of any requirement.

It may be argued that if a borrower is required to hold compensating balances that cannot be withdrawn, the loan amount granted under the credit line may overstate the actual volume of funds that can effectively be used. By the same token, it may appear that the effective interest rate (that is, the interest payment on the proportion of usable funds) will be higher than the contractual rate. Even in cases where such conclusions are valid, the higher cost may be offset by: (1) the value to the customer of the informal guaranteee of loan accommodation under the credit line; and (2) the value of any other bank services received. But these collateral benefits aside, compensating balance requirements may not increase the effective cost of credit to the borrower that traditionally or voluntarily maintains adequate working balances which are equal or greater than the required amount.

Most business borrowers may need substantial working balances. In markets where continuing and often increasing overdraft financing is not the normal method of financing, firms must maintain an average level of deposits for the purpose of bridging the day-to-day gaps between payments and receipts, as well as to meet special contingencies (for example, emergencies and opportunities) requiring immediate cash resources. Actual balances held for this purpose may fluctuate markedly, but since compensating balance requirements are stated in terms of average balances over a period, they may in fact be used to satisfy the firm's working balance needs. Where required balances are equal to or less than the average balances the borrower wants to hold for its working balance needs, the balance requirement will not reduce the effective availability of funds to the borrower.

Thus, in Table 5.1, a borrower that seeks to hold working balances of $200,000 may not be adversely affected by the $200,000 balance requirement. The compensating balance requirement merely obligates the borrower to hold its working balance at the lending bank rather than elsewhere. As far as the lending bank is concerned, the arrangement assures a continuing bank-customer relationship. Customer's deposit adds to the bank's lending capacity and earnings potential, thus encouraging them to offer larger loans or lower contractual rates than those offered to non-customers.

Indeed, if a potential borrower, with a significant working balance need, does not have a formal compensating balance arrangement with its existing bank, but holds large average working balances, another bank may be able to solicit its business by offering a relatively lower contractual rate of interest should the borrower transfer a balance large enough to meet the soliciting bank's balance requirement. Where borrowers already have a compensating balance arrangement that is reflected in loan rates lower than those charged to non-depositors, the scope for this inducement will be limited.[7]

In spite of market pressures to reduce or eliminate compensating balance requirements, there are at least four reasons for such requirements to persist in some developing financial markets. These reasons are: (1) some banks may have a special incentive to require the maintenance of such balances in order to solidify bank-customer relationship, from which the customer obtains collateral advantages; (2) compensating balances may administratively be the most convenient way of paying the bank for services, despite the added cost to the bank for holding reserves against idle deposits; (3) compensating balance requirements may be rendered inflexible by the bank's desire to maintain uniformity of requirements or contractual rates of interest among different borrowers of the same general type; and (4) the upward adjustments in the contractual rate needed to offset any reduction or elimination of compensating balances may be restrained in some cases by limitations on contractual interest rates that management may want to impose in order to preserve selected customer relationships. If borrowers are generally satisfied with their banking relationship, competitive pressures that may cause downward adjustments in compensating balance requirements may not develop.

Nevertheless, bank management may have bank-customer relationship problems in situations where compensating balances exceed borrowers' working balance needs. It is quite probable that customers' rejection of compensating balance requirements in excess of the working balance needs will grow as contractual interest rates and alternative credit providers increase. In response to this rejection, bank management: (1) may educate their customers to accept the compensating balance requirement; and (2) facilitate the creation of financing devices that enable customers to comply with the requirement. In some developed financial markets, compensating balance requirements in excess of working balance needs have resulted in the creation a 'link financing' device that connects the bank, its customer and other financial market participants in an effort to fund these requirements.[8] Liberalized financial markets allow for innovative responses to changing needs.

This device may be illustrated by a simple example. Assume a borrower receiving a $100,000 loan is required by the bank to keep a compensating balance of 20 per cent (that is, $20,000) but wants to use the full amount of the loan to effect payments. Both the borrower and the bank may be satisfied if the borrower can find a third party deposit provider (for example, an insurance company, mutual fund, or pension fund) willing to deposit $20,000 of its own money, perhaps in the form of a certificate of deposit (CD) in the borrower's bank. In this way, the lending bank obtains the compensating balance of $20,000, the borrower gets the use of the entire $100,000 loan, and the deposit provider receives a CD. In some instances, the supplier may provide deposits equal to the full amount of the loan, rather than merely the compensating balances, and subsequently sell part or all of its CD to other investors.[9]

Although the supplier of deposits in a link-financing arrangement may be paid a fee by the borrower, it will also receive interest on the CD held by the lending bank. The combination of fee and interest income sources will be a major inducement to the flow of deposits available for funding increased amounts of term-loans. Notwithstanding the fact that the borrower may have to pay a fee to the deposit provider, link financing may be the least expensive means for the borrower to access the full amount of funds it requires.

If the bank is willing to increase the loan size by an amount sufficient to cover the compensating balance requirement, the added charge can exceed the cost to the borrower of obtaining the deposit through a link-financing arrangement. Where the bank is unwilling to increase the loan size, the alternative to link financing may be borrowing from non-banking entities at a higher contractual rate of interest. For the borrower, link financing can reduce, but cannot eliminate, the cost imposed by compensating balance requirements in excess of working balance needs. For the lending bank, a compensating balance in the form of a CD has the advantage of reducing the volume of required reserve that must be held against the deposit because reserve requirements tend to be lower for term deposits than for demand deposits. They also contribute to the bank's liquidity management if the term of the CD coincides with the term of the loan extended under the credit line.

Evidence in developed financial markets indicates that compensating balance requirements are responsive to cyclical changes in economic conditions. In periods of declining interest rates, when management may want an expansion in loan volume, banks will tend to reduce compensating balance requirements as an additional incentive for actual and potential borrowers. Similarly, during periods of economic stringency and increasing interest rates, management may want to increase balance requirements. Even banks with a policy of fixed ratios of compensating balances to loans or credit lines, regardless of the economic conditions, may pursue the policy more vigorously in periods of rising interest rates and loan demand than in periods of falling interest rates and contracting loan volume. Such variations in the enthusiasm to enforce the policy requirement reflect management's flexibility in adjusting to changing market conditions without changing the contractual interest rate.

Flexibility in the application of balance requirements can, therefore, be a mechanism for transmitting changes in the cost and availability of credit to the market for commercial or business loans. On the availability side, increases in these requirements or in the enthusiasm for enforcing them may immobilize a larger part of loans and deposits in cases where required balances already equal or exceed working balance needs. On the cost side, increases in the required balance ratio will raise the effective interest rates paid by borrowers with small working balance needs.

5.5   CREDIT SECURITIZATION

Granted that banks in developing financial markets are required to finance capital expenditures by term-loans and that compensating balance requirements may alleviate maturity and pricing mismatches arising from the use of shorter-term liabilities to fund longer-term assets, management may be able to reduce undesirable mismatches while providing capital funds to businesses through a continuing process of loan sale, or credit securitization.

Besides the need to manage maturity and interest rate risks, and to generate fee income, loans sales may be motivated by the desire to have the capacity to meet increasing demand for capital expenditure financing. The outright sale of loans, particularly those made to top-quality borrowers may be done on an interbank basis (that is, banks participating in loans originated by other banks). The loan originating banks will earn origination fees and may attempt to retain a portion of the spread.

Loan purchasers may be the smaller banks with high liquidity positions and low loan originating ability. Loan purchasing may be attractive for two reasons: (1) it provides the banks, with little or no previous experience in lending to top quality borrowers, access to such borrowers; and (2) it offers an opportunity for the buyers to earn higher rates of return on their asset portfolios. But if loan sales are on a recourse basis, the originating banks will not achieve the objective of an outright sale, that is to replace the loans with more liquid assets. Credit securitization, which allows for non-recourse loan sales to specialized institutions that fund themselves through the issue of short- or long-term securities, facilitates the achievement of this objective.

In developed financial markets, credits are securitized through four structural components or processes as follows: (1) special-purpose vehicles; (2) pooling of borrowers; (3) credit structuring and enhancements; and (4) repackaging of cash flows. These processes may be transferred to the credit securitization activities in developing financial markets. Figure 5.1 illustrates a basic structure of an asset backed security.

A special-purpose vehicle is a trust or corporation established for the sole purpose of owing the loans. The special purpose vehicle then issues securities that are bought by investors. The intention of this vehicle is to isolate the risks inherent in the loans placed in the vehicle, from all the other risk of the bank originating the loans. Through the special-purpose vehicle, loans to different borrowers are pooled in order to reach a minimum size necessary to justify an issue of securities to the public; and to facilitate the diversification of credit risk.

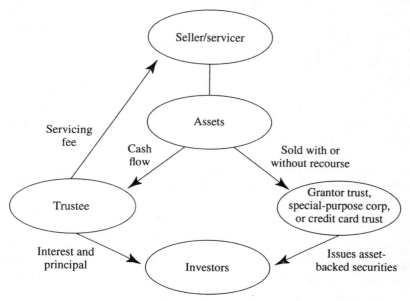

Figure 5.1   The credit securitization process

The loans are pooled, generally into homogeneous vehicles, before being sold to the special-purpose vehicles. This pooling and sale of assets make the loans more transparent, and reduce uncertainties for potential investors. Since the pool is pre-specified, investors know the risk they are absorbing. In fact, they are funding only a clearly delineated existing pool of loans. They are neither funding future discretionary lending or risk taking in which the originating bank may engage, nor are they absorbing interest rate or other risks, that may be borne by the originating bank but are not incorporated in the loan pool itself.

Once the pool of loans and the related collateral are segregated in a special-purpose vehicle, a credit underwriter (for example, a bank, finance company or an insurance company) can assess and underwrite the credit risk in that specific pool of loans and then guarantee the credit risk. Such a guarantee can raise the credit risk of the pool to investment-grade levels. This improved risk profile, in turn, allows large classes of investors, with no skill or desire to assess credit risk, to invest in the securities issued by the special-purpose vehicle.

In some cases, the special-purpose vehicle will repackage the cash flows from the loans and issue tranches of varying maturity.[10] Each tranche will have a different expected life reflecting the expected repayment patterns of the underlying loan. As the loans are paid off by the borrowers, the principal first goes to the first tranche until it is paid off, then to the second tranche until this is paid off, and accordingly to subsequent tranches until they are paid off. This structure enables the loan packager to tailor the cash flows of the different tranches to appeal to particular investor preferences.[11]

Loans with the following characteristics are ideal for securitization: (1) predictable cash flows; (2) consistently low delinquency and default experience; (3) total amortization of principal at maturity; (4) an average maturity of more than one year; (5) several demographically and geographically diverse borrowers; (6) underlying collateral with high liquidation value and utility to the borrowers; and (7) loan interest higher than the market rate of return on the asset-backed security. When measured against these characteristics, overdraft facilities will not be an ideal asset for securitization. Assets that do not have these characteristics may still be eligible for securitization if their credit quality is enhanced. A principal objective of credit enhancement is to ensure that, in the event that the cash flows on the underlying loans may be insufficient to pay the full amount of the credit backed securities on a timely basis, such payments will be obtained from some other source considered reliable.

Since a certain amount of loss can be expected on the assets collateralizing the loans being securitized, credit enhancement is important to improve the quality of the securities issued. Credit enhancement may take many forms, including: (1) limited guarantee by, or recourse to the originating bank or the issuing agency; (2) a standby letter of credit; (3) a reserve or spread account; (4) a surety bond; (5) over-collateralization; and (6) a combination of these forms.[12] Surely, the value of the enhancement will depend on the credit rating of the company providing this service. That company must have a credit rating at least as good as the rating sought for the asset-backed security.

While the credit securitization benefits accruing to individual banks can be categorized as strategic and financial as indicated in Box 5.3, they may be more specifically described in terms of such principal players in the process as: (1) the originating banks or the issuing institutions; (2) the investment banker or underwriter of the related credit-backed securities; (3) guarantors of the credit risk; (4) the borrowers; and (5) the investors.

Banks that are selling loans to a special-purpose vehicle gain a number of immediate benefits. One of the principal immediate benefits is that they can free up equity capital which can otherwise be used to support the assets on their balance sheets. The actual credit risk implied by the regulatory capital requirements for banks, may be much higher than the actual expected credit losses inherent in adequately collateralized term-loans. Thus, banks, with an 8 per cent capital requirement, for example, and an adequately collateralized portfolio of loans reflecting an anticipated loan loss of 1 per cent, will have excess capital of 7 per cent. Selling the loans to a special-purpose vehicle, that in turn issues debt securities which are credit enhanced at a cost that reflects the actual credit risks of the loan, eliminates the excess capital.

There are other benefits to the originating bank. For example, with credit securitization the originating bank accesses a new funding source, and eliminates any interest rate risk it may have from keeping the loan on its balance sheet. Securitization can be a cost-effective way of neutralizing the interest rate risk associated with floating-rate deposits or other liabilities funding fixed-rate loans. It also allows the originating bank to expand its lending, since capital becomes less of a constraint on growth. A not so obvious additional benefit from credit securitization is that the credit-enhanced issues may be a better credit risk than the loans of an originating bank which has subsequently experienced asset quality and other safety and soundness problems. Finally, credit securitization affords

Box 5.3   Credit securitization benefits

Strategic benefits:

- *Loan growth and scale economies*: credit securitization enables banks to increse their financing activity without inflating their balance sheets. It allows for greater economies of scale in loan underwriting and servicing.
- *Barriers to entry*: credit securitization makes it easier for small banks to originate business and other loans.
- *Asset liquidity*: credit securitization makes loans more marketable and permits asset replacement or redeployment.
- *Earnings*: loan scales can be timed so that gains and losses can be recognised at the time desired.

Financial benefits:

- *Asset-liability matching*: the interest rate, maturity, and duration risks associated with financing a specific pool of loans are removed when the loans are sold. For foreign currency denominated loans, any currency risk is also eliminated. The risk-removal attribute of credit securitization is attractive in volatile financial markets.
- *Fee income*: credit securitizaton changes the nature of earnings on a portfolio from spread income to fee income. Spread income is earned by lending at a higher rate than borrowing. In a volatile financial market, spread income is subject to the risk that funds cannot be borrowed or deposits obtained over the life of the portfolio at a rate sufficiently low to generate a profit. Fee income earned by the loan originating bank is immune to interest rate changes, and grows without capital constraint. In effect, the bank is not compensated for its ability to borrow funds or obtain deposits at attractive rates, and to guess interest rate movements successfully. It is compensated for its ability to originate loans at attractive rates and provide cost-effective servicing after the loans are securitized.
- *Financial measurements*: unlike loan funding, loan securitization requires little or no equity underpinning. The reduction of loans on the balance sheet, improves a variety of financial measures such as returns on equity and assets and capital adequacy ratios.

---

the originating bank the opportunity to create new products by freeing it from the constraint of its own balance sheet. Banks that are not inclined to extend medium-term fixed-rate loans to small firms except at substantially high rates of interest may change their position if these loans are securitized. With securitization, interest rate risk is transferred and banks are able to create a product that enables them to earn substantial risk-free interest income and fees.

For the underwriters, guarantors, borrowers and investors the benefits are increased fee income, cost savings, increased credit availability, and investment options. The obvious benefits to the underwriters are the underwriting fees and trading of their inventory. Guarantors of credit risk can charge fees in excess of expected losses without having to extend any loans. In the short-term, credit securitization may offer little benefit to the borrowers. In the longer-term, however, as more assets are securitized, competition may force the originating banks to share the savings from securitization with borrowers by reflecting such savings in lower borrowing costs. A major benefit to the borrowers will be the increasing availability of credit on terms that lenders will not provide if they were forced to keep the loans on their own balance sheet. For investors, the main benefit of securitization is that it increases the volume and variety of their investment options.

The success of credit securitization in developing financial markets will depend on certain specific market conditions.[13] These conditions are: (1) the existence of positive real interest rates and positively sloped yield curves that enhance the appeal of long-term bonds to investors and make them more attractive to market-makers to hold and trade; (2) management's emphasis on the desirability of liquidity and marketability of their banks' assets translated into a shift from the traditional overdraft financing to marketable term-loans which are easily packaged into securities; and (3) the ability of the securities market to raise a significant amount of capital at short notice, and to provide secondary market support because of market depth and liquidity. The banks themselves may be major players in the bond market.

In addition to the market considerations, the success of credit securitization in developing financial markets will depend on the market's perception of the originating bank's ability to originate good quality, properly priced and adequately documented loans.[14] The principal factors that influence this perception are: (1) the bank's asset knowledge; (2) its credit policy and procedures; (3) the predictability and adequacy of the loan portfolio's cash flows; and (4) the bank's ability to service the loans after they are securitized.[15]

For a bank to become a successful originator of loans for securitization, it must be perceived by market participants (for example, the rating agencies, credit enhancers, and investors) as a competent lender with an efficient collection and servicing operation. To execute an efficient and profitable securitized transaction, the bank must have accurate information about its loans and collateral, and must understand its servicing and collection capabilities and costs. The extent of such information and understanding will affect the pricing of the issue and the amount of credit enhancement necessary. A thorough knowledge of the loans being securitized will allow the originating bank or any other seller to provide the information required by the investors, and will demonstrate the bank's lending and servicing competence.

A review of the originating bank's credit policy and procedures is an important element of the due diligence process. The reviewers, including attorneys and accountants, will attempt to verify that the originating bank's policy and procedures are formalized and adequate, and that they are followed by the bank's credit staff. If a bank fails to demonstrate the efficiency of its credit approval practices, and consistency of its staff's compliance with these policy and procedures, the rating of its loan portfolio may be downgraded, thus reflecting on the portfolio's marketability. Bank management in developing financial markets has tended to de-emphasize the importance of formalized credit policy and procedures, because, particularly for privately owned banks, such policy and procedures appeared too constraining.

Cash flows can have a powerful effect on the attractiveness of the originating bank's loan portfolio. Because an overdraft facility does not normally have cash flow predictability, it will not be an attractive asset for securitization. Cash flow predictability, as well as adequacy, will affect the charge-off and liquidity reserve or escrow the credit enhancer will require from the originating bank. Cash flow predictability will be influenced by the: (1) actual maturity of individual loans; (2) expected charge-offs; (3) method of interest computation; and (4) expected prepayment of the loans. For each loan identified for sale, management should specify the contractual maturity and determine the cash flows from principal and interest. However, such cash flows will depend on the method of interest income recognition being used. It may be necessary for all banks selling loans to a single loan pool to have a standardized method of interest income recognition.[16] If the cash flows are sufficiently predictable, then the next issue is whether they are adequate to support the principal and interest at the pass-through rate due to the investors; the fee due to servicer; and the predetermined charge-off coverage required by the credit enhancer.

Although loan sales may be made on the condition that the originating bank continues to service the loans, thus earning the related fees, and the right to any excess servicing cash flows, the retention of servicing rights may not be an automatic but an earned opportunity for the bank. This retention must be earned or granted. Servicing rights are, in theory granted by the investors, who are the new owners of the assets. As these rights and associated income benefits can be forfeited if the bank fails to perform the servicing function efficiently, bank management must understand the normal expectations of the investors, and the specific conditions of the servicing agreements.

In spite of the benefits and the existence of certain general and specific factors that contribute to its success, credit securitization may be subject to severe limitations that influence the speed of its implementation in developing financial markets. One limitation is the shortage of skilled individuals to structure and implement a credit securitization deal. Lawyers, accountants, and other professionals with expertise in credit securitization may be scarce or non-existence in these markets.

Another limitation is the time needed to develop the related documentation. It may take a considerable amount of time for accountants to complete all the details before an attractive pool of loans can be identified, underwritten, and placed with investors. No doubt, the process gets easier over time, as a result of learning by doing. However, any bank wanting to raise funds, through a securitized credit issue for the first time, must invest a substantial amount of resources in loan origination, documentation, servicing and other systems before the issue can be sold.

Finally, the legal and regulatory framework that removes any ambiguity about the rights and responsibilities of the participants in the securitization process must be established and effectively operational. In addition, the regulatory system must be structured to facilitate loan origination and sales. Normally, for a loan to be removed from the bank's balance sheet, regulators may want it to be sold strictly on a non-recourse basis. If there is any recourse, the loan sale treatment for regulatory purposes may be denied and the strategic goal of reducing the amount of capital against assets will not be achieved. In the absence of an effective credit enhancement mechanism, investors will want to have recourse to the originating bank, and if such recourse is available, the regulators will want the loan sale to be included in the bank's capital requirement computation.

5.6 SUMMARY

This chapter has argued that banks have been and will continue to be the principal source of business capital expenditure financing in developing financial markets. In some repressed financial markets, the overdraft method of financing firms permitted lending with no specific purpose and maturity. This financing method has persisted in some developing financial markets. Firms have tended to use their overdraft facilities to finance not only their business inventories, and capital expenditures, but also the personal and private expenditures of their owners and managers. Overdraft limits were set but were often not observed by the debtor firms or enforced by bank management.

The circumstances of developing financial markets with their enhanced credit, liquidity, prepayment, and interest rate risk have suggested new ways of funding business capital expenditures. This chapter has therefore emphasized term-loan financing to ensure a clear purpose and maturity of banks' loan portfolios; compensating balance requirements to alleviate liquidity management problems and to promote bank-customer relationship; loan sales and credit securitization to manage more efficiently interest rate, prepayment, and other risks. It has underscored: (1) the importance of adequate capital for banks wanting to fund their loan portfolios by debt issues; (2) the need for a legal and regulatory framework that facilitated asset origination and sale, and provided capital market participants transparency and confidence in the banks, their management, and the term-loans they originate for sale or securitization; and (3) the relevance, for the success of banks' term-loan financing programme, of formal credit policies and procedures, strict and uniform credit documentation and underwriting standards, and rational loan pricing practices.

6 Managing Credit Risk

In repressed financial markets, banks generated surplus profits in part because market entry restrictions enabled them to overcompensate themselves for the credit risk they took while paying low rates of interest on deposits and borrowing. Deregulation of these markets and the accompanying increased competition between banks and non-bank entities reduced the banks' privileged market position, and eroded their surplus profits. As a result, increased risk-taking and the proper pricing of credit and other risks became central issues for effective management of banks in developing financial markets.

With deregulation, banks soon realized that successful credit risk management lies not so much in avoiding risks as in avoiding surprises. Surprises may be avoided by establishing risk limits and monitoring compliance with these limits. Although banks are required to take some risks for the opportunity to earn profits sufficient to absorb the losses associated with such risk-taking, and to contribute to their capital expansion, no bank would lend if it knows that the probability of repayment is remote or beyond a tolerable risk limit.

This chapter identifies a general challenge, as well as specific challenges in the credit function for bank management in developing financial markets. It focuses on the advantages of establishing formal credit policy guidelines and the credit policy areas to be addressed by the board. It alludes to the policy issues of proper pricing of credit risk but defers the specifics of pricing to a later chapter. Finally, the chapter discusses a set of credit administration and problem loan issues including the need to establish systems and procedures to monitor and control operations, fraud and other risks.

6.1 CHALLENGES

Credit risk is the risk that a borrower will fail to perform according to the terms and conditions of the credit or loan agreement, thus causing the lender to suffer a financial loss on the transaction. This failure may be the result of bankruptcy, a temporary change in market conditions, or other factors adversely affecting the borrower's ability to pay.

A major challenge for credit risk management is to preserve public confidence, while engaging in credit and other banking activities in which losses will occur. Success in meeting this challenge will depend on presenting management as: (1) knowledgeable about the risks inherent in those activities and about the deficiencies in the bank's risk management system; (2) capable of correcting these deficiencies and facing the consequences to the bank's operations when losses occur; and (3) having in place appropriate credit policies and procedures, and a rational system of risk identification, measurement, control, and pricing.

More specifically, bank management in developing financial markets has a number of risk management challenges arising from two main sources: (1) from internal credit policy or credit administration deficiencies that management may be able to correct; and (2) from such external factors as normal business cycles, and a collapse of export prices due to abrupt swings from conditions of excess demand to excess supply, that are beyond the control of management. However, while management may be unable to control the external factors, it must establish an early warning system that facilitates monitoring the impact of these factors on the borrowers' ability to repay. Box 6.1 lists a set of external factors that weaken the financial condition of borrowers, and heighten the risk management challenges for banks.[1]

The risk management process for banks in developing financial markets has many deficiencies that can be corrected by management.[2] These deficiencies, indicated in Box 6.2, include the absence of a formal credit policy, credit classifications, and risk-related credit loss reserves. Most of these deficiencies existed even before deregulation and persisted after deregulation although the probability of loss from lending activities increased substantially, and the need for effective credit risk management became more compelling.

Box 6.1   Financial condition weakening factors

- Persistent government controls of enterprises (for example, licenses, permits).
- External and internal political pressures (for example, trade restrictions, environmental laws).
- Production difficulties (for example, strikes, supply shortages).
- Market disruptions (for example, price collapse, new laws and regulations).
- Instability in business environment (for example, high and unstable inflation, interest and exchange rates).

Box 6.2   Common credit risk management deficiencies

- The lack of a formal credit policy (for example, written policy approved by the board).
- The absence of credit concentration limits (for example, sector, industry and geographic limits).
- Inadequately defined lending limits for credit officers and credit committee.
- Insufficient analysis and review of borrowers' financial condition.
- Excessive dependence on collateral in credit decisions and failure to improve collateral as credit quality deteriorates.
- Inadequate monitoring and control in the credit process including failure to control and audit this process.
- Inadequate credit documentation.
- The practice of indefinitely accruing income on non-performing credits.
- The failure to classify credits in terms of severity of risk and to provide for losses based on such classifications (for example, substandard, doubtful, loss).

6.2   ESTABLISHING CREDIT POLICY AND GUIDELINES

The establishment of a formal credit policy has certain advantages for banks operating in developing financial markets. For example, such a policy: (1) provides standards and reference points that credit officers can use to guide their decisions without frequent referrals to higher management; (2) eliminates the tendency for the concentration of credit decisions on a small number of senior officers, and improves the speed and uniformity of the credit decision process; and (3) defines the bank's objectives in terms of credit risk and return.

The concentration of credit decisions on a few senior credit officers can impede the development of other credit officers excluded from the decision stage, and can contribute to a diversity of lending practices and philosophies within the bank, eventually leading to asset quality problems. A formal credit policy directs the use of the bank's resources and influences decisions about whether or not to lend. Moreover, if a bank is to attain its lending objectives while maintaining the confidence of its depositors and shareholders, its lending must be conducted in an orderly manner as prescribed by the standards and reference points stated in its credit policy.[3]

It should be noted that the establishment of a credit policy does not mean that the board itself has to write the policy. This policy may be formulated and written by senior management. It simply means that the

Box 6.3   Selected credit policy issues

- *Legal considerations*: a statement of the bank's legal lending limits consistent with related laws and regulations.
- *Delegation of authority*: a precise statement on the credit limits of individuals authorized to extend credit and the conditions for extending such credit. Credit limits may be approved by written resolution at least annually.
- *Types of credit extension*: a delineation of the acceptable and unacceptable credit types.
- *Pricing*: the price to be charged for different credit types and different markets. The need for price uniformity within the same market.
- *Market area*: precise definition of the bank's market area to determine the composition of its credit portfolio by type, maturity, and credit repayment plan and consistent with the bank's size, capital, and risk tolerance.
- *Credit standards*: the qualitative and quantitative standards for acceptable credit of different types.
- *Credit approval procedures*: measures for granting sound credits consistent with credit standards. Credit procedures may be covered in a separate manual.

policy when written should be approved by the board not in a perfunctory manner but after careful consideration by each director. Box 6.3 indicates some of the credit policy areas on which the board may focus.

Undoubtedly, the credit policy will reflect the bank's asset management objectives as indicated by its liquidity, risk-return and other ratios. Among these ratios are the maximum credit to deposits, capital to risk assets, credit loss reserves to total credit, and return on asset ratios. Given the deposit and capital levels, compliance with the credit to deposit, and capital to assets ratios will limit the amount of credit the bank can create to the growth of its deposits and capital. Furthermore, given the asset size, a bank with strong historic and perspective earnings will be in a better position to withstand anticipated credit losses than its competitors with a weak earnings performance record. The credit policy of a bank with persistently high return of assets, and high capital-asset ratios may be more permissive than that of a bank with less impressive operating results. While it is true that high earnings imply high-risk lending activities, persistently high earnings by banks operating in competitive markets may suggest the effective implementation of the policy and the monitoring and control of related risks.

Once the credit policy establishes the size of the overall portfolio, it should concentrate on the desired distribution between the various types of credit (for example, commercial, industrial, consumer, trade, agricultural, mortgage, and other credit types) within the portfolio. Among the factors determining the desired levels of these credits are the nature, trends, and stability of the bank's deposits, and the proportions of time, savings, and demand deposits in its total deposits. Although deposit stability, relative shares, and trends are important determinants of a bank's credit portfolio distribution, the needs of the market being served will also influence this distribution. The credit policy may emphasize the granting of mortgage, consumer, and higher yielding loans if the bank has a core of stable savings and time deposits; and short-term commercial or industrial credit and trade finance if the bank's deposits are less stable. In addressing agricultural credit, the policy may recognize the seasonal demand for such credit and the special problems in agriculture that may convert a short-term credit facility to a long-term or non-performing one.

Given the general credit needs of the market being served, the credit policy should indicate the acceptable and unacceptable credit types. As it may be easier to specify the unacceptable types than the acceptable ones, the policy statement on acceptable credit may be broad and less specific than the statement on unacceptable credit. Moreover, because a bank is normally chartered to serve a particular community, the policy position on unacceptable and acceptable credit must be compatible with the bank's overall responsibility to meet the legitimate credit needs of that community. Box 6.4 provides examples of acceptable and unacceptable credit that may be included in a bank's credit policy. Unacceptable credit will vary from one bank to the next but, in general, the policy should include illegal or speculative credit.

Apart from directing the size and distribution of the credit portfolio, and stipulating the acceptable and unacceptable credit types, the board has other specific responsibilities with respect to establishing the bank's credit policy. One of these is to ensure that credit officers to whom lending authority is delegated are technically competent to evaluate and price the various risks, and to extend credits that are collectable and consistent with the bank's credit policy.

The board may delegate lending authority to individual credit officers, groups or combinations of two or more credit officers, and formal credit committees. The selected delegation will be influenced by the competence of the credit officers, size of the portfolio, the type of credit being extended, and market competition. If the competition requires prompt decisions, the individual credit officer may be granted considerable scope. However, since the competence of credit officers may vary widely,

Box 6.4   Acceptable and unacceptable credits

Acceptable credit

- Short-term self-liquidating working capital loans.
- Credit to experienced farmers with identifiable repayment sources (for example, crop loan).
- Credit to finance an inventory of commodities or other inventory or accounts receivable where the collateral is a negotiable instrument (for example, negotiable warehouse receipts) or a perfected lien.
- Non-speculative construction loans with firm refinancing commitments from long-term lenders.
- Various kinds of consumer loans reflecting market demand.
- Term and revolving credits.
- First mortgage on single family homes with adequate equity.
- Credit secured by good quality properly margined (for example, rated) marketable securities.

Unacceptable credit

- Loans to finance a change in business ownership.
- Inadequately collateralized credit to new businesses.
- Unsecured loans for real estate purposes.
- Credit where the source of repayment is public or private financing not firmly committed.
- Credit based on unmarketable securities.
- Term credit of more than a certain maturity.

individual lending authority must be determined by the weakest credit officer, and group or committee credit limits may be the preferred arrangement.

Certain descriptive features of the approval function must be included in the bank's credit policy. These features may indicate a clear definition of a secured and unsecured credit, and other specific credit approval components. Box 6.5 provides examples of these components. In repressed financial markets, credit may be granted because it fits into the government's programme of credit to priority sector, industries or firms. It may also be granted to a particular firm because the firm is wholly or partly owned by the government or the credit itself is guaranteed by the government. In developing financial markets with no, or limited government intervention, credit decisions may be based strictly on risk-return considerations. There should be sufficient policy guidelines to assist management to determine the risk trade-off that ensures the bank's safety and soundness. It is, therefore, important for the bank's credit policy to state clearly the criteria that the credit officers must apply in the credit approval process. Box 6.6 provides some idea of the information that should be

Box 6.5   Credit approval components

- A definition of secured and unsecured credit.
- A definition of the borrowers' total liability to protect the bank against excessive. extensions of credit to affiliates, subsidiaries, principals and related entities.
- The establishment of committees, naming the members, the chairman, secretary, voting procedures and quorum, and lending limits. There may be committees for various types of credit.
- The establishment of joint authority to enable certain credit officers to approve specified amounts of credit.
- The listing of individual loan limits, by credit officer and loan type, amount, and secured and unsecured lending.

Box 6.6   Criteria or information for commercial credit

- For a closely held firm, annual financial statements of its principal and the firm.
- Additional financial information when: (a) establishing a line of credit; (b) repayment ability is doubtful; and (c) borrowers' financial condition has deteriorated and may continue to deteriorate during the term of the credit.
- Credit guarantees by the principals for small or closely held firms.
- Lines of credit considerations for example, compensating balances; payout periods; and separate credit agreement for converting the credit line into a loan with a definite maturity date.
- Criteria to support unsecured credit.
- Promissory note renewal considerations.
- Collateral considerations: When a business credit is collateralized, there are considerations about the collateral that influence the credit amount as a percentage of the collateral and the credit maturity.
- Examples of collateral are: Securities: (a) government and other highly rated securities; (b) listed stocks and unlisted but publicly traded stocks; (c) stocks of closely held companies. Equipment: (a) specialized equipment; (b) readily marketable equipment. Receivables: (a) types of receivables acceptable by assignment; (b) margin requirements on acceptable receivables; (c) notification procedures; (d) time period for the credit. Inventories: (a) floating liens on all inventories; (b) commodity and other loans against bills of lading or warehouse receipts.
- Loan commitments: time limitations; and amount committed.
- Considerations about term credit to firms: maximum term of credit, repayment schedules (monthly, quarterly, semi-annually, or annually) related to the type of collateral and capacity of the borrower and purpose for term credit (for example, purchase equipment, refinance debt; increase working capital).
- Credit agreement restrictions.

obtained and the criteria that are relevant in making a business credit decision.

The bank's credit policy may be supplemented by general and specific guidelines or directives. The general guidelines may deal with such matters as credit concentration, account relationships, compensating balances, and documentation. The specific guidelines may detail the term and evidence of indebtedness for particular types of credit and commitments, credit to collateral ratios, and review intervals for credit lines. Management must ensure that credit officers comply with the credit policy and guidelines by instituting in the credit process a set of control procedures to be observed by the credit officers and reviewed by the bank's internal and external auditors, independent loan reviewers; and a directors' committee, depending on the size and complexity of the credit portfolio.

The guidelines or directives may aim at changing current credit practices. For example, in some markets, a common practice of financing business inventory, accounts receivable, or working capital is through overdrafts on demand deposit or checking accounts. These overdrafts may not be subject to any rigorous annual review, or may not have termination dates and limits observed by the borrower. In markets where banks face fierce competition for deposits, where they have to manage their liquidity by maintaining a relationship between deposits and credit outstanding, and have to achieve minimum capital to asset ratios, the unchecked or inadequately monitored overdraft system of lending may have to be replaced by a more organized system of monitored and regularly reviewed credit lines. The bank's credit guidelines may, therefore, be used to indicate the desired changes in credit practices consistent with changes in market conditions.

In order to achieve consistency in the pricing of various types of credit, the credit policy must include the relevant pricing guidelines. However, these guidelines must allow credit officers some freedom to recognize the inherent differences between borrowers, while requiring that pricing be based upon total yield. Experiences in pricing different types of credit in developed financial markets may be transferrable to developing financial markets. Risk exposure, cost of funds, term of credit or liquidity, and compensating balances are factors that influence the pricing of credit risk. Box 6.7 lists the general and specific guidelines that may be included in a bank's credit policy.

The causes of bank failures in developed financial markets during the 1980s may provide important lessons for bank management in developing financial markets. At least one of these lessons relates to the mispricing of

Box 6.7   Credit guidelines or directives

General

- The bank should not have an undue concentration of credit in any one sector, activity, industry or firm.
- Borrowers should maintain an account with the bank. If a borrower moves out of the bank's primary market area, outstanding credit should be repaid within a reasonable period of time or transferred to the bank where the borrower has an account. Commercial borrowers should maintain compensating balances.
- A credit file should be maintained for each borrower indicating the loan purpose, interest rates, repayment term, lending authority and other relevant information.
- All commercial credit other than cash collateralized credits should be supported by current financial statements.
- Credit to closely held firms must be endorsed by their principals.
- All credit should have a clearly stated plan of liquidation at the time they are made. Quarterly financial statements should be obtained for all major credit lines, and loans.
- Each credit officer should maintain contact with the borrower, to protect the bank's interest.
- Credit must be reviewed on a periodic basis. The review should include changes in the borrower's financial condition, in collateral value, and repayment performance.

Specific

- Short-term credit to firms should be for a term not exceeding 90 days.
- Credit commitment except for credit lines and revolving credit would have a term of 90 days unless there is a stated expiration date.
- The credit to collateral ratio would be stated and would vary on the basis of the collateral held (for example, 95 per cent of savings balances, 75 per cent of vehicle's value, 50 per cent of traded stocks, and so on).
- Unless otherwise stated, lines of credit are for a term of 1 year, and are subject to annual review.
- Credit line confirmation should contain a clause stating that the continued approval of the line is based on the maintenance of a satisfactory financial condition based on financial statements and other related information.
- Credit lines other than revolving lines should be cleared for 30 days during each 12 month period.
- Term credit should have a written credit agreement.
- Credit to directors or businesses in which directors have major interests must be approved by the board and in compliance with regulatory standards.

credit risk, and the reaction of prime borrowers to alternative funding sources offered by the new competitive market environment. The mispricing of credit risk explains the failure of banks in developed financial markets in the 1980s.[4] Such mispricing was determined by observing the risk premiums, based on credit ratings, required by the market for corporate bonds and comparing these premiums with commercial bank yields for loans to borrowers with similar credit ratings. It was discovered that in the bond market, the premium increased considerably as the credit ratings fell below investment grade. In contrast, the yield differential between prime, and higher risk commercial bank borrowers was not substantial and was much smaller than the risk premium between investment and below investment grade bonds.

Prior to deregulation, banks in developed financial markets could have afforded to be less discriminating with respect to the pricing of credit risk than the corporate bond markets because they enjoyed a monopoly on short-term and medium-term commercial credit extension. Hence even though they failed to price their credit risk properly within each rating class, banks did achieve an average yield across their entire portfolios that they considered adequate. Thus, as long as this monopoly position existed, banks were viable.

However, with deregulation in the 1980s and the resulting free market access, increased competition, and bank credit alternatives, the highest-rated most creditworthy bank customers found lower priced borrowing in the bond market, while the lower-rated customers remained with the banks which continued to charge borrowing rates that failed to compensate them for their increased risk. The 1980s represented a period when banks in developed financial markets were exposed to the consequences of their indiscriminate pricing practices. The lesson for bank management in developing financial markets is that management must price their credit to differentiate between their borrowers on the basis of risk and to compensate themselves for the credit risk they take.

The policy for pricing various types of credit may be presented in a general or specific form. The more general the approach, as indicated in broad ranges of interest rates and other charges for different types of credit, the greater will be the freedom of credit officers to price the credit they grant. The more specific the approach, the greater is the probability that customers will be lost over a small percentage difference from the scheduled price or the greater the delay in the approval process as credit officers seek exceptions to the scheduled price. In fact, if too many exceptions are granted the scheduled prices become meaningless. There is also the probability that the minimum price stated in the schedule will become the maximum price charged, regardless of the risk.

Whatever approach is used in the bank's pricing policy, the policy itself will be influenced by a set of basic factors. Among these factors are the inherent risk, deposit balances, liquidity of collateral, repayment term, and the cost of funds and administration.[5] Price will tend to vary directly with these costs. However, as competition limits the price a bank can charge, banks with higher average costs may be unable to increase their price for credit, except by targetting the higher-risk borrowers. Lending to such borrowers may result in serious asset quality problems.

The policy may require the credit officer responsible for extending the credit to continue handling a problem credit but under the supervision of a senior credit officer, or the policy may require the credit to be assigned to another officer under certain specified conditions. It may also stipulate the frequency of reports and follow-up reviews. The credit policy should establish standards for determining delinquent obligations, and outline the procedures for reporting delinquencies to the board. Reporting should be in sufficient detail to assist the board in determining the risk factors, loss potential, and possible courses of corrective action. Moreover, the credit policy should require formal follow-up procedures, and guidelines should be established to ensure that, after a period of delinquency, all credits are presented to the board for review and charge-off decisions.

Just as procedures are followed in the extension and administration of new credits, the credit policy should establish review and follow-up procedures for all charged off assets to maximize the recoverable amount. The policy should also establish practical collection methods and procedures. Changing market conditions, and subsequent business recovery or workout may add some value to what was once evidently a worthless asset. Thus, the policy must stipulate the continuance of a collection system for problem credits from borrowers with recovery potential.

6.3 CREDIT ADMINISTRATION

Credit administration is a staff function. The function aims at formulating credit policy and guidelines, including those for customer relationships, defining credit standards, and establishing appropriate systems and controls that facilitate compliance with the bank's credit policy, and the maintenance of a high quality credit portfolio. Credit administration also provides management information obtained from reviewing the bank's major earning assets. The line function includes lending and new business development. Credit risk will be minimized if the line and staff functions are closely coordinated.

The term 'line-staff' is commonly used by management although its meaning has been vague and subject to debate. For quite some time, the line and staff functions were distinguished by determining which function was essential to the bank's operations (line function) and which one supported these operations (staff function). The line-staff distinction has become increasingly meaningless and complex as managers became increasingly aware that some of the staff functions were essential for the line departments; and that it was possible for someone to have both line and staff responsibilities. In practice, credit administration staff may direct credit officers over whom they may have no authority. Nevertheless, this distinction continues to be used in the literature.

Banks in developing financial markets may be required to provide their customers loans as well as off-balance sheet services that may generate enough non-interest income to justify an unprofitable interest rate spread on some of the bank's loans. As customer relationship moves beyond extending credit into leasing, insurance, cash management, and letters of credit and other off-balance sheet services, bank management may replace the term 'credit officer' by a term that captures the extended activities of the lending officer.

In some banks operating in developed financial markets, the term 'credit officer' has been replaced by such terms as 'calling officers', 'account managers', and 'relationship managers'. The replacement terms imply that the extended credit officer must be familiar with both the availability and details of other services and with the persons in the bank who are specialists in these services. They also mean that there should be identifiable individuals having primary responsibility for specific customers, and adequate information on the bank's credit and related off-balance sheet services.

As competition for prime borrowers intensifies, the vulnerability of banks to asset quality problems will increase. Monitoring of trends and reviewing the banks' overall exposure will be critical functions of credit administration. Prime borrowers, no doubt, will themselves be reviewing the condition of their creditor banks in their attempt to avoid banks which, because of asset quality problems, may be unable to assure them of an uninterrupted funding and related credit services. This review by prime borrowers has been described as a reverse type of credit analysis whereby banks themselves are scrutinized as to their vulnerability to financial distress caused by asset quality and other problems.[6]

Indeed, deregulation will introduce new dynamics in bank-customer relationships as borrowers discover different and more competitive funding alternatives offered by other banks and non-bank sources. Banks that once established their credit price or had that price established for them by the government at an attractive level, may soon find that they are price-takers with low or negative interest rate spreads. Deregulation has emphasized the critical importance of reviewing specific credits, as well as the overall asset quality by banks' credit administration.

In establishing appropriate systems and controls in the credit process, credit administration may focus on, among other things, the organization of the credit function, and the methods for evaluating the repayment ability of borrowers, and the risk inherent in each loan. Implicit in the credit process is an organizational structure with features that vary with each bank according to size, type of credit emphasized, and the characteristics of customers served. A relatively small bank may combine both line and staff functions by requiring its credit officers to perform such tasks as business solicitation, credit analysis, restructuring, review and collection. In a larger bank, these functions may be performed by different departments.

Generally, the credit review system attempts to ensure that all risks inherent in the credit extension are adequately identified and monitored. Box 6.8 indicates the basic steps in the credit review process. There are several risks, other than credit and interest rate risks, in the credit function. Chief among them are operations, fraud, and syndication risks as defined in Box 6.9. Since banks in developing financial markets may not grant a loan in anticipation of liquidating it prior to its maturity, liquidity or marketability risk may be excluded from the risk categories. Until credit

Box 6.8   Credit review measures

Determine if:

- All credits are classified in a manner specified by the bank's credit policy.
- There is an application form for every loan or line of credit.
- Every credit has a specified repayment programme agreed on with the borrower at the time the credit was extended.
- Adequate information is in the credit file in the form of properly prepared financial statements and memoranda by the credit officer containing pertinent information on the borrower.
- Credits are reviewed periodically to try to anticipate deterioration of credit quality.

Box 6.9   Operations, fraud and syndication risks

- *Operations risk*: this is the risk that deficient operating procedures and controls will jeopardize the timely receipt of interest and principal or the priority that should be given to a loan in default.
- *Fraud risk*: this risk refers to the honesty of bank employees and the ability to discourage unauthorized or illegal insider transactions.
- *Syndication and origination risks*: this risk refers to failure to evaluate the borrower's and participating banks' ability to originate high-quality loans when a credit is part of a larger financing activity involving a number of banks.

---

securitization becomes an important component of developing countries' financial system, the credit market of these countries will essentially be a primary market, where credits originated by banks are held in these banks' portfolio until maturity.

The monitoring of all outstanding loans will assist in minimizing operational and credit irregularities. The principal objectives of such monitoring may be to determine if: (1) receipts of interest and principal are collected on a timely basis; and (2) the communication between the staff involved in the credit approval, pricing, review and collection is effective. A bank's safety and soundness can be threatened, if its credit administration fails to move quickly and efficiently in correcting all credit irregularities. For example, a delay in clearing a borrower's payment cheque may result in a loss for the bank should the borrower declare bankruptcy after the issuance of the cheque. This delay may be caused by a communication breakdown between the bank's credit, review and other related staff.

The bank's credit policy must address, as clearly and concisely as possible, the prevention and handling of fraud in the credit function. One method of addressing the issue of fraud prevention is to establish specific standards for credit extended to directors, management, staff and their affiliated interests. The risk of fraud may be minimized if compliance with the bank's credit policy and guidelines is monitored, if the bank's internal auditors are independent of management, and its internal audit and control procedures are designed to identify and report on all insider transactions and conflict of interest situations.

Banks in developing financial markets may join with each other and with banks in developed financial markets to fund an activity or a firm if it cannot be funded by any one of these banks acting alone. When multiple banks are involved, the borrower's as well as the participating bank's credit worthiness must be evaluated. A syndication risk arises in the event that a participating bank fails to meet its obligation, resulting in the weakening of the borrower's ability to perform or in an unplanned increase in exposure of the banks remaining in the syndication. The participating bank may be unable to perform because of capital adequacy, asset quality, liquidity and other safety and soundness problems. A careful evaluation of these participating banks, conducted by each bank's credit administration may minimize syndication risk.

In establishing a system to minimize credit risk and facilitate compliance with the bank's credit policy, credit administration may focus on methods for: (1) evaluating the borrowers' financial needs; (2) assessing credit risk using financial ratios, and cash flow analysis and other methods; and (3) structuring the credit.

The system for evaluating the credit needs of a borrower enables a credit officer to determine if the loan size fits the borrower's repayment ability. A loan that is too small can be as risky as one that is too large. Under-funding may restrain growth, while over-funding may create a debt servicing burden for the borrower. The appropriate amount of credit will, at least, be influenced by the borrower's actual or projected cash flows. Interest and principal are repaid from these flows and from eligible but illiquid assets reflected in the borrower's balance sheet.

It has been argued that operating cash flows provided a better assessment of credit strength than earnings. Moreover, the cash flow to long-term debt ratio has been a reliable predictor of business failure.[7] However, the usefulness of cash flow to determine repayment ability will be influenced by its definition, accuracy, and its combination with other performance indicators such as retained earnings and other profitability measures. At least five accounting ratios representing different dimensions of a business operations can provide useful information on a borrower's repayment ability or the borrower's potential to fail.[8] These ratios are shown in Box 6.10.

The loan structuring system may address at least four loan approval attributes: (1) term, price, and repayment schedule; (2) compensating

Box 6.10   Payment ability or potential failure ratios

- *Cash position*: cash/total or average assets.
- *Liquidity*: current assets/current liabilities.
- *Profitability*: net income/total or average assets.
- *Asset balance*: current assets/total or average assets.
- |*Activity*: current assets/sales.

balances and fees; (3) collateral requirements; and (4) credit covenants as indicated in Box 6.11. The loan term, price, and repayment schedule may be the result of combining the traditional approach that emphasizes that the loan price must reflect the risk characteristics of the borrower, and the more recent portfolio approach which stresses the particular borrower's contribution to the bank's overall credit portfolio's risk. The bank's ability to obtain compensating balances will depend on the size and power of the borrower, market competition, and the nature of the credit transaction. The need for collateral may be influenced by the size, term and creditworthiness of the borrower, and the loan covenants that complement the need for collateral, may be affirmative or negative.

Box 6.11   Credit structuring components

- *Term, price, and schedule of repayments*: the loan price should be based on its risk characteristics. Ensure the low or 'prime' rate covers the cost of funds (for example, the weighted average cost of capital, cost of administering the credit) and an anticipated profit margin. Explore a pricing, term and repayment approach by which the risk of an individual loan is based on credit worthiness consideration, and the particular credit's contribution to the bank's overall credit portfolio risk. Consider the characteristics that are unique to each borrower, for example, new product development, the size of the business, average balances, borrowing frequency, and historical relationship with the bank.
- *Compensating balances*: require the borrower to keep a certain percentage of its credit outstanding in non-interest bearing demand deposit. This enables the bank to realize a higher return and provides a buffer in the event of repayment difficulties. Under competitive market conditions, borrowers may be able to negotiate reduced or no compensating balances.
- *Collateral requirements*: determine whether the loan should be collateralized or unsecured. Unsecured credit may be short-term; collateralized credit may be long-term. If the credit is secured, ensure that the borrower grants the bank the right to sell the collateral and apply the proceeds to the credit in the event that the borrower cannot repay the credit.
- *Credit covenants*: protect the bank against deterioration in the borrower's ability to repay interest and principal by writing restrictive features into the credit agreement. Affirmative covenants make the borrower responsible to submit financial statements, maintain adequate insurance, pay interest and principal as scheduled, and inform the bank of any major changes in the business. Negative covenants require certain performance criteria (for example, liquidity and leverage ratios) and can prohibit the borrower's activities (for example, the purchase of major assets or the payment of cash dividends) if certain performance ratios are not met.

6.4 PROBLEM CREDITS

Normally, a credit becomes a problem when the borrower is experiencing cash flow difficulties. A problem credit, however, may arise although the borrower may not be experiencing such difficulties in its own operations. For example, a borrower may have a foreign currency loan that is in arrears, because it cannot obtain foreign exchange from the central bank to repay the loan, or a borrower, because of its political or government connection, may not want to repay a loan although it has the ability to do so. The borrower with the ability but not the inclination to repay a loan is therefore a wilful defaulter.[9]

It may be noted that while a cash flow problem may be abrupt in its impact, it develops gradually, providing in the process, non-financial and financial warning signs to the officer assigned to that credit. The non-financial signs may include delays in the submission of financial statements at intervals specified by the covenant and spurious explanations for such delays, switching auditors and abrupt changes in business plans. Box 6.12

Box 6.12   Non-financial warning signs

- Evidence of legal action against the borrower by other creditors.
- Deteriorating relationships with trade suppliers.
- Speculative tendencies.
- Acceptance of low profit sales to create volume.
- Loss of key product lines, franchises, distribution rights, or supply sources.
- Changes in the timing of seasonal credit requests.
- A sharp increase in the size of credit requests.
- Notice of insurance cancellation for failure to pay premiums.
- Loss of one or more financially sound customers.
- Commitment to projects promising exceptionally high or unusual profit potential.
- Neglect or discontinuance of profitable basic products or services.
- Delay in reacting to declining markets or economic conditions.
- Lack of visible management succession.
- Credit where more than a single source of repayment cannot be easily or realistically identified.
- Speculative inventory purchases, inconsistent with normal purchasing practices or established maintenance levels of the firm.
- Non-compliance with the terms and conditions of the underlying credit agreement.
- Appearance of other lenders in the financial picture, especially in cases where various assets are subsequently pledged to provide new arrivals with a secured position in preference to the bank's position.

provides a set of indicators of an impending problem credit situation. The financial signs may be revealed through a financial analysis of the business, and by such practices as the rolling over of short-term or seasonal borrowing, and by frequent requests for extension of the maturity date or for temporary overdrafts in excess of approved limits.

Box 6.13 lists the problems that may be revealed by an analysis of the borrower's financial statement. After a problem credit has been identified, the credit officer may: (1) analyze the borrower's problem; (2) consult with the bank's credit recovery units, specialized staff or senior officer, depending on the size and organization of the bank's credit function; (3) recommend an appropriate classification of the credit, and treatment of interest accrual; (4) determine the bank's overall exposure (for example, credit, and off-balance sheet risks) to the borrower; (5) monitor the account activity for over-limits on approved or unauthorized overdrafts; (6) consider collateralizing unsecured exposures, increasing existing collateral, and reviewing credit documentation for any exceptions; and (7) establish a work-out plan for corrective action. The implementation of these measures will require the cooperation of the borrower in providing all necessary information and effectuating appropriate corrective action. It may also require consultation with the borrower's suppliers and major

Box 6.13   Problems revealed by financial statement analysis

- A deterioration in the cash position.
- A slowdown in the receivables collection period.
- Sharp increases in the dollar amounts of accounts receivable or the percentage of total assets.
- Noticeably rising inventory levels or slowdown in inventory turnover.
- A decline in current assets as a percent of total assets.
- Unusual concentrations in miscellaneous assets or intangibles.
- Revaluation of assets for statement purposes.
- The existence of heavy liens on assets.
- Concentrations in non-current assets other than fixed assets (for example, due from affiliates or subsidiaries).
- A high debt-to-worth ratio.
- Disproportionate increases in returns and allowances.
- Rising cost percentages (for example, a small increase may have a big effect on pre-tax profit).
- Rising sales and falling profits.
- Rising levels of bad debt losses.
- Assets levels rising faster than sales.
- A rising level of total assets in relation to profits.
- Significant changes in balance sheet structure.

buyers, as well as, with other banks with which the borrower may have a business relationship. Because of their relative importance measures (3) and (7) should be emphasized.

Banks in developing financial markets may classify their loans, as well as their off-balance sheet exposures, as a function of default risk. The classification of the bank's assets may be based on the repayment status of the credit, the repayment capacity of the borrower, and the cash value of the collateral. In addition, credit risk may be classified objectively on actual performance, and subjectively on the borrower's financial condition and repayment ability.[10] A system that classifies credits as performing and non-performing, current and past due, or on the aging of overdue credits rather than on the risk of default, may not adequately reflect the bank's asset quality. In fact, such a system permits the removal of a problem credit from the classification of say non-performing after one payment of overdue interest.

Box 6.14 describes credit classifications that may be adopted by banks in developing financial markets. Moreover, while it is important to have an adequate classification system, it is even more critical to monitor its implementation particularly ensuring that specific reserves are consistent with the classification categories indicated in the system. As competition for

Box 6.14   Credit classifications

- *Sub-standard*: Objective criteria: Non-performing credits which are past due for more than 30 days but less than 180 days or credits with 25 per cent of their value considered loss. Subjective criteria: Credits that display well defined credit weaknesses (for example, cash flows inadequate to service the credits, under capitalization, or insufficient working capital, absence of adequate financial information or collateral or other documentation).
- *Doubtful*: Objective criteria: Non-performing credits which are at least 180 days past due but less than 360 days; and are not adequately secured by legally foreclosable collateral. Subjective criteria: credits that demonstrate all the weaknesses inherent in credits classified substandard with the added characteristics that the timely collection of the credit in full is uncertain; realizable collateral values under forced liquidation are insufficient to protect the bank from loss; and potential loss is estimated to exceed 30 per cent of the credit.
- *Loss*: Objective criteria: Non-performing credits that are 360 days or more past due and not well secured by legally foreclosable collateral; credits to insolvent firms with negative working capital and cash flow. Subjective criteria: Credits which are considered uncollectible and of such little value that continuation as a bankable asset is not warranted.

the most creditworthy borrowers intensifies and banks accommodate the less creditworthy borrowers, it may be necessary to establish reserves for losses in anticipation of charge-offs. Such reserves would suggest prudent management. In developed financial markets, the general reserves against losses tend to be about 1 per cent of net outstanding credits as specified in equation (6.1). This percentage may serve as minimum general reserves for banks in developing financial markets, in addition to the specific reserves included in the asset classification system.

$$NC = TC - (ACL + UEI) \qquad (6.1)$$

where:

NC = net outstanding credit
TC = total gross credit
ACL = allowance for possible credit losses
UEI = unearned income on existing credits

Both general and specific reserves impose discipline in the credit process and compel banks to reflect their true financial condition. No specific reserves are required for credit considered current although general reserves, based on the assumption that even the highest quality credits have a probability of default, may be appropriate. Table 6.15 shows suggested specific reserves for classified credits. These reserves may be used to adjust the bank's capital accounts when determining its capital adequacy condition.

Furthermore, it is normal for management to establish acceptable charge-off guidelines for various types of credit depending on the bank's risk/return trade-off strategy. The greater the risk taken by the bank the higher will be the anticipated problem credits and acceptable charge-off

Table 6.15   Specific reserves for classified credits

- *Sub-standard credits*: Minimum specific reserves of 25 per cent of the aggregate sub-standard classifications.
- *Doubtful credits*: Reserves of 50–90 per cent of the doubtful classifications based on the length of time the credit was overdue (for example, reserves of: 50 per cent of credit overdue from 180–225 days; 60 per cent for credits overdue from 226–70 days; 70 per cent for credits overdue from 271–315 days; and 80 per cent for credits overdue from 316–64 days).
- *Loss*: Reserves of 100 per cent of the loss classifications.

Box 6.16   Suggested charge-off ratios: per cent of outstanding balances

- Revolving credit   0.50 – 0.75
- Installment credit   0.50 – 0.60
- Loan and discount   0.15 – 0.25
- Mortgage loans   0.10 – 0.15

percentages. For example, a revolving credit line to a borrower involved in a product subject to substantial market changes may have a greater charge-off ratio than mortgage loans for single family homes. Box 6.16 provides guidelines for what may be considered acceptable charge-off ratios for four types of credit.[11]

Once the problem credit situation is determined, a senior credit officer, usually senior to the one handling the account, may review the credit and discuss a plan of action before approaching the borrower. In some cases, it may be prudent to move the account from the originating officer to another officer who is not close to the borrower, or to a problem credit unit that may be more inclined to implement all aspects of the work-out plan even-though they may be unpleasant. However, the originating credit officer may have a better understanding of the borrower including its management capabilities. In addition, the originating officer's continuing involvement in the credit may improve his or her competence in resolving other problem credits. Thus, if the credit officer's identification with the borrower is not considered too close, and this officer can report on the problem credit situation in an objective manner, it may be sensible to retain the officer in the process under close supervision by a senior officer throughout the work-out period.

An important consideration in the work-out plan is whether to keep the firm in business or to permit its liquidation. Available information of the firm's management, product, and competition may suggest that the problem is a temporary one and can be resolved within a predicable time period if the existing credit is restructured. However, certain factors, such as the long-term inability of the borrower to compete, a decline in the demand for the firms's products due to economic and technological changes beyond the control of the firm's management will certainly influence the decision to permit the continuance or liquidation of the firm. However, if the plan requires the firm's liquidation, the timing of such liquidation will be critical in minimizing any loss to the bank. Time is needed to ensure there are no documentation deficiencies that will weaken the bank's legal claim against the borrower.

If a decision is made to permit the borrower to continue its operations temporary or otherwise, the following measures may be included in the work-out plan: (1) eliminate or reduce every expense possible, only essential expenses may be allowed and these must be kept to the minimum; dividend payments must be stopped; (2) reduce inventory and carefully analyse accounts receivable; (3) dispose of all assets that are not essential to the firms's operations; (4) improve cash flow by delaying accounts payable if possible; further extend the current maturity of any debt that is subordinated to the bank's debt; and (5) encourage management to obtain new equity from owners and other sources. Diligence and creativity must be reflected in any work-out plan intended to keep a financially fragile firm in business.[12]

If liquidation is considered to be the only appropriate course, the plan must indicate how management will proceed. Before the bank proceeds to liquidate, it must: (1) establish that the borrower has defaulted on the credit; (2) ascertain that it has all the collateral on the firm that it can obtain; and (3) have available at its disposal those professional resources (for example, attorneys and accountants) required to protect and defend its interests.

A liquidation may be formal or informal, both aiming at speed, efficiency and cost savings. The informal method allows for the sale of the firm's assets and the distribution of the proceeds to the firm, the bank and other creditors, on the basis of an agreement between the firm and its creditors. The formal method requires the assignment of assets to a third party responsible for liquidating them and distributing the proceeds. The borrower may not want to follow any of these methods and may elect to file for voluntary bankruptcy or reorganization. If either of these methods is chosen, the bank may request its attorneys and credit administration to follow the situation closely, and comply with the legally prescribed bankruptcy requirements. In some developing countries, where bankruptcy laws are undeveloped or non-existent, the choice may be restricted to an informal liquidation of the firm.

6.5 SUMMARY

This chapter has focused on risk management of commercial credits because such credits tend to have greater inherent risk than mortgage lending and installment loans to households. In most developing countries agricultural credits are provided mainly by financial institutions specially established to service the agricultural sector. The chapter has also identified the general and specific credit risk challenges in developing financial markets. These challenges arise because of the existence of certain factors in developing economies that weaken commercial borrowers' ability to perform and heighten the risk inherent in the lending process. It has identified some of these factors. In addition, it has specified the risk management areas to be addressed by a bank's credit policy and guidelines, and the characteristics of acceptable and unacceptable credits that may be included and avoided respectively in the bank's asset portfolio.

In addition, the chapter has argued that the credit approval system, and the criteria on which approvals are based, must be carefully defined, and has provided examples of these criteria. It has acknowledged the tendency for credit risk to increase in developing financial markets. The principal reason for this tendency is that banks in these markets often lose their most creditworthy borrowers while attempting to maintain or improve their operating results. At the same time, the product and factor markets in which the customers operate tend to become more competitive, and the economy more unstable. The chapter has therefore emphasized the support role of credit administration, the importance of credit review and follow-up, and the need for carefully implemented strategies to minimize asset classifications and their effects on the safety and soundness of banks.

7 Credit and Deposit Pricing

The deregulation of financial markets in developing countries has changed the operational environment of banks in substantial ways. The high and volatile interest rates that accompanied deregulation have caused firms with excess balances to demand effective cash management services, and required banks to price their loans to reflect the risk inherent in these loans, the shareholders' demand for a competitive return on equity, and the increased cost of funding. In repressed financial markets the loan pricing system was a simple one that recognized the stable nominal interest rates on deposits and fixed spreads. Although the pricing standards in repressed financial markets (for example, contractual interest rates, fees and compensating balances) continue to be relevant in developing financial markets, these standards are modified and new standards added. The principal objectives of the new pricing standards are to enable banks in developing financial markets to cope with the: (1) increased competition between themselves and non-bank providers of credit, deposit, and other financial products and services; (2) reduced level of customer loyalty; (3) expanded supply of competitively priced saving and borrowing instruments; and (4) urgent need to price the risks inherent in the banks' lending activities.

This chapter focuses on the pricing of consumer installment loans and revolving credit, consumer deposits, and commercial or business loans. It examines the approaches bank management in developing financial markets may adopt in pricing their products, recognizes the importance of high and stable deposit balances, and identifies a set of measures these banks may implement to achieve and maintain high average deposit account balances. In addition, the chapter reviews the role of profitability analysis to determine the contribution of individual borrowers to a bank's operating results and illustrates the role of this analysis in a bank's loan pricing system. Finally, the chapter demonstrates a loan pricing system that recognizes banks' capital asset ratios, desired return on equity capital and the marginal cost of funds.

7.1 PRICING APPROACHES

Management may have the choice of adapting a full cost or marginal cost pricing system. Under certain circumstances both systems may be used.

Management may be criticized for supporting a pricing system based on estimated full costs plus what is considered a reasonable profit. In pricing the bank's products, management may want to consider such relationships as total costs versus total revenues, marginal costs versus marginal revenues, and market demand characteristics. While this criticisms may be sound, there is validity in the position that banks may attempt to recover the full costs of their products, plus an adequate compensation for effort expended and funds invested in getting these products on the market. The difficulty with the full cost approach to pricing, however, is its failure to accommodate many factors, other than full production costs, that are important pricing determinants.

Despite this failure, bank management when using the full cost approach may be more confident of their ability to determine the actual, standard or projected costs of their products than to ascertain the potential prices of their products based on analyses of market demand characteristics that are uncertain and beyond their control. Moreover, no bank can be operationally successful in the long-term if the revenue derived from its products does not exceed the products' full costs. Thus, management must know the bank's full costs, and when its products are being sold at a price below full cost. In addition, management must ensure that within a given period, the bank receives full cost reimbursement, together with a reasonable profit on most of its products, if the bank is to maintain its long-term viability.

In some situations, the marginal costs of a bank's products may be more relevant for pricing purposes. Marginal costs are the additional production and sales costs that may be saved in the event that the product is not brought to the market. In introducing a new product the marginal costs may be the: (1) costs of information and expertise; (2) variable costs that would have been saved if the product were not produced; (3) charges on any new fixed assets used to produce the product; and (4) additional selling, delivery, and administrative costs involved in the production. The additional cost of the capital required to finance the production and sale of the product may also be included. If the marginal revenue from sales exceeds the marginal costs, it may be better for the bank to produce and sell the new product than not to do so. However, management must consider factors other than marginal costs and revenues before proceeding.

One of these factors is the excess of revenue derived from the product over the cost of producing it. Given the market price, it can be argued that only marginal costs are relevant in deciding to produce or sell a product. If the market price is not given, management may set a price to equalize the product's marginal cost and marginal revenue. Such an equalization, however, assumes a knowledge of the market demand for the product, or the shape of the product demand curve. If market demand at various prices can be ascertained the probability of underpricing will be minimized.

Figure 7.1 illustrates the situation where market demand, marginal costs, and marginal revenues for bank products (for example, credit and deposits) are known. It also depicts the equilibrium price and quantity of products under two different competitive environments that may exist in developing financial markets. The two demand situations highlight the bank as a price-taker indicated in Figure 7.1 (a), and as a price-setter as in Figure 7.1 (b).

Figure 7.1(a) is based on the assumption that the market for the bank's products is highly competitive and consumers are indifferent as to the

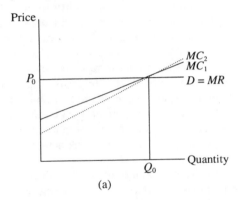

(a)

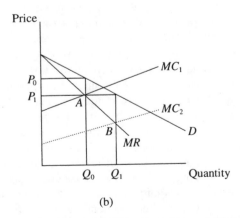

(b)

Figure 7.1   Product demand for (a) price-takers and (b) price-setters

bank from which they buy these products. The demand function is horizontal over the relevant price range indicating that the bank can sell as much of the product as it wishes at the current market price, P_o. In this case where the bank is a price taker, its reaction to the market is to set its output (for example, the CDs it wants to issue, or the loans it wants to make) so that its marginal cost and marginal revenue are equal. Marginal cost will tend to rise as the bank increases its promotional activities to expand its product's market share. At the same time, given the quantity produced, the bank's profit will increase only by lowering marginal cost as indicated in MC_2.

Figure 7.1(b) is based on the assumption that demand for the bank's product will expand as the bank lowers the price. The bank will lower the price to point A, where marginal cost and marginal revenue are equal. At point A, unlike the case of the price-taking bank, MC_1 is lower than the product price, P_o. Given market demand, the price-setting bank can increase profits while lowering the product price by reducing marginal cost. At point B, the price-setting bank increases profits while lowering its product price and increasing the amount sold.

A price-setting bank can also increase its profits if it has the power to segregate its markets and charge different prices for similar products in each market. For instance, a bank may find that the demand for its long-term, low downpayment consumer loans is relatively insensitive to price because borrowers demanding such loans are more likely to be in greater need of funds and thus less sensitive to loan rates than payment terms. At the same time, the bank may find that its short-term, high downpayment loans are very sensitive to price, as its higher income borrowers are willing to access other banks offering lower rates.

Figure 7.2 depicts the two loan demand situations. D_1 shows a loan demand function that is relatively insensitive to price, while D_2 shows a loan demand function that is highly sensitive to price. With D_2, the bank will be unable to sell its products if they are priced above the market price or will not gain by selling at a price lower than the market price, when it can sell any amount at the market price. Given the bank's marginal cost, it will set prices in the two markets where MC intersects MR in each market. The price established in the market with the D_2 function will be P_2 and the price in the market with the D_1 function will be P_1 which is higher than that of P_2.

An important implication of Figures 7.1 and 7.2 is that the pricing strategy for banks in developing financial markets must be influenced by the extent to which the banks themselves are price-setters in the market they serve. Management may have to consider the impact a price reduction will

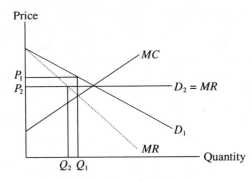

Figure 7.2   Price discrimination

have on the quantity of product demanded and on the change in revenue resulting from such a reduction. Profits will be enhanced as marginal revenue equals marginal costs, as output increases, and as management segment the market and set higher prices in the market with a lower price sensitivity.[1]

Another implication of Figures 7.1 and 7.2 is that management should know both the marginal costs and full costs of the bank's products sold in different markets. Under competitive market conditions, it may not be possible to charge prices that even cover full costs, let alone that provide a profit. In such a situation, a knowledge of marginal costs can establish the floor price for the products while incurring losses. Knowledge of the full costs of these products will assist, however, in showing the extent to which the floor price received is covering these costs; and in encouraging management to target prices that will reimburse the bank for the full costs to the extent possible. Accepting prices below full cost may therefore be a strategic short-term pricing decision.

It may be sensible to charge, at least in the short-run, less than the full cost of a product to utilize equipment and staff capacity, and to maintain or increase market share. Here, the marginal cost involved is the major cost consideration, although the product's full cost is still an important limiting factor. But a point will be reached where a product may be eliminated even though the revenue it generates exceeds its marginal cost and provides some contribution toward the remaining costs. This point is established when staff, facilities, and management efforts being expended on this product can be more effectively deployed to other products which enhance the long-term profitability of the bank. A product's survival will therefore depend on its price being enough to cover its marginal cost and to make, as determined by management, a satisfactory contribution to the bank's profitability.

On occasions, management may have to decide whether to maintain an existing product or to replace it with a new product, and what may be the price of the replacement product. In the case of a price-setting bank offering a new product, the major factor is the probable price that the bank's customers will want to pay for the product. Full cost may be a minor factor, since the price that equalizes the product's marginal cost and marginal revenue will be in excess of the product's full cost. However, management may have to reduce the product's price if this price fails to widen the market or make the product competitive. In such a situation full cost becomes an important factor to the extent that it offers resistance to the lowering of price beyond a certain point.

Taking into account the bank's production capacity, Table 7.1 illustrates how full and marginal cost analyses, under competitive market conditions, can assist in determining the relative contribution of products to a bank's profitability or operating cash flow, and the products that may be given

Table 7.1   Cost and sales analyses

	Product A $	Product A %	Product B $	Product B %
Full cost analysis				
Price	2.00	100	2.50	100
Full cost	1.80	90	2.40	96
Net income	0.20	10	0.10	4
Marginal cost analysis				
Price	2.00	100	2.50	100
Marginal costs	1.60	80	2.00	80
Marginal contribution	0.40	20	0.50	20
Full and marginal cost analysis				
Price	2.00	100	2.50	100
Marginal costs	1.60	80	2.00	80
Marginal contribution	0.40	20	0.50	20
Fixed costs	.20	10	.40	16
Net income	0.20	10	0.10	4
Sales and marginal cost analysis				
Sales	(2 units) 4.00	100	(1 unit) 2.50	100
Marginal costs	3.20	80	2.00	80
Marginal contribution	0.80	20	0.50	20

promotional priority. A comparison of the prices and full cost of products *A* and *B* will suggest that the bank may promote product *A* over product *B* since the net income contribution of *A* is larger than that of *B*. When marginal cost (which is assumed to equal marginal revenue in Table 7.1) is separated from full cost, product *B* appears to be the one that may be promoted because its marginal contribution to the bank's profits is higher that than of product *A*. However, the marginal cost of each product amounts to 80 per cent of the product's selling price indicating that whichever product is sold the marginal contribution per sales will be $0.20. Thus, with respect to marginal cost, it does not really matter which product is promoted.

When decomposing full cost into marginal and fixed costs, it is evident that product *B* uses the fixed cost components (for example, facilities, equipment, and so on.) twice as much as product *A*. On the assumption that the same facilities or other fixed assets are involved in producing each of these two products, then 2 units of *A* can be produced and sold for the same use of facilities as 1 unit of *B*. Assuming that fixed cost is the limiting factor in the case of products *A* and *B*, and that demand exceeds the bank's productive capacity, product *A* may be produced in preference to product *B*. However, it may be necessary to continue producing product *B* to maintain loyalty of customers whose demand will be needed when the bank has unused capacity and market conditions slacken. Given market prices, full cost, marginal cost and income contribution are not the only considerations for producing one product in favour of another. Changes in productive capacity relative to demand, and maintaining competitiveness are also important factors.

7.2   PRICING CONSUMER LOANS

Consumer loan pricing is affected by a number of factors. Principal among these factors are the loan size, maturity, prepayment, and insurance. The average cost and price of a consumer loan will tend to fall as the loan size increases. In fact, it may be necessary to charge extremely high lending rates to make small consumer loans profitable for a bank. The smaller the loan size the greater must be the contractual rate of interest to ensure a respectable net return. As the loan size increases, the contractual rate required to generate a given net return will tend to fall.[2]

Although loan rate ceilings, if they exist, may permit significantly high interest rates on smaller consumer loans, because of the size of the interest rate required to make such lending profitable, banks wanting to avoid the image of a high-rate lender to small borrowers may establish minimum-sized consumer loans which they are willing to extend. However, it may be feasible to accommodate some small loan requests, if these are from repeat borrowers for whom loan origination and collection costs are low. In general, banks in developing financial markets may want to charge substantially higher interest rates for smaller loans or avoid making such loans at all if these banks are to be profitable.

The required interest rate on a consumer loan may be lowered not only as the loan increases in size but also as it increases in maturity. The lower interest rate for longer maturities may be explained by the fact that the loan origination cost can be recovered from higher finance charges spread over a longer period of time. Thus, a bank may charge lower interest rates for consumer loans with longer maturities, than those with shorter maturities. Notwithstanding, banks tend to charge higher contractual rates for loans with longer maturities than for loans with shorter maturities.

There are at least five reasons for the tendency to charge higher rates for longer maturities. These reasons are the: (1) greater risk of loss that may be associated with borrowers wanting loans with longer maturities, (2) probability that borrowers wanting longer maturities to minimize their payments may be less rate sensitive than borrowers wanting shorter maturities, (3) high prepayment of longer-maturity consumer loans makes for higher interest rates as contractual maturities become irrelevant for calculating probable net returns on these loans; (4) need to cover the liquidity risk for longer maturity loans by charging a premium rate of interest on such loans; and (5) requirement to price inflation and interest rate risks in an environment of high inflation and interest rate expectations.

Although longer maturity loans tend to be riskier, banks may be encouraged to make these loans because they contribute to profits and attract new customers. For instance, longer-maturity loans allow borrowers to adjust their loan payments in a manner consistent with their own budget constraints, resulting in an increased demand for such loans. The increased loan demand, in turn, enables the bank to charge higher loan rates and fees. Even if higher interest rates are not charged, longer maturities tend to generate higher net rates of return than shorter ones at any given interest rate. Furthermore, longer-maturity loans may attract younger low-income borrowers to the bank.

Loan prepayment poses two important problems for bank management in developing financial markets. These problems are the: (1) uncertainty of realizing the planned net return on loans extended; and (2) exposure to interest rate risk. Loan prepayment contributes to loan underpricing if the potential of such prepayment is not considered when setting the loan contract price. Given loan origination and other costs, prepayment will reduce the bank's receivables outstanding and increase these costs relative to such receivables. With an unplanned increase in relative costs, the bank's net return based on the loan contract price will be reduced or become negative as a result of prepayment. As far as interest rate risk is concerned, if the bank hedges its consumer loan portfolio by issuing liabilities with similar average maturities, an interest rate decline can induce unexpected prepayment and unfavourable interest rate sensitivity gaps.

Bank management must therefore recognize the potential for consumer loan prepayment and factor this potential in their pricing decision. For example, management may impose explicit prepayment penalties, or charge non-refundable loan origination fees if market competition permit.[3] Using the Rule of 78, or other appropriate method, management may also reduce the interest rate rebates on prepaid loans. The Rule of 78 computes a less than proportionate interest rate on debts that are repaid before their maturities.[4] Whenever the Rule of 78 is used for the early retirement of a debt, the fraction of the original loan that is to be rebated can be determined by:

$$F_r = \frac{L(L + 1)}{N(N + 1)} \tag{7.1}$$

where:

F_r = the rebate factor
L = the number of remaining payments
N = the number of payments

The interest payment factor (F_p) for the Rule of 78 is:

$$F_p = (1 - F_r) \tag{7.2}$$

Credit insurance is an extra charge that may be imposed on consumer loans and can provide an important revenue source for banks in developing financial markets. It also helps to reduce losses on what may otherwise be problem loans. Credit insurance tends to be profitable because most borrowers outlive the term of their loans and claims on the insurance are infrequent. Thus, premiums tend to be high relative to the insurance risk.

In addition, premiums are normally computed on the initial and not on the declining value of the loan.

The pricing of consumer loans may also be influenced by non-interest rate factors that may reduce or alter default risk. These factors include down payment and collateral requirements and late-payment fees. The higher the down payment and collateral on a consumer loan, the smaller is the default risk. However, while these enhancements may reduce default risk, they may also reduce consumer loan demand, and average loan size. By encouraging borrowers to meet their loan obligations on time, late-payment fees can help to reduce debt collection costs and potential losses.

Together with consumer loans which may be repaid by monthly install-ment, the bank may extend revolving lines of credit to its customers. It may be cheaper for a bank to extend credit lines to its small creditworthy customers than for it to provide a series of small loans to such customers over an extended period. This is because origination costs for a revolving credit are incurred once, when the line is established, while for a series of small consumer loans they are incurred for each loan processed. However, there are certain factors that should be considered in pricing revolving credits. Among these factors are the cost of updating information on the customer's creditworthiness, and the probability that customers with re-volving credit lines may hold lower deposit balances than customers with installment loans.

In pricing revolving credit lines, bank management may want to con-sider the costs to the bank of these lines compared to the costs of extend-ing a series of small consumer loans, the costs of updating credit line customers' credit information, and the penalties for low deposit balances. Thus, revolving credit lines may be made easily available at a price lower than that of small installment loans. However, the price of these lines must be sufficiently high to cover their costs and have some relationship to the expected use of the facility. Given the origination costs, a credit line that is occasionally used may be charged a price higher than one that is frequently used. The cost of updating customer credit information may be recovered by the imposition of a credit line maintenance fee. In addition, a high monthly fee imposed on revolving credit line customers with low deposit balances may encourage these customers to maintain prescribed minimum balances in their deposit accounts.

7.3   PRICING DEPOSITS

Banks in developing financial markets compete in prices to attract differ-ent types of deposit, more particularly large certificates of deposits (CDs).

Deposit pricing strategies may aim at attracting the required amount of deposits at the minimum net costs to the bank. These costs include interest, and non-interest expenses, net of fees and service charges. Banks tend to avoid imposing services charges on large CDs, although such charges are common for demand deposits. The cost of obtaining funds by selling large CDs at a specified interest rate can be determined by that rate together with the related deposit insurance premium, deposit service costs, and reserve requirements as indicated in Equation (7.3).

$$CD_c = \frac{(CD_i + CD_{ip} + CD_{sc})}{(1 - CD_{rr})} \qquad (7.3)$$

where:

CD_c = CD costs
CD_i = CD interest rate
CD_{ip} = CD insurance premium
CD_{rr} = CD reserve requirement

Equation (7.3) indicates that CD_c will vary directly with interest rates, insurance premium, expenses incurred in servicing depositors' accounts, and reserve requirement.

If the issued CDs are covered by deposit insurance, interest rates will be determined by the market, and banks will be mainly price-takers. In other words, under competitive market conditions, if a bank's competitors increase their interest rate on deposits, the bank will obtain less funds by offering a lower interest. However, if the CDs are not insured, banks that are perceived as less risky may be able to compete deposits away from other banks while offering lower interest rates on these deposits. In developing financial markets, with no or limited deposit insurance and with banks achieving different safety and soundness standards, undoubtedly, there will be price-setters and price-takers for CDs and other deposits.

In repressed financial markets, depositors may receive standard interest rates irrespective of the size of their deposits. As these markets are liberalized and banks compete for funds, the deposit market may be segmented between a large number of small savers who are indifferent to interest rate changes, and a smaller number of large savers who are interest rate sensitive and are prepared to place their deposits with banks that offer higher interest rates. Figure 7.3 illustrates the pricing strategy that a bank may

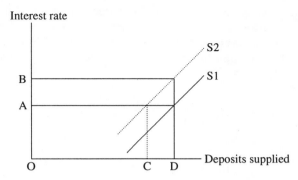

Figure 7.3   Pricing strategy for different savers

follow to retain the deposits of both price-sensitive and price-insensitive savers. When financial markets were repressed, the bank depicted in Figure 7.3 was supplied with OD amount of deposits at OA interest rate. As banks compete for deposits by increasing interest rates, some savers required higher interest rates to maintain their savings, otherwise they were prepared to reduce the available savings, as reflected by the new supply curve S2, unless interest rates increased to OB. Thus, by changing its deposit rates to accommodate the rate-sensitive savers, the bank maintains its initial deposit supply of OD. Banks in developing financial markets may maintain such interest rate differential between consumer deposits by issuing certain minimum-sized CDs to their rate-sensitive savers.

With the deregulation of interest rates, banks will have greater scope to vary the interest rate and term of the deposits they offer their customers. A bank may design one variant of a deposit account for rate-sensitive customers, charging full fees for the use of the account, but offering competitive interest rates. It may also design another variant of a deposit account for fee-sensitive customers, charging no fees or crediting the value of minimum balances against fees while paying below market interest rates.

Surely, within relatively wide limits, banks with well informed and creative management can become price-setters rather than price-takers by designing deposit accounts appropriate for rate-sensitive as well as for fee-sensitive depositors. Given some degree of price-setting ability, bank management may have at least three strategic options for consumer deposit pricing in developing financial markets. These options are: (1) pricing to save taxes, particularly where income taxes are high and consumers are interested in the after-tax returns on their deposits; (2) pricing to encourage balance maintenance; and (3) split-rate pricing.

The after-tax net return on a customer's deposits is a function of the customer marginal tax rate, the nominal interest paid on the deposits, the amount of the deposits and, and any non tax-deductible fees paid to the bank. The relationship between these variables are expressed in Equation (7.4).

$$NR = (1 - t_j) \times (i \times D) - BF \qquad (7.4)$$

where:

NR = after tax net return
t_j = customer j's marginal tax rate
i = nominal deposit rate
D = deposit amount
BF = bank fees (non tax-deductible fees for bank services)

Assume a depositor is in a 30 per cent tax bracket and maintains an average deposit balance of $5,000 with the bank. On the basis of Equation (7.4) the customer will earn the same after tax net return of $297.00 if the bank paid a 10 per cent interest and levied a monthly service charge of $4.50 as if the bank levied no service charges and paid an interest rate of 8.46 per cent on the deposit balance. Thus, the 30 per cent tax bracket customer will have an incentive to maintain a deposit relationship with the bank if the deposit rate is at any level over 8.46 per cent and the service charge is zero. Moreover, the bank's monthly net cash outlay will be significantly lower in the case of the 8.46 per cent and zero service charge situation, than in the case of the 10 per cent and $4.50 service charge situation. The 10 per cent and $4.50 monthly service situation results in a net monthly outlay of $37.17 (monthly interest of $41.67 less $4.50 service charge). The 8.46 per cent no service charge situation results in a monthly outlay of $35.25.

Modify the above example to allow for a customer in a lower tax bracket, say a 10 per cent tax bracket, with a $5,000 deposit balance, a 10 per cent interest rate paid on this balance, and monthly charge of $4.50 levied for services used by the customer. Based on Equation (7.4) the customer will be better off with a deposit rate in excess of 8.8 per cent with no service charge than with the rate of 10 per cent and the $4.50 monthly service charge. However, at the 8.8 per cent interest rate, the bank's monthly cash outlay for the interest it pays on the deposit is $37.67, and its monthly cash outlay for the 10 per cent deposit interest less the $4.50 service charge will be $33.00. Thus, the bank will not gain by attempting to induce lower tax bracket depositors to accept lower interest rates on deposits in lieu of fees. Bank management in developing financial markets must take into account their customers' marginal tax rate to determine the appropriate combination of interest rate to be paid on deposits and fees to be levied for banking services.

Because larger deposit balances facilitate the covering of fixed costs and reduce the probability of overdrafts, banks may price their deposits to encourage the maintenance of increasingly larger deposit balances. For example, on a $5,000 deposit a bank earns a 2.5 per cent spread between its average return on assets and its interest expense, and has $4.00 monthly servicing costs (for example, postage, mailing, and computer services) associated with this account. The 2.5 per cent spread, equivalent to $10.42 per month, will be more than adequate to cover the servicing costs. If the account balance falls to $500, the monthly spread value will be $1.04 which will be considerably lower than the servicing costs.

If a reduced spread, resulting from a small interest rate increase, encourages the maintenance of minimum deposit balances, the fixed costs associated with carrying an account will be covered more easily, than in the case of a higher spread and smaller balance maintenance. Since they allow more earnings to be retained by the bank from the spread between interest income and interest expense, larger accounts are usually more profitable than smaller ones.

Split-rate pricing is another strategy banks in developing financial markets may implement to encourage the maintenance of minimum deposit balances. This pricing arrangement allows for different rates of interest for different ranges of deposit balances, the higher the balance the higher the interest rate. For example, the bank may offer a rate of 5.50 per cent on the first $5,000, 5.75 per cent on balances between $5,000 and $10,000. Any amount over $10,000 earns 7.00 per cent. A depositor will therefore earn an average of 5.625 per cent on a deposit balance of $10,000. Moreover, for every $1.00 deposit over $10,000, the depositor earns 7.00 per cent. If the bank paid a standard rate of 5.50 per cent on deposits regardless of the deposit size, the difference between the average split rate and the standard rate will be 0.125 per cent on a $10,000 deposit. Split-rate pricing provides depositors an incentive to maintain larger average balances and allows banks to compete aggressively by increasing interest rates for incremental deposits without a significant increase in their deposit cost.

7.4   PRICING JOINT PRODUCTS

Banks in developing financial markets may have to offer a wide range of products or services to maintain or improve their relationship with customers. Such relationships may be worthwhile only if they are profitable, and this profitability may be measured by the difference between the total revenues earned on all products and the total costs incurred in providing the products. Joint product pricing may be used in the pricing of consumer deposit and credit and in the pricing of a package of products.

The joint product pricing experiences of developed financial markets suggest that the method of pricing consumer deposit and credit is to offer loan rate discounts to depositors. These discounts may range from 0.25 per cent to 3.00 per cent depending on the size of the account balance, and number of deposit accounts. The basis for loan rate discounts to depositors is to promote deposit growth that is profitable after taking all expenses into account. An issue for management is the proper accounting treatment of these discounts. If loan rate discounts are instituted to promote deposit growth, then such discounts may be treated as a deposit marketing expense. Failure to treat the discounts in this manner may underestimate the earnings on the bank's loans, and the costs of its deposit growth. Moreover, the recognition of the loan rate discount as a deposit marketing expense enables the bank to consider whether some other marketing approach may be more cost effective.[5]

Should management decide that loan rate discounting is a cost-effective marketing approach, it may consider the options that increase the usefulness of this approach. One or a combination of three options are relevant. Loan rate discounts may be offered only to: (1) new depositors in full recognition that existing depositors may demand equal treatment, (2) depositors with a long-term (1 year or more) relationship with the bank, or (3) borrowers who repay their loans by deductions from their deposit with the bank. Option (3) may be the most effective in promoting deposit growth in as much as it requires the borrower to maintain a deposit relationship at least during the term of the loan. Another advantage of this option is the probability of loan losses will be reduced because of the automatic debiting of loan repayment from the borrower's deposit account.

The pricing of loans to promote deposit growth may be influenced by the age distribution of the bank's actual and potential customers. It has been argued that there are stages in the lives of these customers when they may borrow heavily or save aggressively to smooth their consumption patterns over their life cycle.[6] Younger customers tend to borrow heavily to achieve the level of consumption consistent with their expected future income. These same customers at middle age tend to repay debt and increase savings to provide for the occasion when their income falls after retirement. Despite a lower income at retirement, they maintain their income levels by a process of using their savings accumulated during middle age. In developing financial markets, unemployment and low income levels of the younger customers may impose severe restraint on their ability to borrow. The middle class may be unable to save because of high personal income tax rates and the ravaging effect of inflation on disposable incomes; emigration might even have reduced the middle class to an insignificant segment of the population. The retired population may have no savings to maintain consumption higher than afforded by their meager pensions, unless supplemented by remittances from abroad.

This life cycle hypothesis of these customers' behaviour may not be of much assistance to bank management in developing financial markets attempting to price loans to attract deposits or to target the bank's loan rate reduction programme to a particular market segment. Periodic surveys may be conducted by the central bank or a group representing the financial industry to determine the composition of consumers' assets and liabilities and their use of financial services. The survey results may provide an empirical basis for determining the types of financial service demanded by customers and the characteristics of the users of these services.[7] The survey results may not fit any *a priori* position on consumer behaviour and may be country or even region specific. Whatever the survey results, bank management may want to market their loan rate discount programme to consumers who are potentially large suppliers of funds and who are sensitive to small interest rate differentials. The loan rate discount programme will be effective if it is tied to the maintenance of minimum balances on savings accounts.

The loan rate discount programme need not be associated with minimum deposit balances alone. It may be a part of a credit and service package that includes safety deposit boxes, insurance, money orders, and other financial services for a single monthly fee. The benefits of an inclusive credit and service package are that it can increase the bank's fee income, and reduce its interest expenses without causing a reduction of deposit balances. These benefits can be realized if the bank's credit and service package is used by high-income customers with a preference for paying a small or no monthly fee for the package to receiving high interest on their deposit balances. Once the bank and the high-income customers are aware of the potential tax savings of free or low-cost services, it may not be difficult to attract high-income depositors by offering these services rather than high interest rates on large deposit balances.

7.5   PRICING COMMERCIAL CREDIT

Although consumer installment loans and revolving credit lines will continue to be important components of banks' credit portfolios, the increasing privatization of firms and the resulting expansion of the economies being liberalized may raise the proportion of commercial loans in the credit portfolios of banks in developing financial markets. As these loans and the related credit risks expand, bank management will have to become increasingly cognizant of the fact that the optimal loan pricing is one that maximizes the bank's market value or shareowners' interest in the bank. In other words, the loan pricing system may aim at maximizing the returns on the bank's equity capital.[8]

One method of determining whether the commercial loan portfolio creates enough income to maximize the bank's market value is for management to conduct a loan profitability analysis of each credit extended, and if possible adjust the loan price to meet the income maximization objective. Of course, the success of any such price adjustment will depend on whether the bank is a price-setter or a price-taker in this credit market segment. Loan profitability analysis attempts to obtain an estimate of the customer's contribution to the bank's earnings by reviewing, in a systematic manner, all revenues obtained from the customer and all costs incurred by having this customer and its related business with the bank.[9]

A basic assumption of loan profitability analysis is that the bank customer is provided a comprehensive set of banking services from which the bank obtains interest, deposit balances and fees. The analysis is based on information relating to the customer's contribution to the bank's balance sheet, and to the bank's income and expenses. Table 7.2 profiles the contribution of a firm with a 1-year 15 per cent fixed interest loan, and funds with a transfer price of 12 per cent per annum. The profile indicates that on average 8 per cent of the loan was funded by the customer's own balances, and loan commitment fees provided 25 per cent of the total income generated from the customer. Income before cost of funds amounts to 20 per cent of net borrowed funds and compares favourably with the 15 per cent loan rate. The 5 per cent difference, or the effective rate of return, amounting to one-third of the loan rate, can be explained by the value of the free balances and the loan commitment fee. Profitability, after allowing for a 12 per cent transfer price for funds amounts to 7.1 per cent on net borrowed funds.

Management may consider at least three factors in determining the appropriate transfer prices in the bank's loan function. These are: (1) the cost

Table 7.2   Loan profitability analysis

Sources and uses of funds	$	$
Average loan balance		100 000
Average collected demand balance	10 000	
of which investible balances	8 000	
Average time balances	–	
of which investible balances	–	
Total investible balances		8 000
Net borrowed funds		92 000
Income		
Gross interest income on loans		15 000
Fees on loan commitment		5 000
Other fees	–	
Total income		20 000
Expenses		
Interest on deposit balances		–
Cost of services provided		1 500
Total expenses		1 500
Income before cost of funds		18 500
Transfer price of funds		12 000
Profitability		6 500

of borrowed funds used to fund the transaction; (2) the target rate of return on the bank's equity capital; and (3) the risks inherent in the transaction.

The cost of borrowed funds can easily be determined in the case of fixed-rate lending. This cost may be linked to the CD or some other money market rate depending on the relevant maturity and funding opportunities available to the bank. For loans with well defined repricing terms, the direct cost of funds is also easily determined. The direct cost of a loan priced on the basis of the 3-month CDs rate can be easily estimated. However, for prime-based loans, this cost may not be as easily determined as in the case of fixed-rate, or variable-rate lending with defined repricing terms. A system of pool-rate pricing may be established for prime loans. This system entails establishing a funding pool, determining the cost of the pool, and transferring this cost to the bank's portfolio of prime loans.

The second factor in determining the appropriate transfer price is the bank's leverage and target return on equity. Management must establish the target return on equity, determine the margin over the cost of borrowed funds that will yield this return, and incorporate this margin in the transfer price. Given the planned leverage ratio, the margin that will contribute to the target return on equity may be easily determined.

The third factor relates to adjustments for credit or default risk. The transfer price system may require the bank to recognize loan loss rates associated with different types of lending and to include these rates in the cost of funds. The risk adjustment factor may consist of an expected loss rate linked to a particular type of loan and a compensation for actually taking such risk. This compensation may be viewed as either an increase in return for taking greater than average risk, or a differential allocation of capital across different loan types.[10]

Interest, deposit balances, and fees have always constituted the income side of any lending relationship. After deregulation, fee income has been emphasized. One of the reasons for the increased emphasis on fee income is the reduced availability of free or low-cost deposit balances. During financial repression, firms maintained their demand deposit balances at their major banks. In fact, these banks really had no need to set minimum deposit balances since the balances themselves were usually substantial, and they were often all the cash, in the form of demand deposits, the firms maintained anywhere. These balances were dictated more by available funds than by any plans to restrict them to a level commensurate with services the banks provided. Interest rates were too low to compensate for any serious cash management effort by the firms, which in turn were charged affordable and stable rates on their bank borrowing. In fact, banks in repressed financial markets had a sure formula for success. Loans and investments were funded primarily with demand deposits, which paid no interest, and to a lesser extent with low-rate savings accounts.

The high interest rates that accompanied financial liberalization, and the demand by firms for cash management services, combined to change the comfortable life bankers enjoyed in repressed financial markets and foreshadowed the competitive and complex pricing arrangement prevalent in developing financial markets. Higher interest rates made it worthwhile for the borrowing firms to invest their excess balances previously maintained in interest-free demand deposits. To maintain their deposit levels, if even at a higher average cost, bank management tended to encourage some of the firms to reduce their excess balances at other banks in order to concentrate them at their own banks. With these balances on which interest is paid, banks could expand their commercial loan volume more rapidly than without them.

Even if the banks are compelled to borrow short and lend long in the new deregulated, high interest rate, and intensely competitive commercial credit market, they can maintain their profitability by implementing variable interest rates to reduce or eliminate the interest rate sensitivity gaps between their borrowing and their loans. Thus, so long as the funding and the demand for bank loans are not shifted to non-bank entities or to new markets (for example, the commercial paper market), banks would continue to be profitable since a substantial supply of funds would be purchased and lent at a spread.

However, several factors could operate jointly or separately to disturb this profitable scenario common particularly in the early evolution of developing financial markets. Among these factors are the: (1) development of a commercial paper market comprising the prime borrowers and investors with excess balances; (2) establishment of new and stringent capital adequacy standards by bank regulators; (3) demand by banks' shareholders for stable and competitive rate of return on their investment; and (4) proper recognition of the risks inherent in the banks' loan portfolio in the pricing of their lending and off-balance sheet activities.

The experience of developed financial markets with regards to the competition by banks for the excess balances has shown that such competition resulted in a reduced availability to the banks and a shifting of these balances to the commercial paper market where prime borrowers issue commercial paper at rates lower that the banks' lending rates and firms with excess balances buy these paper at rates higher than those offered by the commercial banks. A growing commercial paper market, therefore, provided firms not only an alternative funding source but also attractive short-term investment instruments.

Commercial lending in developing financial markets, like in other financial markets, involves five major types of credit: seasonal, asset conversion, cash flow, asset based and project related credits. A borrower may have credit that combines features of these various credit types – seasonal and cash flow loans may have asset based features. Retailers and wholesalers tend to be candidates for seasonal or asset based credit; manufactures, for asset based and cash flow credits; and public utilities and regulated entities, for project related credit. Each credit type, no doubt, has a different risk profile. Box 7.1 describes the different types of credit.[11] A bank's commercial loan pricing system must be sufficiently adequate to capture the risk associated with the various types of credit, while increasing the bank's profitability and return on equity capital.

The prime rate, or the base rate, is an important element in commercial loan pricing. Prime rate is the rate charged by commercial banks for credit extended to their best customers. This rate provides the base on which the commercial interest rate differential between the prime rate and any other rate of interest charged for a commercial loan is an approximate measure

Box 7.1   Credit types

- *Seasonal* : seasonal bank credit is extended to meet the peak, short-term credit needs of firms or to fill a seasonal gap between the transformation of the firms inventory, funded with suppliers' credit, to finished products for sale, and the collection of the proceeds of sale of the firms' products. Seasonal credit is extinguished at each production cycle.
- *Asset conversion*: asset conversion credit is credit, on an ongoing instead of a seasonal basis, to fill the gap between suppliers' credit and the collection of proceeds from the sale of the manufactured products. An asset conversion credit tends to be ongoing, and its cycles tend to overlap.
- *Cash flow*: cash flow credit tends to be long-term loans to finance the purchase of plant and equipment, or to support increasing levels of current assets with life cycles of 1 year or less.
- *Asset based*: asset-based credit is credit collateralized by assets with a residual value (for example inventory and accounts receivable financing) which the market will transform into cash to pay the creditors in the event of financial distress. Asset-based credit is short-term financing extended on a permanent basis to support a high level of essentially liquid assets that provide the collateral for the credit.
- *Project related*: project-related credit is credit that combines the characteristics of a cash flow credit with those of an asset-based credit.

---

of the premium for the additional risk involved. The term 'base rate' has grown in popularity in developing financial markets. The base rate is the rate around which commercial loan pricing varies mainly as a function of risk. Thus, a firm may borrow below or above the base rate depending on whether it is a low-risk or high-risk borrower.

Commercial loan rates may be fixed for the term of the loan or they may be variable. Variable rates may be adjusted at certain predetermined intervals and in terms of changes in an agreed rate, be it the base rate or some other market rate reflecting the bank's cost of funds. Whether a fixed or variable rate is charged will depend on the bank's and the borrower's interest rate expectations and their respective abilities to transfer the interest cost. If, in a rising interest rate environment, borrowers can transfer increased interest cost to the prices of the goods or services they produce or if interest cost is an insignificant element of their total costs, they may be indifferent if the contractual rate is variable or fixed. However, with the volatile and upward-trending interest rates that characterized developing financial markets, borrowers may prefer fixed interest rates and lenders, variable ones.

To meet the demand for commercial loans, banks may access the money market with its active buying and selling of short-term funds. This access provides information on the marginal cost of funds and facilitates the pricing of commercial loans. For example, banks can establish their base lending rates by determining a spread over the marginal cost of funds required to guarantee a competitive return for their stockholders, after allowing for specific loan loss provisions or specific credit and other risks.

Thus, in determining the price of a commercial loan, management may start with a set of basic information. Such information may include: (1) the required capital to asset ratio, and the earnings value of capital; (2) a competitive return on equity capital; (3) an interest rate spread sufficient to cover the capital/asset ratio requirement; (4) the marginal costs of funds; and (5) the proportion of non-interest operating expenses that can be assigned to the origination and servicing of the loans, as well as the taxes to be paid on income derived from this loan.[12]

The system of pricing commercial loans must be flexible enough to reflect changing market conditions and the different risk and conditions associated with each borrower. This flexibility is particularly required with the origination of large commercial loans intended for sale to or participation with other banks or for credit securitization. In fact, the success or failure of a loan sale or participation may be influenced by the adaptability of the initial pricing arrangement to changing market conditions. The loan documentation must reflect this flexibility. For instance, participants in a loan may want to change the interest base of the loan from a prime interest rate based loan to a money market rate based one; they may want to provide pricing incentives to encourage borrowers to reduce their leverage ratios or improve their capitalization; they may even want to have the flexibility to impose penalties, by charging higher premiums over the base rate, should the borrower fail to meet certain performance standards.

Table 7.3 illustrates a system for pricing commercial loans. This system is endowed with some degree of flexibility to the extent that the loan price may be modified to reflect the marginal cost of funds, the risk of individual borrowers, the size of the loan, and the existence of compensating balances. Adjustment for risk may be reflected in varying the required spread.

Adjustment for loan size may be shown in the reduced average cost of loan origination and loan servicing and, therefore, in lower non-interest expenses; and adjustment for compensating balances may be indicated by a reduction in the cost of funds in an amount equivalent to the earnings value of the balances. A large loan to a borrower with a high credit rating, alternative funding sources, and deposit balances with a bank, will have a different price from a small loan to a new and highly leveraged firm with little or no compensating balances in the bank.

Table 7.3   Pricing a commercial loan

Assumptions	%
Required capital to asset ratio	8.25
Competitive return on equity capital	20.00.
Marginal cost of funds	12.00

Required spread
to cover capital ratio and desired return on capital
= .0825 × .20 = .0165 = 1.65%

Cost of funds

Marginal cost of funds	12.00	
− earnings value of capital	.75	
= cost of funds on loan	11.25	

Price determination

Cost of funds	11.25
+ non interest operating expenses	.65
+ taxes	.30
total expenses	12.20
+ required spread	1.65
= commercial loan rate	13.85

Adjustments that recognize low risk borrowers with large compensating balances may result in the failure of the bank to achieve a spread large enough to generate a competitive return on equity. Management may improve the bank's return on equity by generating more fee income for activities that do not increase the bank's assets. As far as the bank's commercial lending activity is concerned, fees may be obtained from the unused portion of a firm commitment to lend, and loan origination especially if the intention is to sell the entire loan or to sell participation in it. In fact, some borrowers have opted to pay fees to their banks for services in lieu of holding compensating balances. The option has been exercised because, in countries where reserve requirements are high, compensating balances increase the cost to customers by more than they increase the yield to the bank. Thus, charging the borrower directly by including the cost of services in the loan price tends to be more cost effective for the borrower and the bank.[13]

Normally, fee income is generated from off-balance sheet activities, which are activities that do not involve the creation of assets or the taking of deposits. Such activities, which carry credit risk themselves, include commercial and stand-by letters of credit, commitments to lend, third-party guarantees, interest rate or currency swaps, repurchase agreements, foreign exchange and other contracts. In pricing its off-balance sheet services, a bank may consider the risk involved in having to meet its off-balance commitments on behalf of its customers, as well as the impact of this risk on its capital adequacy and required return on equity capital.

7.6 SUMMARY

The chapter has emphasized the role of marginal cost and marginal revenue in a bank's product pricing and has stressed the importance of full cost pricing for the long-term viability of banks operating in developing financial markets. It has argued that, under competitive market conditions, banks may be unable to charge prices that even cover full costs, let alone realize a profit. In such a situation, a knowledge of marginal costs would set the floor price for the products while incurring losses. A knowledge of the product's full costs would assist in showing the extent to which the floor price received has covered these costs, and in encouraging management to target prices that would as far as possible reimburse the bank's full costs. Accepting prices below full cost would therefore be a strategic short-term pricing decision.

The chapter has explored the pricing of consumer loans and deposits and the pricing of joint products such as consumer deposit and credit, and a package of products. It has emphasized the role of loan size, maturity, prepayment, insurance and such factors as down payment and collateral requirements and late payment in pricing consumer installment loans. Moreover, the chapter has argued that a bank's costs of granting credit lines to their customers may be lower than its costs of extending a series of small consumer loans.

It has shown that the pricing of deposits would be influenced by market interest rates, deposit insurance premium, deposit service costs, and reserve requirements and has recognized that in any market, there could be rate-sensitive and rate-neutral savers. It has argued that deposit rates should accommodate the rate-sensitive savers, while requiring these savers to maintain minimum-sized deposit balances on which higher interest rates would be paid. In addition, the chapter has argued that, given some degree of price-setting ability, banks in developing financial markets have at least three strategic options for consumer deposit pricing: pricing to save taxes; pricing to encourage minimum balance maintenance; and split-rate pricing.

In the area of commercial loan pricing, the chapter has indicated that the pricing system should aim at maximizing the rate of return on the bank's equity and consequently maximize the bank's market value. It has suggested that a method of determining whether a bank's commercial loan portfolio created enough income to maximize its market value was to perform loan profitability analyses, and adjust the loan price on a case by case basis to meet rate of return targets.

8 Managing Asset and Liability Risks

In repressed financial markets, banks faced little or no price competition, and experienced high profitability. Deposit interest rates were fixed and so were interest rates for some loans granted through government directed credit programmes. Rates on these loans ensured a positive and attractive interest spread. Rates on other loans were not fixed by the authorities and banks also recorded substantial spreads that were not competed away because of market entry restrictions. The supply of investment securities for savers and investors was limited, and the markets for these securities were shallow. Exchange control regulations restricted the freedom of banks to operate in foreign currencies, and fixed exchange rates isolated them, to a large measure, from exchange rate risks. With interest and exchange rates fixed, and the central bank providing discounting facilities in the event of a liquidity crisis, the major risk to be managed was credit risk. But even in this area, risk was minimized by the government directed or supported credit programmes. In fact, risks were low and returns were high for banks operating in repressed financial markets.

In developing financial markets, the variability in exchange rates and interest rates affects market prices and the value of banks' asset and liability portfolios; the supply of investment securities increases, while securities markets become deeper and more liquid. Because of competitive pressures, and stricter conditions for accessing central bank liquidity support, problem banks in developing financial markets tend to fail and to be liquidated more easily than they did in repressed financial markets. With the removal of entry barriers, some banks establish offices in other developing financial markets to complement their domestic borrowing and lending activities. Banks in developing financial markets, therefore, have to manage not only credit risk, but a number of other risks, including interest rate, exchange rate, liquidity, settlement, and transfer risks. The effective management of these risks assists in stabilizing the banks' overall cash flow, and in ensuring their profitability and viability.

The complexity of financial risk, no doubt, argues a strong case for an identifiable and dedicated risk management function in a bank's organization structure. Such a function should be: (1) comprehensive to include asset, liability and off-balance sheet risks; (2) based on reliable information and scientific risk management techniques; and (3) delegated to asset-liability managers or committee depending on the size of the bank. In examining the asset-liability management components, this chapter focuses on information, policies, risk management and assessment.

8.1   INFORMATION AND POLICIES

Given the tendency for high interest rate volatility and intense competition in developing financial markets asset-liability management attempts to use an explicit and coordinated approach to the management of both sides of a bank's balance sheet. The objective of this approach is to ensure that there are asset-liability managers and an asset-liability committee (ALCO) that manage the bank's balance sheet in such a manner as to minimize the exposure of its earnings, liquidity, and equity to changes in market conditions. The attainment of this objective may be manifested in such results as stable net interest margins, optimum earnings, adequate liquidity, and effective control of financial risks.

In order to achieve these results, the asset-liability managers and the ALCO must be guided by policies that specifically address the bank's overall asset-liability management goals and risk limits, and by information that relates directly to its asset-liability positions. Examples of the related information are: (1) historical, current and projected data on the bank's asset-liability portfolios, including any projected additions, maturities, and repricing; (2) interest rates and yields on its current and projected portfolios; (3) market limitations on the bank's ability to adjust its product prices; and (4) changes in the bank's balance sheet caused by customers' decisions to prepay their loans, withdraw their deposits before maturity, and transfer their business to other banks.[1]

Experiences in developed financial markets have indicated two major difficulties inherent in the asset-liability management process. These are the failure to: (1) adopt meaningful policies; and (2) implement the policies once they are adopted.[2] It is the responsibility of the board to recognize that a formalized asset-liability management policy is the cornerstone of all other bank policies; and to instruct the ALCO to develop a meaningful asset-liability management policy for its approval. Once this policy is approved the board is obligated to support and encourage its effective implementation.

Undoubtedly, the effective implementation of a bank's asset-liability policy will mainly be the result of teamwork among the bank's senior management staff, given the required information and technical competence of this staff. Some banks, particularly the smaller ones, may have the policy of transferring their officers during their banking careers to various management functions within the bank. Other banks, particularly the larger ones, may train their officers to function within specific areas for their entire careers and consequently, investment officers will focus on their investment portfolios, commercial loan officers on their commercial loan portfolios, installment loan officers on their installment loan portfolios, operations officers on operations, and none of these officers will be concerned about the bank as a whole. Although this narrow approach to banking may improve the effectiveness of each functional area, it may hinder the achievement of a coordinated approach that is essential to effective asset-liability management.

The ALCO can foster the required team spirit. ALCO members may include heads of the bank's lending, investments, marketing, and financial management departments. The bank's chief executive or president may serve at least in an ex-officio capacity to the committee, and any member may be the ALCO's chairman. Each member will bring his or her specific perspective on achieving the bank's overall objectives. However, the officer in charge of the bank's financial management function will be expected to play an important role in the ALCO deliberations. It is the financial manager who will ensure that the bank has a specific policy for overall asset-liability management, and that this policy addresses the goals and risk parameters covering such areas as investments in securities, liquidity, money market assets, funds acquisitions, hedging, and foreign exchange trading. Moreover, the financial manager may choose the appropriate techniques for analysing and controlling interest rate risk, and take the lead in educating non-financial managers on the ALCO about the theory and techniques of asset-liability management.[3] For effective risk management results, a massive effort must be made to improve the information available to, and competence of ALCO members.

Depending on the size of the bank, the variety of its asset and liability activities, and the sophistication of the markets in which the bank operates, the asset-liability policy may be a simple or a complex one. Two basic policy areas that must be addressed for effective asset-liability management are the: (1) ALCO authority, purpose, membership, and functions; and (2) performance targets (for example, net interest margins, return on average assets and equity) that must be achieved.

In general, the policy must recognize that the manner in which a bank structures its assets and liabilities will determine its interest rate risk position. The most common example is that of a bank that funds longer-term fixed-rate assets with shorter-term or variable-rate liabilities. Since yield curves tend to have an upward slope much of the time, with short-term rates lower than long-term rates, this bank will make a profit by borrowing short-term funds and lending them on a longer-term basis. With this strategy, the bank assumes interest rate risk. In other words, if short-term rates rise, the bank's cost of funds will increase, while the rate earned on its longer-term assets will remain relatively fixed. In certain circumstances, the spread between asset yields and liability costs can become negative. Even if the spread remains positive, the bank's net interest income may be insufficient to cover its overheads, creating losses that erode capital.

Whether a given interest rate risk position actually leads to problems for a bank will depend on movements in interest rates. Should the yield curve remain upward sloping and interest rates remain unchanged, the strategy of borrowing short and lending long will be a continuing source of risk-free profits. But the yield curve would not always be upward sloping, and surely interest rates would change. It is, therefore, the effect of potential rate changes on a bank's asset-liability activities that must be of concern to risk or financial managers.

The primary determinant of a bank's exposure to interest rate risk is the extent to which assets and liabilities are mismatched. Mismatching refers to the timing difference between the changes in interest rates received on a bank's assets (namely interest income) and paid on its liabilities (namely interest expense). In practice, banks tend to exhibit some degree of mismatching and exposure to interest rate changes. In countries with market-determined rates, asset and liability managers are confronted daily with the effects of rate changes. It is, however, important to recognize that interest rate risk also exists in countries with administered rates, even when those rates have remained fixed for long periods. Any number of factors can lead to a change in those rates, and such a change will affect the financial condition of the institutions operating in that market, depending on their interest rate risk position. Often the consequences of rate changes (for example, interest and exchange rate changes) would be traumatic for bank managers with little or no related experience, information or techniques.

Effective asset-liability managers can use several risk measurement techniques in an attempt to assess how future earnings might be affected by potential interest rate movements. Normally, each measurement technique would be based on simplifying assumptions, and thus each technique has its limitations. Thus, informed judgement is required to interpret the risk measures. Fundamental to interest rate risk measurement is timely and accurate information on the interest rate repricing dates of the bank's assets and liabilities. Knowing when the interest rates on all assets and liabilities can be changed is critical to determining the bank's interest rate risk position.

The most commonly used information depicts the different volumes of assets and liabilities whose interest rates can be reset within various future time periods. This report, commonly referred to as an interest rate gap report, represents the gaps in the timing of rate resettings on assets and liabilities. Netting assets against liabilities in the various future time periods produces the gap for each period. By multiplying a hypothetical rate change by the size of the gap, management obtains a measure of the sensitivity of future net interest income over the future time period corresponding to the gap. Gap reports are typically used to estimate potential changes in net interest income over the near term, generally the next few quarters or next year. But gaps reports tend to be fairly imprecise and sometimes misleading.

Simulation models project future net interest income under a variety of different interest rate scenarios. The models use the same type of information found in gap reports, as well as information on the current interest rates associated with existing assets and liabilities. Starting with this information on repricing dates and existing rates earned and paid, and adding assumptions about future interest rates, simulation models project future interest income and expense under a variety of different future interest rate scenarios. The result can be a fairly good measure of the sensitivity of the bank's net cash flow or earnings to interest rate changes.

Regardless of the type of measurement technique used, an important factor in a bank's ability to assess interest rate risk is the timeliness and accuracy of the information upon which the measurement process is based. The most important information relates to the interest rate repricing dates associated with existing assets and liabilities and related current interest rates. Typically, this information is obtained from the automated or manual accounting and processing systems used by banks to track the various assets and liabilities. As a practical matter, many banks in developing financial markets may not have the basic information necessary to complete a gap report, and fewer will have the information required for a good simulation model. For these reasons, the highest priority is to improve the timeliness, accuracy, and completeness of the basic risk management information.

Interest rate risk management positions may be categorized here as strategic, tactical, and trading. Strategic positions typically arise from a bank's lending and reflect the practice of banks to lend long and borrow short. Moreover, strategic positions tend to remain stable, and thus require less active management. Alterations in strategic positions are usually accomplished by conscious adjustment of the loan and deposit mix, often by altering the pricing or marketing strategy in an effort to increase or decrease the volume of loans or deposits, or modify their repricing dates.

Tactical positions arise primarily from a bank's investment and funding activities in the money, capital and perhaps derivative markets (for example, futures and swaps). These positions characterize many securities firms, but also exist, to varying degrees, in commercial banks. Since tactical positions usually involve liquid instruments obtained from primary and secondary markets, these positions can be adjusted rapidly in response to unexpected interest rate movements or changed expectations. Thus, tactical positions often reflect conscious risk taking in anticipation of short-term or medium-term interest rate changes. Banks also use tactical positions to offset undesired strategic positions until the product mix can be adjusted. Tactical positions require daily management.

Trading positions, which may at times be large, are taken in anticipation of very short-term rate movements (from a few minutes to a day or two). In order to run large positions, the trader must be assured that they can be closed in a matter of minutes. For this reason, trading positions are usually limited to money and capital market instruments with high secondary market liquidity, and to active derivative markets. Trading positions must be managed constantly, and be closed or reduced to policy prescribed levels at the end of the business day. Of course, these levels will be minimal or zero.

As asset-liability managers are responsible for monitoring and controlling the bank's interest rate risk, they must have a clear understanding of the strategic positions, as reflected in the amount of risk acceptable to senior management and the board. Ordinarily, the size and nature of acceptable strategic positions are periodically reviewed by them in the context of long-term business plans and economic trends. In larger institutions operating in developed financial markets, senior management may grant asset-liability managers explicit authority to take tactical positions within specified limits. Tactical positioning is then taken by asset-liability managers based on their short-term and medium-term interest rate projections. In those few institutions with trading operations, senior management and asset-liability managers may establish explicit positions and stop loss limits for traders running trading positions. Adherence by the traders to these limits is routinely monitored by the asset-liability managers.

Liquidity management is another important component of asset-liability management. Liquidity is the ability to meet anticipated and contingent cash needs – the risk is measured by the probability that these needs may not be met. Cash needs arise from deposit withdrawals, liability maturities, and loan disbursements (for example, new loans and the drawdown of outstanding lending commitments). Cash needs are met by increases in deposits and borrowings, loan repayments, investment maturities, and the asset sales. Inadequate liquidity may lead to unexpected cash shortfalls that must be covered at inordinate costs, thus reducing profitability. In the worst case, inadequate liquidity can lead to the bank's insolvency. On the other hand, excessive liquidity can result in low asset yields and poor earnings performance.

Liquidity is managed to enable the bank to maintain its required reserves at the central bank and sufficient liquidity for the cash needs of its customers. An overriding goal of liquidity management is to ensure that cash needs can always be met at reasonable cost. These needs may be met by the maturity or sale of assets, the acquisition of deposits, or additional money market funding. Depending on the size of the bank or the sophistication of the money market in which the bank is a player, the process of liquidity management may be separated into asset management or liability management.

As a general rule, small banks and banks operating in underdeveloped money markets tend to emphasize asset management when managing their liquidity positions. This emphasis may be explained by their limited ability to raise money market funding and to generate additional deposits to meet sudden, unexpected cash flow shortfalls. The focus of the asset management approach is on the: (1) maturity structure of the bank's deposits and borrowings; and (2) estimates of loan and other asset growth. The intention of this focus is to ensure that, as far as possible, cash outflows can be met from cash inflows associated with maturing assets. For unexpected needs, a stock of high-quality liquid assets is maintained. However, these assets are ordinarily obtained from active secondary markets that provide assurance that the assets can be quickly sold at low discounts or otherwise easily converted into cash. In addition, banks relying on asset management will often arrange committed lines of credit from other institutions as a back-up source of funding for extreme emergencies.

In order to minimize their portfolios of high quality but low yielding liquid assets, larger banks with greater access to developed financial markets may rely more on liability management than on asset management for liquidity control. In times of need, these banks raise additional funding in large volumes, primarily through the money markets. For these banks liquidity management primarily involves the expansion, diversification, and quantification of sources of additional funding. Expanding the number of funds providers familiar with the bank and willing to invest in its money market instruments serves to increase the likelihood that funding would be available when required. Diversification among the types of funds providers stabilizes funding capacity and minimizes funding concentrations that will increase the bank's vulnerability to problems being experienced by a major funds provider. Bank management in the more advanced developing financial markets that rely on liability management must have an acute awareness of the potential fragility of both the money markets and the financial condition of the major funds providers in those markets.

Some banks in developing financial markets accept foreign currency deposits directly through their foreign currency offices or subsidiaries or through transfers to their home offices. For banks with domestic and foreign currency liabilities, liquidity must be managed for each set of currency denominated liabilities. For domestic currency liabilities, the bank would be able to access the central bank for liquidity support – either by pledging eligible collateral or by borrowing on an unsecured basis. If there are any convertibility restrictions on the domestic currency, banks with foreign currency liabilities must pursue the most conservative liquidity management practices to meet the cash needs of their foreign currency depositors.

As a practical matter, it is a relatively routine process to manage liquidity in a healthy bank operating in a stable environment. More challenging is managing liquidity in an unstable environment. To prepare for the liquidity consequences of such an environment, asset-liability managers should develop contingency plans. Contingency plans contemplate worst-case scenarios and establish strategies to deal with such events. In addition to developing contingency plans, asset-liability managers may implement appropriate measures to improve liquidity when a bank is likely to encounter financial difficulties. For example, liability maturities can be extended to reduce potential cash needs over the near term. However, to be able to implement such measures asset-liability managers must be fully informed about the condition of the bank, and more particularly about the quality of its loan portfolio.

It is often the case that asset-liability managers are informed of serious asset quality problems only days or even hours before knowledge of those problems becomes widespread. Managers responsible for the loan portfolio tend to obscure deteriorating credit quality until it reaches a critical point. Good internal communication is critical, because asset-liability managers can use in an effective manner the period between the time the problem is identified internally and the time it becomes known externally.

Adequate liquidity is often influenced by the public's perception (for example, depositor and borrower perception) of the financial and management strength of the bank. If the bank's condition is seen as deteriorating, usually because of significant loan losses, extraordinary liquidity demands will arise. Depositors will withdraw deposits, or not renew them when they mature. The capacity of the bank to raise funds in the money markets, at any cost, will eventually decline as creditors reduce or eliminate their available lines of credit. The reduced availability and increased cost of funding, may be accompanied by a surge in drawdowns under outstanding loan commitments. Borrowers may respond to the bank's potential failure by accessing their credit lines to ensure that they have the funds they need in the future. They may also access their credit lines to offset their bank deposits that may not be readily withdrawn. Thus, a deterioration in the market's perception may seriously impact a bank's liquidity position. The ability to measure and monitor liquidity risk is therefore an important management requirement.

A typical liquidity report provides details on all cash flows associated with existing assets and liabilities. Since some deposits may not have contractual maturities, estimates of their cash flows may be based on an analysis of past trends. Similarly, estimates of cash flows available from loans should recognize that many loans may be rolled over at maturity. The liquidity report may also include estimates of potential loan and deposit growth, taking into consideration commitments and guarantees, and seasonal trends in loan and deposit volumes.

An effective liquidity measurement system will depict a best-case and perhaps several worst-case funding scenarios. Under at least one worst-case scenario, asset-liability managers may estimate the impact of a sudden deterioration in the quality of a bank's loan portfolio on the market's perception of the bank. In fact, an unsatisfactory asset quality affects the bank's liquidity position not only through its adverse impact on market perception but also through the resulting reduced cash flows associated with the non-performing, renegotiated or otherwise troubled assets. The measurement of liquidity must, therefore, be based on a cash flow analysis designed to identify the time and size of current and potential funding requirements taking into account such conditioning factors as market perception, asset quality, commitments and contingencies. Liquidity of banks in developing financial markets may not be completely measured by the simple balance sheet ratios. Such ratios afford only an incomplete measure of liquidity. Moreover, the quality of the liquidity measurement will depend on the timeliness of information on maturities of existing assets and liabilities, and on the quality of the analysis of past and projected trends in assets and liabilities. For many banks, the initial steps in improving their liquidity management may be to ensure the accuracy and timeliness of the maturity information available from their accounting and operational systems and the reliability of the analysis of these trends.

8.2   MEASURING RISK

Risk management presumes a clear definition, and a method of measuring the risks to be managed. Risk is a difficult concept to grasp and a great deal of controversy has surrounded attempts to define and measure it. A common definition of risk, however, is one that is stated in terms of probability distribution. This definition associates risk with the probability of not achieving an anticipated outcome, be it an expected return on investment, a targetted level of non-performing loans, net interest income, or overall cash flow.

To be useful, any measure of risk should have a definite value. One such measure is the standard deviation that summarizes the dispersions about an expected value or expected outcome. A bank's overall risk can, therefore, be defined as the probability of failure to achieve an expected value and can be measured by the standard deviation of this value. In addition, the expected value must serve as a comprehensive indicator of the bank's performance under changing market conditions.

It may be useful to review a set of basic concepts that facilitates a clear understanding of this definition. The concepts are probability distribution, expected value, and standard deviation. The probability of an event is defined as the chance, or odds, that the event will occur. For example, a financial manager may forecast a 40 per cent chance that short-term interest rate will decrease – a 60 per cent chance that it will not. If all possible events, or outcomes, are listed, and if a probability is assigned to each event, then the listing, together with the assigned probabilities, is defined as a probability distribution. A weighted average of outcomes is obtained by multiplying each possible outcome by its probability of occurrence and summing the results. This weighted average is the expected value. The variance of the probability distribution is obtained by determining the deviations of each possible outcome from the expected value, squaring each such deviations, multiplying the squared deviation by the probability of occurrence for its related outcome and summing these products. The standard deviation is found by obtaining the square root of the variance.

Table 8.1 illustrates the probability distribution of an interest rate scenario, expected rates of return on capital, and standard deviations about

Table 8.1   Probability distribution, expected value, and standard deviation

Interest rate scenario (1)	Probability of interest rate scenario (2)	Rate of return on capital (3)	(4) = (2) × (3)	
Bank A				
Decrease	0.4%	20%	8.0%	
Unchanged	0.2%	10%	2.0%	
Increase	0.4%	20%	0.8%	
			Expected value:	10.8%
			Standard deviation:	14.1%
Bank B				
Decrease	0.4%	15%	6.0%	
Unchanged	0.2%	10%	2.0%	
Increase	0.4%	80%	3.2%	
			Expected value:	11.2%
			Standard deviation:	8.3%

the expected value for Bank A and Bank B. These banks are operating in the same developing financial market but have different activity focuses, and cash flows as reflected in their rates of return on capital. Moreover, Table 8.1 shows that with a 40 per cent chance of an interest rate decrease, both banks will experience high rates of return on capital. This is explained by the tendency that a decrease in interest rates will lower the interest expense for both banks, increase loan demand, induce higher interest income, reduce loan loss provisions, and increase the market value of their investment securities portfolio. But the return has been higher for Bank A than for Bank B, both of which have started from a position of a 10 per cent return as indicated in the unchanged interest rate scenario.

With an interest rate increase, the banks experienced a decline in their rates of return perhaps due to an increase in interest expenses, a rise in loan charge-offs, or a decline in the market value of their investment securities portfolio. Bank A's return, resulting from the rate increase, is much lower than that of Bank B, possibly, because of the greater sensitivity of the former bank's asset portfolio to a high interest rate environment. For example, Bank A may have a large portfolio of investment securities, the price of which declines with an interest rate increase or a portfolio of non-performing loans resulting from the impact of high interest rates on the repayment capacity of its borrowers.

It may be noted, however, that the rates of return for Bank A vary far more widely than that of Bank B as reflected in the standard deviation differences. The standard deviation of Bank B's rates of return is almost half that of Bank A. As far as the rate of return indicator is concerned, Bank B, therefore, reflects a lower degree of risk than Bank A. For a normal distribution, the larger the size of the standard deviation, the greater the probability that the actual outcome will vary from the expected outcome (for example, an expected value such as an average return on a bank's asset portfolio, or a level of net cash flow).

8.3   A COMPREHENSIVE INDICATOR

A comprehensive indicator of a bank's performance may be described as its net cash flow, and risk may be measured as the volatility or standard deviation of this cash flow.[4] The cash flow indicator refers to the flow of funds arising from the bank's operations. This indicator, however, can be interpreted in different ways. For example, it can be interpreted as: (1) net income after taxes plus depreciation for a given period; (2) income after taxes and before depreciation; or (3) revenues less cash expenses for the period.

Table 8.2 illustrates the net cash flow computation based on these three interpretations.

Essentially, a bank's net cash flow from its operations is the sum of its net income after taxes, its depreciation, amortization of deferred charges, and other major non-cash expenses.[5] Measuring the volatility of these sources, identifying the reasons for such volatility and controlling it, are the essential elements of financial risk management.

Net income from operations is an important component of a bank's cash flow. It is the income residual after all interest and non-interest expenses have been paid. Thus, the goal of maximizing and stabilizing a bank's cash flow is mainly one of maximizing and stabilizing its net income. Net income volatility associated with interest rates, exchange rates, and market price fluctuations, therefore, serves as an important measure of risk management effectiveness. That part of a bank's own cash flow not related to net income, although important, is simply a recovery of capital invested. Whatever the existing cash flow, a negative net income will represent only the conversion of assets. A negative net income and a positive cashflow, therefore, represent a process of liquidation and not one of advancement. Furthermore, changes in the net income component of a bank's cash flow may reflect management's success or failure in controlling the various types of risk to which the bank has been exposed. Fluctuations in net income may, for example, reflect the management of interest rate and

Table 8.2 Cash flow computation $000

Net income after taxes plus depreciation:

Net income	870	
Plus: Depreciation	50	
Cash Flow	920	

Income after taxes and before depreciation:

	Per income statement	*Cash flow*
Income before depreciation and taxes	1 500	1 500
Less: estimated depreciation	50	
Taxable income	1 450	
Estimated taxes	580	580
Net income	870	
Income after taxes and before depreciation (cash flow)		920

Revenues less cash expenses:

Revenues	9 000
Less: cash expenses	8 080
cash flow	920

market risks, the management of credit and transfer risks, changes in loan loss provisions, and gains and losses on securities held.

Bank management in developing financial markets, must become increasingly informed about the various methodologies, strategies, and tactics that can be used for effective risk management. Interest rate risk, for example, may be minimized by the application of a set of asset-liability management methodologies used in developed financial markets; market risk may be minimized by a set of portfolio management strategies and tactics; and credit risk may be reduced by improving the bank's credit policy, procedures and practices.

Reported net income for some banks may be distorted and may be seriously misleading for risk management purposes. This is not because banks in these markets report their income on an accrual rather than on a cash basis.[6] Mainly, it is because of their practice of accruing interest on non-performing assets, and providing credit in the form of inadequately controlled overdrafts.[7]

Normally, interest income represents the major element in a bank's net income and is calculated on an accrual basis. This means that interest due on loans and securities is calculated for the period covered by the bank's income statement, whether or not the interest has actually been paid. However, although a portion of a credit may be overdue or non-performing loans for a significant period, the related interest may continue to be accrued and included in the bank's operating cash flow. This practice distorts the bank's real cash flow.

In most developed financial markets, interest accrual on non-performing assets is discontinued after a specified number of days (for example, 90 days) of non-performance. A carefully designed asset classification system will assist management in identifying various categories of assets on the basis of their actual and potential credit and transfer risks, and provide guidance for adjusting accrued interest, establishing general and specific reserves, and writing-off non-performing assets. Effective risk management demands the implementation of such a system for banks operating in developing financial markets.

Surely, the accrual of interest on non-performing assets can endanger a bank's long-term viability. With this practice, new funds derived from deposits and borrowing will be used to pay accrued interest, other operating expenses, taxes and dividends, while the opportunity to apply these funds to the financing of sound and profitable assets will be missed. This has been the experience of some state-owned banks with their high asset growth that reflects the practice of interest capitalization, or interest accrual on non-performing loans. Computing interest on uncollectible interest over an indefinite period makes net cash flow a misleading risk management indicator and must be disallowed by management.

Overdraft financing by banks in developing financial markets also distorts reported cash flow. This type of financing tends to succeed where the bank reviews, in a rigorous manner, the account performance and collateral held, and has a policy of demanding full repayment in the event of unanticipated credit risk or transfer risk. In many developing countries with the overdraft system as part of their colonial heritage, credit reviews may not be rigorous, overdraft agreements may not be formalized, and a system to enforce repayment may be absent. In these countries, interest may be charged to the overdraft account although the balance on this account has exceeded the agreed limit and the account may be inactive, in terms of deposits to it, for some time. The result is an increase in the bank's income, its asset size, and the customer's overdraft balances. Overdraft financing, without a reliable system of review, control, and recovery of outstanding balances, distorts net income, cash flow, and assets.

Table 8.1 has applied the concept of standard deviation to illustrate the volatility of rates of return under certain interest rate scenarios. The same concept can be used to measure the bank's cash flow volatility and compare this volatility over time or with that of other banks operating in the market. With the volatility of Bank A's net cash flow being higher than that of Bank B, as indicated in Figure 8.1, Bank A has a higher risk profile than Bank B.[8]

8.4 RISK TOLERANCE POSITIONS

Depending on management's tolerance for risk, banks in developing financial markets may hold a number of risk management positions. Management with a high tolerance for risk, as reflected by the size of standard deviation of a bank's net cash flow from operations, may expect to be compensated by high returns or high cash flow, and vice versa. In other words, returns as measured by net cash flow may tend to be positively correlated with the bank's overall risk tolerance. With financial liberalization, bank management is required to address unaccustomed risks and in the process, to decide on the banks' risk-return position in the market. Of course each bank may have a different risk position reflecting

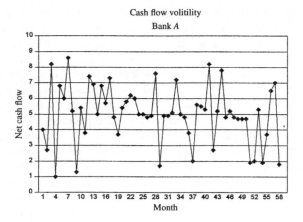

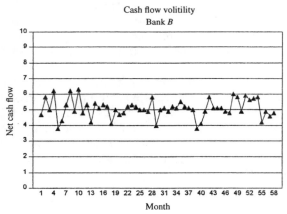

Figure 8.1   Cash flow volitility

management's tolerance for risks. Figure 8.2 illustrates possible risk-return positions of banks operating in a repressed financial market with low risks, and in a developing financial market with significant risks.

Position *A* is consistent with the repressed financial market scenario, with its low risk and high cash flow. Positions *B*, *C*, and *D* represent the risks and expected cash flow for banks operating in competitive markets. In these three markets, position *B* records the lowest risk and position *D* the highest expected cash flow, while positions *B* and *C* have the same cash flow but the risk at position *C* is higher than that of *B*. Positions *C* and *D* have the same risk profile but the cash flow on position *D* is higher

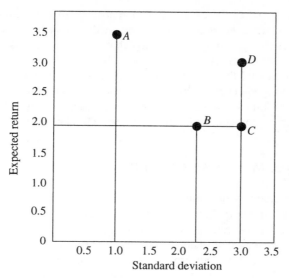

Figure 8.2   Risk return positions

than that of position *C*. Remember it is assumed that position *A* is not available under competitive market condition. Decisions will, therefore, have to
be made with respect to which of the remaining positions the banks will
want to hold. It is easy to eliminate position *C* because the same cash flow
can be earned with lower risk at position *B* or a higher cash flow can be
achieved for the same risk at position *D*. Thus, *B* and *D* are the available
options among the three assumed competitive market positions.

This illustration makes the point that banks in developing financial
markets cannot simultaneously maximize their cash flows while reducing
their risks as might be the case in a repressed financial markets. A bank
can only trade-off risks for cash flow and maximize this flow within its
risk tolerance position. An objective of risk management, therefore, is to
ensure that a bank's overall risks remain within acceptable limits and the
actual cash flow is consistent with the expected cash flow given these
limits. To achieve this objective, management will be required to understand the major risk factors that affect a bank's profitability or its operating cash flows.

Generally, however, a bank's risk exposure depends, in part, on the
volatility of interest rates and asset prices in the developing financial
market, the bank's maturity/sensitivity gaps, the duration and interest rate
elasticity of its assets and liabilities, and the ability of management to

measure and control the exposure. In the absence of risk hedging instruments, bank management, having established its risk tolerance position may protect that position by ensuring that fundamental risk mitigating components (e.g. structures, systems, policies and procedures) are in place. Specifically, these components may include the: (1) establishment of a risk management committee and appropriate policies and procedures, including risk limits; and (2) development of effective system for identifying, measuring, and controlling interest rate, and other risks.

8.5 RISK ANALYSIS APPROACHES

The management of the bank's investment portfolio to minimize market risk may be more complicated than the management of its credit portfolio to minimize interest rate and credit risks. This is because of the complex nature of investment decisions particularly in an environment of high interest rate volatility, and limited availability of financial risk hedging instruments. Furthermore, a bank's investment manager has to consider the yields on investment securities, cost of funds, and all risk parameters to maximize net investment income. Maximizing the difference between the bank's cost of funds and yield on investment, is central to the investment function which, in turn is integral to the bank's overall asset-liability management. Three main approaches – gap analysis, simulation modelling, and duration analysis – are available for assessing the trade-off between risks and return or operating cash flow. These approaches may be used separately or on a combined basis to achieve a full understanding of the trade-off.

Gap analysis is one of the most widely used risk management approaches in developed financial markets. It measures the difference between a bank's assets and liabilities which will be repriced or will mature within a predetermined period. With an expected interest rate increase, a bank will have a risk exposure, as reflected in a probable decline in its net interest income, if its liabilities subject to repricing exceed its assets subject to repricing. It will also have a similar risk exposure if the level of interest rate is expected to fall and its assets subject to repricing exceed its liabilities subject to repricing within a predetermined period.

Table 8.3 provides a simple illustration of gap analysis. This illustration shows a bank with $325,000 of assets and liabilities that will be repriced or will mature at certain specified intervals. Based on this analysis, income will decline during the first two periods (0–90 and 91–180 days) if interest rates are rising and will increase if they are falling. A risk exposure to falling interest rates occurs during the 1–5 year interval because the posi-

Table 8.3   Maturity-repricing gap $000

Assets/ Liabilities	0–90 days	91–180 days	181–365 days	1–5 years	Total
Assets	–	25	100	200	325
Liabilities	100	125	100	–	325
Gap	–100	–100	0	200	0

tive gap indicates that assets are being repriced at that period. For the 181–365 days period the bank has no interest rate exposure because of the repricing equality of its assets and liabilities.

One of the attractions of gap analysis is the ease in estimating, by way of a simple equation, the expected change in net interest income resulting from an interest rate change. This equation is:

$$\Delta NII = Gap \times \Delta i \tag{8.1}$$

where:

NII = net interest income
i = interest rate

On the basis of Equation (8.1) if interest rate for assets with maturities of 0–90 days increase on average by 3 per cent, and rates for assets with maturities of 90–180 days increase on average by 2 per cent, while rates for instruments with other maturities remain unchanged, the change in net interest income for the bank with sensitivity gaps depicted in Table 8.3 will be a negative $5,000.

Other attractions of maturity/repricing gap analysis are: (1) the gaps can be easily and inexpensively obtained from the bank's asset-liability reports; (2) the analysis, which is based on fewer assumptions than the simulation modelling and the duration analysis, is easy to explain to management, and (3) the analysis captures repricing mismatches. Because these mismatches can at least indicate interest rate risk, gap analysis provides a useful initial step in understanding the impact of interest rate changes on a bank's cash flow.

While the simplicity of the gap analysis assumptions is an advantage, the assumptions themselves have certain inherent weaknesses. Examples of these assumptions are that: (1) the entire yield curve will shift in the same direction and degree as the interest rate changes – a parallel shift in the yield curve; (2) all assets and liabilities subject to repricing will be fully and simultaneously adjusted to the change in interest rate; and (3) such adjustment will occur at the commencement point of the maturity/repricing intervals. These assumptions and their inherent weaknesses hinder the usefulness of gap analysis as a sole risk management tool.

At least three requirements must be considered when developing a model that will simulate the impact of interest rate changes on a bank's assets and liabilities. These relate to the model's assumption and the relevant information or data input, the processing of the model, and the generation and analysis of the model's results or output. The input requirements consist of such information as interest rate attributes, and maturity/repricing related to on- and off-balance sheet transactions. However, while every effort must be made to obtain sufficient information for a reliable model, too much time and resources can be spent on this exercise, resulting in costly delays in developing the model. A reliable simulation model can be developed on the basis of skillful approximation of the relevant data combined with technical competence of the staff involved.

The processing of a simulation model mainly attempts to determine whether the model adequately captures the bank's current and projected condition and operating cash flow, taking into account the different interest rate and market price scenarios. The intuition and judgement of staff responsible for analysing the impact of market forces on the bank's condition and cash flows and the staff's ability to provide a reasonably realistic basis for their interest rate and price assumptions, and their balance sheet strategies, are important factors in determining the model's adequacy. The more varied are the assumptions and strategies, the more diverse will be the output results. In fact, if the model is tested with four different balance sheet strategies and four different interest rate assumptions, the result will be sixteen sets of projections. This can lead to an overload of information, thus increasing the complexity of the risk management decision. Nevertheless, one of the most effective outputs from the model will be a decision matrix that shows the bank's projected cash flow from operations under alternative strategies and assumptions.

Simulation modelling may be combined with variance analysis to improve management's ability to measure and control its interest rate risk. By conducting a variance analysis between a bank's actual and forecasted financial results on a regular basis, management will hone its skills in developing forecast assumptions and refining the accuracy of the model on which the forecasts are based. However, because of the variety of assumptions used in projecting a bank's financial condition and operating cash flow, the impact of individual risk factors on the actual outcome cannot be easily isolated. In such a case, management may consider using a step-wise simulation analysis that measures the impact of a single factor while controlling all other factors. For example, the impact of an interest rate change on a bank's earnings may be estimated by first holding other changes constant. Once this estimate is obtained, assumptions about other factors such as loan prepayment speeds, loan volume, deposit flow can be accommodated in a step-wise manner.

A simulation model has its advantages and disadvantages. The main advantages are the model's ability to project the bank's balance sheet and operating results under different interest rate and price assumptions, and different strategies; and its ability to capture changes in the bank's operating environment. In developing financial markets these changes are many and complex. The model's disadvantages lie in the several assumptions, as well as the required minimum competence level of staff to make it operational. In fact, simulation modelling for banks operating in developing financial markets with their high interest rate and price volatility, intense competition and uncertainty will require several balance sheet, interest rate, and other assumptions, alternative balance sheet strategies, and technically competent staff to verify, interpret, and report the model's results to management. There may be a substantial shortage of such staff in these markets.

Duration analysis provides another approach for measuring the interest rate risk inherent in a bank's balance sheet. It estimates the average amount of time required before the discounted value or the present value of all cash flows (for example, principal and interest) can be recovered by an asset holder, be it a bank or a bank depositor. Duration is therefore a measure of the effective maturity or length of the cash flow streams associated with different financial assets and liabilities. A basic duration equation is:

$$D = \frac{\Sigma(PV \times t)}{TPV} \qquad (8.2)$$

where:

D = duration
PV = present value of cash flows
t = period
TPV = total present (market) value of cash flows.

An important concept based on Equation (8.2) is that of interest rate elasticity, which estimates the change in market value of a bank's balance sheet or its capital resulting from a percentage change

$$IRE = \frac{-D}{1 + i} \qquad (8.3)$$

in interest rate. This elasticity is derived from Equation (8.3) where:

IRE = interest rate elasticity
D = duration
i = market interest rate or discount rate.

Table 8.4 illustrates an application of duration analysis to a bank's portfolio of investment securities with a book value of $1 million.[9] The securities are 8 per cent annual coupon bonds with a maturity period of 5 years. In this illustration, the securities portfolio has a duration of 4.31 years and an interest rate elasticity of −3.99 per cent. These results indicate that although the maturity period of the portfolio is 5 years the effective maturity of the portfolio's cash flow stream is 4.31 years; and that an interest rate increase of 1 per cent, will cause a decrease in the portfolio's market value by about 4 per cent. By extending the duration to include all assets and liabilities, it is possible to estimate the impact of an interest rate change on a bank's capital.

A bank may hold its investment securities to maturity, or designate them as trading securities or as securities available for sale.[10] A decision to

Table 8.4   Duration and interest rate elasticity computation

Period years	Market rate %	Cash flow	Discount factor	Present value $000	Present value × period $000
1	8	80	.926	74.00	74.00
2	8	80	.857	69.00	138.00
3	8	80	.794	63.00	189.00
4	8	80	.735	59.00	236.00
5	8	80	.681	735.00	3 675.00
Total		1 080		1 000.00	4 312.00

$$D = 4\,312/1\,000 = 4.31 \ years$$
$$IRE = -4.31/1.08 = -3.99\%$$

hold the portfolio to maturity implies that the bank will not be affected by interest rate changes or prepayment risk. However, because of a number of factors, management may not hold the portfolio to maturity but, instead, may designate it as being available for sale. Among these factors are: (1) actual and anticipated changes in market interest rates and related changes in the portfolio's prepayment risk; (2) an increase in the need for liquidity due to a rise in deposit withdrawal or in loan demand; (3) changes in the availability of and the yield on alternative investments; (4) changes in funding sources and terms; and (5) changes in exchange rate.

Normally, securities available for sale are reported at fair market value with unrealized gains or losses reported as a separate component of the bank's capital accounts. Based on Table 8.4, a 4 per cent decrease in the market value of the bank's $1 million securities portfolio associated with a 1 per cent increase in interest rates will result in a loss of $40,000 and, ceteris paribus, a corresponding reduction in the bank's capital.

Duration analysis has its advantages and disadvantages. Among the advantages are: (1) its emphasis on market valuation; (2) its concern with the long-term effect of interest rate changes on asset portfolio, compared to gap analysis and simulation modelling that focus on the short-term impact; and (3) the ease in interpreting its IRE results. The disadvantages of duration analysis relate mainly to the interest rate assumptions that are implicit in the analysis. For example, because the interest rate risk function may be non-linear, the accuracy of the analysis must be limited to small changes in interest rates. Furthermore, the use of the analysis is limited by the ability of management to forecast changes in the discount rate. Such changes are required to enable the making of appropriate risk minimizing adjustments in the bank's balance sheet and operating cash flow.

The complex and interrelated risk factors that affect a bank's profitability, combined with the disadvantages of gap, simulation and duration analysis, suggest the need for other analytical tools. One of these tools is regression analysis that, in its most simple terms, measures the relationship between one dependent variable, and one or more independent variables. Suppose a bank wants to determine the relationship between the interest rate on prime loans and that on CDs, the interest rate on CDs and that of Treasury bill futures, or the interest rate on CDs and the flow of funds into CD accounts. Regression analysis will require establishing propositions of the particular relationship and translating these propositions into mathematical form.

The propositions may be that: (1) after the CD rate rises beyond a certain level and if CDs provide the major source of funding, the interest rate on a bank's prime loans is an increasing function of its CD interest rate; (2) the interest rate on CDs is an increasing function of the Treasury bill futures rate; or (3) the flows into CD accounts are an increasing function of the CD interest rate. The relationship specified in proposition (1) may help to establish the stability of a bank's interest margin; the one specified in proposition (2) may help to determine the effectiveness of hedging a bank's funding costs with financial futures; and that in proposition (3) may indicate the ability of the bank to meet its funding needs based on its current pricing policy.

The translation of these propositions into mathematical form may be more complex than establishing the propositions themselves. Here the analyst is faced with a bewildering variety of possible specifications of the propositions. Should the relationships be linear in the variables or non-linear, and if non-linear should they be logarithmic, polynomial, or some other specification. Furthermore, even when the form of the relationship is specified there is still the problem of specifying the time lags in the equation. Does the flow of funds into CD accounts in the current time period, for instance, respond to a last period change in CD interest rates or several previous changes in such rate? The conventional response to these difficulties is to postulate, in the first instance, as simple a form as possible for these relationships.[11] Thus, the above propositions may be formulated in the following model:

$$\Delta PL_i = \alpha_0 + \beta_1 \Delta CD_i \qquad (8.4)$$

$$\Delta CD_i = \alpha_0 + \beta_1 \Delta TB_{fi} \qquad (8.5)$$

and

$$\Delta CD_b = \alpha_0 + \beta_1 \Delta CD_i \qquad (8.6)$$

where:

CD_i = interest rate on three-month certificate of deposits
CD_b = flows in CD accounts
PL_i = interest rate on prime loans
TB_{fi} = 90-day Treasury futures rate

and where the *a priori* restrictions on the model may be expressed by:

$$\alpha_0 > 0, \ \beta_1 > 1$$

These three relationships together with the restrictions constitute the linear regression models that can be estimated, using time series data, to obtain simple correlation and beta coefficients. The correlation coefficients indicate the linear relationship between the variables while the beta coefficients measures the relative sensitivity of the dependent to the independent variables. Thus, if CDs are used to fund prime loans, strong positive correlation between the interest rates of these variables will no doubt be estimated. In addition, the beta coefficient will indicate the change in PL_i for every 100 basis point change in CD_i. Thus, if a 100 basis point change in CD_i results in a 150 basis point change in PL_i as indicated by the beta coefficient, then a portfolio of prime-based loans funded by CDs may be exposed to a considerable amount of basis risk.

Regression analysis can improve the gap, simulation, and duration models by refining the assumptions of these models through the application of the interest rate sensitivity results indicated by the beta values. Given an appropriately specified regression model, the limiting assumption of gap analysis, that all assets and liabilities subject to repricing will adjust fully to changes in market rates, can be modified to reflect the sensitivity of the respective asset and liability items to interest rate changes based on their beta coefficient values. The application of the beta coefficients to the asset/liability balances of the gap report will, therefore, result in a beta-adjusted gap report that more adequately reflects the actual interest rate risk of a bank's balance sheet and operating cash flow. Similarly, the beta coefficients can be applied to the interest rate adjustments in simulation models, and the cash flow calculations in duration models. In fact, the objective of beta analysis is to measure the interest rate sensitivity of the bank's investment and funding rates, and to improve the accuracy of its risk measurement models.

8.6 RISK FACTORS

The efficient management of risks inherent in a bank's activities depends on a clear understanding of the major factors affecting these activities. This understanding may be developed by identifying the risk factors and measuring their impact on the bank's operating cash flow under a range of interest rate scenarios. Management can then decide on the risk it will assume or hedge, given the interest rate expectations, the technical competence of available staff, and the bank's objectives. There are at least six major risk factors facing bank management in developing financial markets. These are: (1) maturity repricing mismatch; (2) spread changes between asset-liability rates and market rates; (3) changes in production volume and product mix; (4) yield curve rotations; (5) choices in the balance sheet; and (6) off-balance sheet activities.

Of course, gap analysis is concerned with measuring interest rate risk resulting from an imbalance between a bank's assets and liabilities within a given period. A clear understanding of the maturity/mismatch risk factor will require management to distinguish between a static and a dynamic gap measure. While the static gap measure fails to reflect the reinvestment of assets and the renewal of liabilities, the dynamic gap measure reflects these activities.

Net interest margins can be compressed as a result of the differences in the interest sensitivities of a bank's assets and liabilities. Such a compression is referred to as basis risk. Assume that a bank has a portfolio of adjustable rate loans funded by adjustable rate deposits and the repricing intervals of these loans and deposits are matched. However, the indices to which the loan and deposit rates are linked are different. The loan interest rate is linked to a cost of funds index while the deposit interest rate is linked to the Treasury bill rate. Moreover, there may be significant lag between the cost of fund index and the Treasury bill rate – the index may change less often than the Treasury bill rate. In this situation, it is quite possible that the spread changes between the bank's assets and liabilities may not reflect changes in market interest rates. In fact, net interest margins can be compressed with rising interest rates.

The bank may also have greater basis risk than its competitor banks with asset-liability repricing indices that tend to move in line with each other and with overall market rates. Since basis risk can have significant cash flow implications, bank management must monitor and control this risk in its balance sheet in general and its investment portfolio and funding in particular. Basis risk analysis will help the making of timely decisions on holding Treasury bills, or extending credit based on a cost-of-fund index.

Interest rate changes have a direct impact on the volume and mix of a bank's assets and liabilities. The more frequent are these changes the greater may be the variability of the bank's cash flow. Under competitive market conditions, when rates are increasing the growth in loan and deposit volume tends to level off or decline. Loans become more expensive for borrowers that may prefer fixed-rate loans, and deposit flows may fall as depositors seek higher yields in alternative financial instruments. Bank management in developing financial markets with their high interest rate volatility may be able to reduce the cash flow impact of interest rate changes by changing production volume and product mix.

Management must also be aware of the phenomenon of yield curve rotation. This phenomenon recognizes that interest rates do not normally change by the same degree or in the same direction across different maturities of the yield curve. The phenomenon's importance lies in the fact that any change in one segment may not be accompanied by similar changes in other segments of the yield curve. For example, if the yield curve indicates the rate of interest on 3-month bonds at 5 per cent but some financial institutions believe that the short-term rate may rise and as such increase their 12-month deposit rate say from 5.5 per cent to 6 per cent, three-month CD holders may not necessarily switch to 12-month CDs because the rate is higher and is not expected to change. They will most likely switch to instruments of similar maturities offering higher yields.

Since money is a commodity with interest rate as the price, under competitive market conditions, bank asset and liability yields compete with the yields on products of like maturities at other financial institutions. These products are therefore sensitive to changes in the segment of the yield curve with the same effective maturities. The assumption of parallel shifts in the yield curve is inherent in gap and duration analysis. Simulation analysis has the flexibility to analyse yield curve rotation risk. Because of the impact of yield curve changes on a bank's cash flow as reflected in its investment securities prices and its net interest income, management in developing financial markets should develop timely information not only on yield curve changes but on yield curve rotation risk.

There are several choices that are inherent in a bank's balance sheet. Two of these choices are commonly exercised by borrowers and depositors in competitive markets: (1) borrowers may repay their fixed-rate mortgages earlier than agreed because they expect mortgage rates to fall; and (2) depositors may close their savings and chequeing accounts because of better services being offered by non-bank financial firms. An implication of the choices is that interest rate risk is not symmetrical as implied by gap and duration analyses. Earnings may be hurt more by a rate change in one direction than assisted by a rate change of the same magnitude in the opposite direction. For instance, a 1 per cent increase in interest rates may cause a 4 per cent contraction in loan demand and ultimately a reduction in earnings. But a 1 per cent decrease in interest rates may induce no new borrowing from the bank though it may encourage bank depositors to find alternative investment instruments that offer better yields.

Even in repressed financial markets, banks are engaged in off-balance sheet activities. In developing financial markets, however, the range and volume of these activities tend to expand. Examples of these activities are loan commitments, forward foreign exchange transactions, financial futures, guarantees of various types, and fiduciary services. Markets for forward exchange and financial futures contracts as well as for fiduciary services might not be well developed in some developing financial markets. However, in most of these markets loan commitments and guarantees are commonplace and increasing.

Bank management may be encouraged to expand their off-balance business because of two main reasons: (1) to maintain or increase their cash flow, given their capital base and any compression on their interest margins due to competitive factors; (2) to cope with the constraints imposed on their balance sheets (for example, regulatory pressure to improve capital ratios) while improving rate of return on assets.

The risk inherent in a loan commitment is similar to an actual loan in that the bank must be prepared to fund certain loan requests under the line. Management may protect the bank from liquidity and interest rate risks by subjecting the line to the availability of funds, and by pricing the loan at the time of funding. Management may also offer standby letters of credit and loan commitment services that guarantee their customers performance with third parties.[12] Although off-balance sheet risks are not apparent on the balance sheet, they must be included in the risk management of banks operating in developing financial markets, particularly those which are undercapitalized.

8.7   SUMMARY

This chapter has emphasized that effective risk management in developing financial markets begins with: (1) established risk management policies to guide risk management behaviour and information to facilitate the effective implementation of these policies; (2) a clear definition of risk, and (3) the instituting of systems for identifying, measuring and controlling the various risks inherent in these markets. It has defined a bank's overall risk as the probability of failure to achieve an expected value and has suggested that this risk could be measured by the standard deviation of this value. The expected value was defined as net operating cash flow, considered a comprehensive indicator of a bank's performance under changing market conditions. In instituting effective risk management systems, bank management might consider the various risk management approaches used by banks in developed financial markets. The chapter, therefore reviewed a set of the more commonly used approaches and in the process identified their advantages and disadvantages.

An important risk management decision relates to the bank's risk position. The chapter has identified a number of risk positions bank management could take and has argued that, unlike the case of management in repressed financial markets, bank management in developing financial markets would not be able to maximize their returns while reducing or maintaining their risk positions. As bank management in these markets could only trade-off risk for return as reflected in the bank's cash flow, a major risk management objective would be to ensure that the bank's overall risk remained within acceptable limits and to minimize the variance between its actual and expected operating cash flows. To achieve this objective, management would be required to identify, measure and control the factors that explain the risk inherent in the bank's activities. The chapter has identified and discussed some of these factors.

9 Managing Human Resources

As financial markets become more competitive and as interest and non-interest expenses rise, the effective use of human resources becomes increasingly important. In banking, where human resource costs are usually exceeded only by interest expense, optimum human resource use is necessary if profits or cash flows from operations are to be maximized. Therefore, banks in competitive markets will have to identify and implement measures that will enable their staff, to exploit their full potential and enthusiasm as a team and as individuals. These measures may be specified in the bank's overall human resource plan.

Bank management may be faced with the challenges of technology and regulation and the difficulty in finding or preparing staff to meet these challenges. Moreover, as domestic financial markets become more internationally integrated, the productivity of staff and equipment becomes crucially important. Finally, as the banking business grows geographically, the human resource capability will have to expand to meet the new and increasing demand that accompanies such growth. Therefore, bank management in developing financial markets will have to recruit not only tellers and loan officers as was normally the emphasis in repressed financial markets, but also staff with skills in securities and foreign currency trading, with expertise in particular economic sectors and industries, and with knowledge of the business practices and needs of the domestic and foreign market locations where the bank operates.

This chapter reviews some of the challenges of effective human resource planning and utilization, identifies a set of objectives on which bank management in developing financial markets may focus, and describes measures that may be implemented to achieve these objectives. Among these objectives are to: (1) organize the bank's human resource management function in a manner to achieve its mission and objectives; (2) utilize the bank's human resources as effectively as possible; and (3) develop the bank's corporate culture and specific skills to achieve its performance goals. The chapter argues that bank management in developing financial markets may encounter special problems in attempting to achieve effective human resource management and highlights some of these problems.

9.1   HUMAN RESOURCE PLANNING

The human resource management practices of repressed financial markets may be incapable of meeting the challenges that face banks in developing financial markets. Among these challenges are the need for compliance with increasingly complex prudential regulations and public reporting requirements; for technology; and for expertise in non-traditional fields. Each bank may rise to the challenges in different ways. Some banks, steeped in the management tradition of repressed financial markets, may be inclined to stick to the narrow personnel emphasis on replacement hiring, training, promotion, and compensation determination.

Other banks may have the broader view that human resource planning and management must have the right individuals in the right jobs today, but also provide today for the needs of the future.[1] The broader view centres on management's determination of the size and type of staff required to achieve the bank's future goals; as well as the skills and competence of the bank's existing staff. Moreover, this determination implies that the bank has the human resource forecasting capabilities that provide information on the new skills needed, the amount and quality of training, or existing staff required to achieve the bank's objectives.

The broader view stresses that knowing the bank's goals and objectives is not enough. Knowing the difference between human resource needs, and skills available to meet these needs is also an important management challenge. At times, the skills and competence of staff are often under-utilized and any new objectives management may have may be achieved by a more efficient utilization of such staff. It is therefore important to have access to complete personnel data (for example, education, work history, and performance evaluation) to assess the bank's ability to venture into new activities with its existing work force.

As in any other market, a principal objective for banks in developing financial markets is to operate efficiently and profitably. This objective can be attained if banks provide the products and services that are in effective demand and do so by utilizing competent staff and appropriate technology. An organization structure that facilitates the achievement of this and other related objectives will tend to focus on the manpower needed (for example, aggregate number of employees, and required skills) and define the levels, jobs, and tasks for each employee.

With financial liberalization, the banking environment becomes more complex as reflected mainly in the product mix, and customers' demand for more efficient services and innovative products. This complexity is also indicated in the increased willingness of customers to switch to the most efficient providers, as well as in the increased scrutiny of the bank's performance by market participants, and bank regulators and supervisors. An effective response to these challenges is for management to organize the bank's human resources to achieve specific results. In doing so, the bank's human resource plan will have to specify the desired results, define staff responsibilities and individual job functions, indicate the size of staff and types of skills, and assist in reorganizing the bank and its related functional units to achievement these results.

9.2   ORGANIZATIONAL RESTRUCTURING

The bank's organization structure will be influenced by its mission, strategy and tactics to achieve its business objectives. A problem for any bank attempting to restructure itself to cope with the challenges of competitive markets, is management's inability to specify the appropriate products or services, rationalize the bank's leadership or supervisory structure; and define the responsibilities of functional units and their employees for achieving specific results. Generally, this problem is rooted in the fact that the management process derived from a repressed financial market environment adapts rather slowly to the dynamics of a developing financial market.

Box 9.1 lists a set of organizational challenges to be addressed by bank management in developing financial markets. In dealing with the challenge of organizational restructuring and human resources effectiveness, management may focus on improving the operating systems at the branch, regional office, and head office levels. The major objective of this improvement may be to enable the bank to demonstrate to the market, its regulators and its employees that management has a strategic direction and ability to achieve its objectives because of the existence of clearly defined authority levels, appropriate technology, information, performance monitoring, and internal control systems.

To improve the bank's operating systems, management will have to specify the strategic objectives of each functional unit and define the measures appropriate to achieve these objectives. For example, at the branch level, management may emphasize improved customer service that may include branch rationalization or relocation. A specific service area may be over-banked or a branch relocation may be necessary to reflect the changing demographic and economic circumstances. Banks operating in geographically large countries or with an operating presence (for example, branches and subsidiaries) in foreign financial markets, may establish

Box 9.1   Organizational issues

- Inadequate identification of primary market areas, or inappropriate products and services.
- A leadership structure that permits some supervisors to report directly to the board and bypass the managers to whom the supervisors should report.
- Unspecified duties or responsibilities of functional units for achieving specific or targeted results, and fragmentation between units creating overlapping and inefficiencies.
- Absence of certain basic conditions for effective management (for example, human resource planning, internal controls and audit, training and technology).
- Inefficient coordination of work flows between organizational units (for example, domestic and foreign branches, head office).
- Out-of-date managerial processes (for example, a bureaucratic management that emphasizes procedures and record keeping rather than, profitability, customer service, staff training and innovative products).
- Absence of performance standards, performance monitoring, and culturally specific incentive programmes.
- Inadequate management information to guide an effective restructuring, staffing, and product and service development.

regional management systems that permit a set of offices or subsidiaries to report directly to regional sub-units of head office.

Normally, a principal objective of the regional management system is to improve the effectiveness of head office supervision by delegating responsibilities to strategically located units. Meanwhile, at head office level, management may concentrate on strengthening leadership and internal controls, and monitoring results in terms of clearly measurable performance standards. In addition, head office management may focus on human resource planning and implementation, appropriate technology and operating systems, and the delineation of authority levels, information and decision flows.

Surely, management will have to prioritize the various measures that will alleviate or remove the constraints on achieving the bank's objectives. These measures may aim at: (1) developing the basic organizational units responsible for implementing the bank's strategic plan and for managing its current operations; (2) reviewing the bank's branches and subsidiaries, and its regional management, with the intention of rationalizing, and improving their operations; (3) coordinating the bank's various functional units, and establishing effective leadership, supervision and internal controls; and (4) improving the quality of information used in management decision making. The implementation of each of these measures will require the retention of skilled and competent staff and the maintenance of adequate staffing levels.

Strategic objectives that may exert an important influence on the bank's organization restructuring programme and its skill requirements are essentially concerned with improving its competitive ability and profitability. Two examples of these objectives are to: (1) develop a customer base consisting of firms conducting domestic or international business; and (2) emphasize investment or foreign exchange trading activities thus requiring the establishment of a treasury unit. Management may also want to establish head office support units in areas that will improve the safety and soundness of the bank's operations. Examples of such areas are management information and other systems development, policies and procedures for specific activities, internal control and auditing. The head office support units should facilitate the implementation of a comprehensive approach to human resource management requiring analogous units or skills at the regional or branch level so as to expand the availability of skills throughout the banking organization.

A bank with branches and subsidiaries may remove functional fragmentation and overlapping by being specific about the expected performance of each unit and by creating a structure that coordinates the operations of these units to achieve the strategic objectives. In other words, management's restructuring of the bank's branches and subsidiaries may be aimed at enabling these units to achieve their performance targets by delivering, in their respective market areas, their products and services as efficiently as possible.

Removing inefficiencies in the bank's operating structures and improving the quality of service may require management to reform certain functions (for example, accounting, information, and documentation) and processes in each of the bank's operating units. Building efficiencies in these areas will require a commitment to optimize the use of information, technology and staff, and the existence of integrated management and effective leadership. Management will also have to identify leadership deficiencies and correct them. Leadership may be deficient at all levels (for example, at the board, senior and middle management, and regional and branch management levels). This deficiency may be explained by the absence of clearly defined roles and responsibilities of employees, and the existence of an organization structure that fails to coordinate these roles and responsibilities, and to reward effective performance.

Management may design and implement a customer service programme that ensures a uniform demonstration of a positive customer service culture throughout the bank. In repressed financial markets, banking products and services were standardized, choices between banking institutions were limited, and customer loyalty was enduring. Competitive market conditions demand the correct treatment of customers particularly in terms of appropriate products and services, office layout and location, minimum customer service standards, and the willingness and ability of staff to exceed these standards. The instituting of performance standards and measurement is directly relevant in evaluating employees' contribution to the bank's operating efficiency and competitiveness.

9.3 EFFICIENT RESOURCE UTILIZATION

A basic condition for effective management is that human resources must be utilized as efficiently as possible given the cultural and other constraints. The efficient use of these resources presupposes a continuing dedication to maintaining an optimum number of employees, and mix of skills in each of the bank's operating units. The task of maintaining the level of staff and mix of skills consistent with the bank's profit maximization objective is certainly not a simple one for bank management. Finding the appropriate skills, or staff with the potential to acquire such skills in time to respond to the need for operational and other changes, creates significant performance pressures on management. Moreover, management may be subject to substantial social and political pressures to retain staffing levels although it may be commercially sound to reduce such levels.

The political pressures may be exerted by government officials wanting their relatives and friends to be hired, retained or even promoted in state-owned banks or private banks depending on government business for their viability. The social pressures may be more subtle to the extent that excess staff may be older employees with children to educate and family to support, and with limited prospects of finding alternative employment. The fact that the staff may be unionized, that they may not be responsible for their under-performance, or that they were unaware that their performance fell below the stipulated standards, will aggravate the social pressures and restrain management's ability to effect personnel changes.

With staff compensation representing a significant proportion of a bank's operating costs, overstaffing can cause a drain on its profitability.[2] It can also create a situation of underemployment among all employees, or overemployment among the few competent ones. Ordinarily, overstaffing will not contribute to superior customer service. Instead, it will reduce the work load of all but a few workers. Persistent overstaffing due to political or social pressures may create a corporate culture that accommodates tardiness at the time when competitive market conditions demand prompt and efficient delivery of products and services to customers.

Underemployment tends to hinder the development of competence and fosters mediocre performance even among staff with the potential to excel.[3] Management of overstaffed banks may therefore be forced in a position of recruiting future managers and supervisors from a workforce bred in a low-performance culture. The negative effect of overstaffing on operating and other objectives can be long-term indeed. The alternative will be to recruit, when necessary, high performers from other banks and financial institutions at the cost of further overstaffing and low morale of existing aspirants.

In some banks, overstaffing may coexist with understaffing. The understaffing may be due to the lack of particular skills to meet the expanding demand for non-traditional products and services, or to ensure operating efficiency. Together with an increased transactions volume requiring improved technology and related skills, management will have to deal with risk management issues for the bank as a whole (for example, asset-liability management) and for certain specific areas (for example, credit risk, and regulatory risk). The bank may be understaffed in technological, communication, information analysis, and risk management skills, and overstaffed in clerical, secretarial, and administrative support.

Although it is true that skills deficiency may be found in any bank, this deficiency tends to be more significant for banks in developing financial markets. The critical human resource needs for banks in these markets will be found at the supervision and management of the credit, treasury, trade finance, human resource management, technology, and audit function. Banks that replaced the repressed financial market legacy of an oversupply of clerks, secretaries and administrators, with the required amount of skilled and productive staff directly contributing to efficiency and profitability will be the ones to lead the competition for customer support and market share.

Box 9.2 indicates the content of three quantitative techniques normally used in estimating the staffing requirements of a bank and its functional units. The staff optimization benefits derived from quantitative analysis can be substantial relative to the cost of conducting such an analysis. In fact this pay-off can be significant for banks with a branch network where a large proportion of staff, say about 80 per cent to 90 per cent, is normally located.[4]

To replace the human resource legacy of repressed financial markets, management will have to be decisive about the bank's staffing require-

Box 9.2   Techniques for estimating staffing requirements

- *Workload analysis*: break down the functional unit's work into discrete parts (for example, processing of deposits, or a specific type of credit application, developing a training programme, or establishing an electronic data processing programme). Estimate, in work hours, the amount of time required to complete a particular unit of work or output. Project the number of such work units that will be produced in the year. Multiply the number of work units to be produced in a year by the time per unit in order to obtain the total amount of work hours for that work unit in that year. Divide the work hours derived for the year by the available work hours per person per year to obtain the number of employees required for the particular unit of work or output for the year.

- *Relationship analysis*: relate one factor with another, either to forecast workloads and then use this forecast to project staffing requirements, or to forecast staffing requirements directly. (Examples of relationships for this analysis are between the number of: (a) customers in a branch, and customer service staff, (b) installment loans, and installment credit staff, (c) branch audits conducted, and (d) borrowers, and credit officers.) Identify the relationships and calculate them for say, the previous 3-year period. Project the change in these relationships in the current year as a result of such events as automation, improved work flow, work simplification, improved training and so on. Use the relationships to project staffing requirements for the particular functions for the year.

- *Modelling*: build two, three or four 'model' functional units (for example, branches, other offices, subsidiaries) representing a cross-section of the main types of functional units in the bank. Perfect these models in particular areas of interest (for example, customer service, processing efficiency, internal control, credit documentation, analysis, collection and so on). Implement one model or the other in the rest of the equivalent functional units of the bank. Develop relationships between the volume of different types of standard transactions and staffing requirements. Use these relationships throughout the system as appropriate (for example, as they apply to branches, other offices and subsidiaries) to match staffing requirements with specific products, services, and work volume of any unit.

ments and take the necessary steps to fulfill these requirements using objective business criteria. For example, management must ascertain the number and types of jobs required to meet the bank's objectives, the right staffing levels, and the minimum knowledge, skills and abilities for each job. Management may estimate that the bank needs a total of say 1,500 jobs, allocated between head office, branches and subsidiaries and categorized in number and types, such as the number of credit officers, their credit specialization, and location in the respective units. In addition, the minimum qualification is specified for each position in each functional unit. The importance of identifying the skills requirements for each unit and functional area cannot be overemphasized. Professional judgement, combined with quantifiable analysis can enhance the reliability of the results.

With the staffing requirement determined, the next step is to obtain the mix of skills for the various functional units. Given an objectively defined staffing requirement, a well considered job description can assist in determining the required mix of skills. If a bank does not have job descriptions, particularly for its skilled staff, management may have to use other methods of ascertaining the bank's skill requirements. One method is to establish the job levels in each functional unit and the skills required for each of such levels. In the credit function, for instance, skills may be required for credit documentation, analysis, approval, collection, and work-out situations. Because of skill deficiencies in the market as a whole, many of the bank's functional units will be inadequately staffed. Job specific training, therefore, becomes an important element of a bank's competitive strategies.[5]

For banks with a pool of potential talents, a major reason for training will be to exploit this potential through skills upgrading programmes. These programmes should be based on clearly defined performance requirements for specific functions and jobs within these functions. Training for jobs in the electronic data processing function may aim at upgrading the quality of skills for computer systems operations, and supervision. For computer systems, the emphasis may be on improving or establishing performance standards in equipment maintenance, software improvement, and security procedures; for operations the emphasis may be on the accuracy of data input and output; and for supervision the emphasis may be on the continuing efficiency and reliability of the process, relationship with computer service providers, and the quality of information generated for management decision and customer service.

9.4   WORK PERFORMANCE AND CULTURE

The effectiveness of human resource management will be influenced by the bank's corporate culture. A corporate culture that stresses high and sustained staff performance and encourages the retention and attraction of skilled professionals will foster management and operational effectiveness. However, the corporate culture is normally constrained by the overall culture which differs considerably between societies. While various definitions of culture exists, widespread agreement has been reached on three aspects of culture. These are: (1) culture is not innate, but learned; (2) the various facets of culture are interrelated – that is, if culture is disturbed in one area, every other area will be affected; and (3) culture defines the boundaries of different groups. The overall culture has a profound effect on corporate management in any given country. Put simply, culture is the way of doing things in the society, community or firm. It is reflected in the attitude of management and staff to work, technology, and to change in general. Although culture can be the most constraining and uncontrollable variable when attempting to change attitudes of staff accustomed to the repressed financial market environment, the bank's long-run survival under competitive market conditions will depend on the nature of its employees' reaction to the change necessary for the bank's operational success.

On a continuum showing employees' attitude to change, a bank may have a conservative or traditional culture that continues to accommodate the attitudes and practices of the repressed financial markets, or a progressive culture that effectively adapts to the demands of a competitive market environment. The criterion for placing a bank at a point on this continuum is the amount of resistance to change – the lower the resistance, the higher a bank will be placed on the continuum and vice versa. An understanding of the process of moving along the continuum can facilitate the creation of a corporate culture that enables the bank to adapt to the changes in the developing financial market environment. To adapt a bank's corporate culture to the changing market environment, management must focus on such organization characteristics as authority and decision making; decision making and delegation; work ethic and motivation; supervision; and hiring and firing.

An integral part of a corporate culture is the nature of the relationship between management and staff. Each culture has its expectations for the roles of manager or supervisors and staff. Participatory management may be encouraged in one culture and discouraged as incompetence in another. Employee initiative and leadership may be praised and copied in one culture but regarded as selfish and destructive to group harmony in another.[6] There appeared to be nothing inherently natural about the way managers and staff are supposed to interact. Every society has a heritage that has created expectations for individuals in certain positions. Clashes between the corporate and societal cultures must be minimized – the new ways of doing things in the bank must at least proximate traditional expectations. An understanding of existing relationships and expectations must therefore be the basis for effecting changes in the bank's corporate culture.

It is true that financial market liberalization occurs in countries with different cultures. In some of these countries, management authority in business is inherited. Management positions, even in banks with public ownership, are occupied by certain 'established' families, resulting in authority being conferred on the person rather than the position. In other developing countries, a manager may command respect by virtue of position, age, or influence. In developed countries, management authority tends to be based on achievement, contribution to the firm's strategic objectives, or on fair handling of staff. Despite the differences in the origin or basis of authority, a set of common principles that guide management-staff relationship in banks operating under competitive market conditions must be found.

Among these principles that influence managers, authority and decision making is the one that requires management, at all times, to look and behave like management. This principle recognizes that strength and competence will influence the staff's response to change. But the elements of strength and competence may vary between cultures. In some cultures, these management attributes take the form of resoluteness and knowledge, while in others, they are derived from unique entrepreneurial, financial and political achievements, or intellectual leadership. But there are culturally imposed limits on the exercise of management authority regardless of the source of such authority. These limits must be known and incorporated in the corporate culture. At all cost, counter-cultural behaviour by management must be avoided. Such behaviour sends confused signals and engenders employees' underperformance.

The process of decision making and delegation in a bank, as in any other business, may range from authoritarian and centralized to participatory and democratic. An authoritarian management style prohibits delegation of authority and may impede expeditious and informed decision making. Centralized decision making tends to be common in several countries with financial liberalization programmes. At least in the early stages of financial liberalization, centralized approval of routine transactions may be normal. As these transactions grow in volume and complexity, delegation becomes necessary for operational efficiency. Moreover, even where attempts are made to delegate authority within the bank, the bank's customers may insist on seeing senior management or the head person, instead of seeing the subordinates with delegated authority. The subordinates themselves may continue to seek the head person's approval before taking any action.

A basic principle of human resource management is that employees must be involved in the work process in the ways they understand. The contribution of employees unaccustomed to participatory management will be insignificant if the bank, without prior employee conditioning, adopts the practice of participatory management. Over time, through employees' training and observation, participatory management may be instituted. Where the culture is rooted in a tradition of participatory decision making or is based on a belief in the natural harmony between humans or the perfectibility of human relationships, participatory management may be an integral part of the bank's corporate culture.[7]

The infrequent changes in interest and exchange rates, a loyal client base, government guarantee programmes, and the overall lack of competition and regulatory constraints, may in part explain the tendency for a relaxed and non-aggressive attitude of bank management and staff in repressed financial markets. The management of extraordinary risks, the need to comply with regulatory stipulations with regards to capital adequacy, asset quality, liquidity and other measures, and the challenge to succeed are events that compel new attitudes to work. The work ethic for developing financial market must therefore be one of increasing performance and productivity, aggressive and informed management, and adaptability to change. The motivating factors may be adequate rewards for effort, opportunities for upward mobility, and training to cope with the technological and other changes. However, employees' adaptation to these factors will be determined by the cultural elements that influence motivation, attitudes, and performance in particular cultures. It is not unusual for employees' interest in their jobs to be less important than their interest in their private enterprises that may be financed by the bank itself. The relative unimportance of their bank jobs may be reflected by a high rate of job absenteeism. To respond successfully to the competitive market pressures, bank employees will have to be more disciplined and productive. Discipline is necessary to reduce conflict of interest, to minimize insider transactions, or to cope with the temptation to misappropriate the bank's resources, and to devote working hours to productive efforts. Despite the competitive pressures, there may be certain underlying attitudes that are unchangeable, at least in the short-run.

In some cultures, employees are wedded to their companies, in other cultures they are job rather than company oriented, still in others they are neither job nor company but individual oriented.[8] In paternalistic cultures, where relationships and loyalties are personalized, management tends to elicit performance by using personal influence and working through specific individuals. Employees' evaluation may be based on their loyalty, or their willingness to perform personal favours for their superiors rather than on their actual job performance. In these situations, the line between friendship and business may be unclear and the impact on the unfavoured but highly skilled worker may be demotivating at least.

In order to adjust the work ethic to the dynamics of market competition, management will have to identify the unique characteristics of each culture that can be used to motivate productive effort. For example, in cultures where competition is the norm, management has an important responsibility to specify the objectives and goals of inter-staff, inter-office, and inter-bank competition, and to ensure that the definition of winning is firmly understood. Competitive rules must be established, communicated and enforced. In cultures where cooperation is the rule, the task of management is to encourage inter-staff harmony while promoting inter-bank competition. Finally, in cultures where employees may have no personal job ambition or work-group loyalty, management may motivate results by associating the employees' contribution to the bank with their contribution to the excellence of performance of their families, country or other areas of specific interest to them. Incentives and rewards for effort vary between cultures. Where inter-staff competition dominates, a financial bonus for outstanding performance may motivate the over-performer and other staff to increase their effort. Where the culture emphasizes cooperation and group harmony, a financial bonus may humiliate the receiver and confuse the other team players. As the market grows more competitive and dynamic, bank management, in adapting to the market and in motivating their employees, must be aware of the many alternatives to financial rewards as a motivator to performance. There are financial as well as non-financial incentives to performance if applied in a culturally specific manner. Examples of these incentives are financial bonuses, job security, vacations, gifts, sports or health facilities, services, prestige, recognition and appreciation, and opportunities for upward mobility and training. The guiding principle is to maintain consistency between the incentives and the cultural values.

As the transition from a repressed to a developing financial market proceeds, and even in the circumstances of a developed financial market, decision mistakes will be made on such matters as products and services, systems, technology, and staffing. Managing under competitive market conditions, with incomplete information and inadequately trained staff, will require a corporate culture that tolerates mistakes and provides for their correction and inclusion in the bank's institutional memory. Such tolerance will facilitate a process of learning by doing, the avoidance of previous mistakes, or the accessing of answers to issues already resolved.

The bank's ability to retain skilled employees can be influenced by the way management deals with such staff relative to the competition. In the cultures of most of the countries that are deregulating their financial markets, the preservation of dignity is a paramount value. Employees, particularly the most skilled of them (for example, accountants, computer specialists, credit officers, and others) who lose self-respect, or the respect of others, dishonor both themselves and their families. A single harsh word by a manager or supervisor may result in employees leaving their jobs for other similar or better jobs offered by a more tolerant competitor. If the employees are unionized, the result may be more severe than the loss of scarce skills. It may be a loss of production and customers as well.

A disciplined work force is required for a bank's profitable survival under competitive market conditions. Employees must maintain regular bank hours, provide quality service to customers, demonstrate honesty and avoid conflicts of interest. In repressed financial markets with permissive regulatory and supervisory standards and deficient enforcement capabilities of these standards, management and staff may use the bank's assets and time for their personal benefit, even to the extent of starting small businesses with credit from the bank. Such practices persisted because, among other things, public information on the bank's performance was unavailable or carefully sanitized by its private owners. Under competitive market conditions, the emphasis is on profitability based on sound banking principles and practices and public information on these practices. Recruitment, hiring, promotion, transfer, discipline and firing – all contribute to creating a corporate culture that stresses profitability and service through employee competence and integrity.

9.5 ACHIEVING PERFORMANCE GOALS

As the bank expands and the market environment grows more complex, the need for active, insightful and effective human resource management becomes more pressing, and expected performance results more difficult to accomplish. Achieving performance results will be based on the work ethic in the bank, and on management's ability to exploit the opportunities offered by market freedom, and technology. The work ethic in turn is influenced by the societal and corporate culture. Management's response to market and technological opportunities will depend on the bank's ability to attract and retain highly qualified staff with the ability to select the technology and apply it in a performance enhancing manner. Modern technology will allow the bank's staff to create more wealth more efficiently.

The bank's ability to attract and retain competent staff depends on its employee reward programme. Although any reward system must be culturally specific, the need to enhance performance in a changing market environment will require management to review its employees' reward programme, with the objective of informing management about the strategy for changing the bank's remuneration system, controlling costs, improving allocation of existing payroll expenses, matching or exceeding competitive or other levels of remuneration, or enhancing incentives. The questions that may be relevant for the review are listed in Box 9.3.[9]

Technology management has an important role in enhancing performance and increasing competitive advantage. Exposing banks to technology transfer has been an important consideration for their privatization and, in part, explains the preference for joint ownership with banks in developed financial markets. Undoubtedly, bank management in developing financial market has realized that technology can assist in identifying and achieving a range of strategic possibilities for the bank and its functional units. To achieve performance goals technology must be viewed as an asset to be

Box 9.3   Reward analysis questionnaire

- *Quality staff*: into which jobs does the bank need to attract skilled staff? Does the remuneration programme permit the bank to do so? How does the bank's remuneration system and overall work environment, including its corporate culture, compare with those of its competitors?
- *Employee retention*: does the bank have a employee retention problem (that is, is the bank losing skilled staff to its competitors)? Has the bank lost employees because of inadequate remuneration?
- *Employee motivation*: does the remuneration programme motivate high performance at all levels?
- *Target culture*: what types of work culture does the remuneration system foster? Does the work culture being fostered represent what management expected? To what extent does the remuneration system foster the bank's corporate culture?
- *Organization reinforcement*: does the remuneration system reflect the relative importance of the jobs in the bank? Are enough incentives available for individual employees' career development and growth?
- *Business plans and unit goal accomplishment*: what is the link between the performance of individual employees, functional units, or the overall bank, and the bank's remuneration programme? Would a more direct link improve the concentration and motivation of unit management and staff to realize their goals?
- *Cost control*: are the bank's remuneration expenses effectively managed? Do employees fully appreciate the many components of the bank's remuneration package and respond accordingly, in terms of increased effort, to these components? How does the bank's payroll expenses to asset ratio compare with those banks in its peer group?

acquired, managed and increased. However, the acquisition of technology, like that of any other assets, exposes the bank to risks relative to the expected rewards. Management must be well informed about the technological, financial and human resources issues before launching the bank in the modern era of technology.

Management in developed financial markets has recognized that technology intensive banks generally demonstrate high growth rates, and even banks with established market positions may gradually find themselves outflanked by competitors with superior product or process technology. This outflanking may occur in spite of the fact that the new technology may create new markets and threaten traditional technology only progressively, that is through one sub-market at a time. Technological innovations by banks can pose serious threats to traditional ways of doing business by substantially improving competitive advantage. In other words, late or inadequate management responses designed to permit participation in the new technology may lead to a loss of market position from which recovery may be difficult, and on occasion, impossible. Appropriate and timely management responses will be assisted by the availability of staff with the skills to monitor, manage, and exploit technological changes.

It is true that technology adapts readily to the standardized characteristics and expanding volume of banking transactions. It is also true that because of the rapid changes in banking technology, uninformed decisions on technology adaptation can effect the bank's future survival. Management's response to this reality will lead to several primary technological decisions to maintain the bank's long-term viability. These decisions may include: (1) the establishment of a mechanism to assess the technology for maintaining the bank's competitive strength and to monitor technological changes in other banking markets; (2) the conduct of a strategic evaluation of the type of technology needed, this evaluation may encompass such areas as the desired capital-employee ratio or production process, technical personnel requirement, and output-product mix; and (3) the optimum method for obtaining the technology, whether through technology transfer or through research and development.[10] Together, these decisions constitute the essence of technology management. The major purpose of these primary decisions is to act early enough to ensure that the bank has the needed technology, whether through external acquisition or internal development.

Box 9.4 provides a framework for technological management of banks in developing financial markets.[11] This framework delineates management response to technology as positive and managerial, or active and

Box 9.4   Technological management framework

Activity level	Positive: management orientation, wide scope, lower risk and gain	Active: entrepreneurial orientation; limited scope; higher risk
Monitoring technological change	As a purchaser, learn to use technology	Purchase technology with the intention to manufacture this technology
Managing technological change	Guide the bank through the effects of change, and adapt new technology	Adapt and develop new technology
Exploiting technological change	Introduce new products and services based on adapted technology	Sell technology domestically and to other developing financial markets

entrepreneurial. Given the limited availability of needed skills and the degree of unfamiliarity with the application of technology to banking operations in these markets, the relevance of a positive management orientation indicated in the framework cannot be overemphasized. In spite of these limitations, some banks may take the entrepreneurial approach by establishing separate technology subsidiaries. This approach should be taken with the greatest of caution and only by adequately capitalized and staffed technology subsidiaries.

9.6   PERFORMANCE APPRAISALS

A system of employee performance evaluation or appraisal is required to complement the other components (for example, technology, skills, and corporate culture) of competitive advantage. Under competitive market conditions, an important goal of human resource management is to use employees' abilities in jobs that have meaning and maximize the employees, real contribution to the bank. This goal implies the matching of jobs with persons, resulting in improved productivity and employee satisfaction.

In an environment where skills are in short supply, the attitude of employees regarding what they think they can contribute to the bank and what they desire from management may be very different from what it was under repressed financial market conditions. Bank management in developing financial markets may have to be more accommodating to the views of their employees, particularly the ones with the desired skills and competence. For these employees, the bank's objectives may have no great significance unless management accepts their skills and talents, and makes a true effort to put these capabilities to work in the right positions. These are positions where the employees can see their career goals accomplished, and management can see a need that contributes to the bank's competitive ability fulfilled.

The formulation and effective implementation of human resource policies that recognize an employee's knowledge, ability, and performance must be pre-eminent. Performance measurement and appraisal criteria are important implementation considerations. In the initial implementation of a performance appraisal system, simple subjective measurements as 'achieve' or 'exceed' performance standards may be all that can be implemented. The appraisal criteria may also be subjective and may include such components as the quality of work, how much is produced, cooperation of the employee, initiative to help wherever needed, knowledge of the job, and dependability based on attendance and attitude.

A subtle problem management may have in recruiting skilled employees is the individualism of these employees in part derived from their acculturation in the developed countries where they received their training and acquired their skills and attitudes to work. Often a more involved review of abilities and performance must accommodate this individualism. It is important for management to understand that the individual seeking employment brings not only skills, experiences and knowledge, but also attitudes, outlook and philosophy, and in most instances, a desire to obtain a position that utilizes his or her particular skills and fulfills his or her personal aspirations. While it may be difficult for management to fit talents to job, the more exacting problem is to continue this fit in future years of service. Employees will demand greater fulfillment from their jobs as their careers develop. They will also want to be evaluated on objective rather than subjective criteria.

Bank management in developed financial markets has realized that as the phenomenon of individualism strengthened with the scarcity of certain skills and the striving for job satisfaction, employees tended to demand greater participation in decisions that affected them.[12] Management has also realized that employees wanted no greater participation than that of being involved in the appraisal of their performance. After all, employees are aware that their appraisal results can influence the benefits they receive (for example, salary increases, fringe benefits, promotion and training).

Assuming that the corporate culture does not tolerate participative decision making, bank management may have to adjust this culture by establishing an appraisal process that permits supervisor–employee discussion. Participative performance appraisals are increasingly becoming the rule rather than the exception. Skilled staff in short supply will expect nothing less, they will certainly prefer to be employed in banks with participatory performance-oriented personal development policies and practices.

Individually tailored development requires the involvement of the bank's personnel and planning units, and a thorough analysis of each employee. This analysis may be based on information obtained from personnel records, and in-depth discussion with the employee. After employee information is obtained the needs of the bank must be explored to facilitate the fit between skills and needs. Normally, the bank's current needs are not too difficult to identify; its future needs are. The specification of the bank's future staffing needs (for example, where certain positions are or will be vacant, the type of job responsibilities, and suggestions for future performance requirements for the positions) must be done by a unit of the bank knowledgeable and versatile in this area.

9.7   THE TRAINING FUNCTION

The training function includes a set of inter-related activities and processes as indicated in Box 9.5. The commitment of management to training cannot be overemphasized. This commitment must be based on a clear understanding of what objectives management wants to achieve and the role of training in achieving them. For instance, management should specify performance objectives satisfactory to the bank's board, and its stockholders. These objectives should be clearly defined and subject to accurate

Box 9.5   Activities in the training function

- *Training*: any developmental activity that expands knowledge and skills related to the banking functions and services.
- *Programmes*: any internal or external materials, format or other teaching aids used in the training process.
- *Feedback*: a process of informal and formal evaluation to determine training effectiveness.
- *Organizational development*: a process of determining overall bank goals and strategies and unifying the various functional units to achieve the bank's strategic objectives.

measurement. Normally, these measurements will be stated in financial terms (for example, increase in loans, deposits, and per share earnings, or decrease in interest or non-interest costs). The essential point is for management to have targets against which individual performance can be assigned and then measured. As employees demonstrate success or failure in achieving the targets, criteria for training programmes can be established.

Moreover, some management objectives and goals will be short-term while others will be long-term. The term structure of these objectives and goals provides important information for the bank's training function. Management should know the lead time it has to develop the knowledge and skills required to achieve the bank's objectives. An example of these objectives is discovering the most profitable customer base for the bank's future expansion. If the marketing plan should indicate the kinds of skills required to identify and penetrate this base, a training programme can then be implemented to develop the relevant skills.

Management must have an enlightened and proactive approach to the training function. In other words, management must see the training function as an investment aimed at acquiring the skills required for the bank to achieve its product, service and growth objectives. This approach will require budgeting for training staff, funds for training materials, employees' absence from the job to attend training sessions. However, like any other investment, management must review the bank's investment returns from the training function, as indicated in the training results, relative to the bank's operating plans. By requiring the quantification of training results, management will be sending a clear signal that training can and does have a return especially when the function aids management to achieve its objectives.

The location of the training function in the bank's organization can be a major management decision. There has been a tendency for bank management in repressed financial markets to locate the training function in the operations department because the emphasis was on operational activities such as cashiering, manual proofing, and ledger balancing. As banks grow and become increasingly exposed to the forces of competition, the need for a separate personnel or human resource unit becomes apparent. The responsibility of this function expands from the training in operating tasks to attracting, developing, motivating and retaining qualified staff.

In spite of the external forces that impel the need for a separate human resource unit that includes training as one of its activities, management still has to determine the appropriate time to create this unit. Of course, there is no precise answer to this timing issue. Surveys in developed financial markets have suggested that when a bank reaches $100 million in assets, the opportunity for this unit begins to emerge.[13] But much will depend not only on asset size but also on the organization and operational issues such as: (1) the available funding for human resource development; (2) the existing and prospective size of its primary market area; (3) the product and services the bank intends to supply to this area; the bank's technological focus; and (5) its current and anticipated functional units in domestic and foreign markets.

The qualifications and size of the training staff are also factors that influence the effectiveness of the bank's training function. At least the training staff should be individuals with the skills, ability and knowledge that enable them to understand the bank's objectives and assist in building the staff's competence to achieve these objectives as efficiently as possible. Box 9.6 indicates a few characteristics of an effective training manager. As far as the number of trainers required to conduct an effective programme is concerned, a bank may require only one competent full-time employee assisted by managers and supervisors from the bank's other functional units.

Additionally, the size of the full-time training staff depends on the training unit's ability to produce effective training programmes that help the bank to meet its skill requirements. In some cases, it may be better to acquire outside training support than to design an in-house training programme. It may also be sensible to hire training staff as needed for specialized training needs. In the final analysis, the decision to have a full-time training staff of one or more will depend on the: (1) training task to be accomplished; (2) human resource issues to be addressed; (3) time constraints on instituting certain services or establishing certain functional

Box 9.6   Characteristics of a training manager

- *Orientation*: financially oriented and not just a behavioural theorist.
- *Capability*: capable of providing a catalytic influence.
- *Change agent*: an understanding of the meaning of change on the bank and its staff and an ability to facilitate such change.
- *Focus*: less concerned with programme than with assisting in the identification and solution of performance problems.
- *Recognition*: willingness to be recognized through evaluation that reflects improved staff performance resulting from training programmes.
- *Skills*: skills in oral and written communication, training methods, and subject matter.
- *Tenacity*: ability to investigate new methods and approaches to assist the bank to achieve increasingly higher staff performance.

Box 9.7   Training impediments

- Management's failure to understand how training benefits the bank.
- Trainer's failure to define the training problems based on a proper 'needs analysis'.
- Failure to be explicit about: the training programme's objectives, the creation of these objectives, and the personal benefits to the trainees taking the programme.
- Management's failure to reinforce the bank's training efforts on a periodic basis.
- Failure to update training material to reflect changes in the bank's objectives.

---

units; and (4) availability of suitable candidates for the training position or positions.

In its haste to implement a training programme, bank management may fail to consider the impediments to an effective training function. This failure, if it occurs, is generally the result of a lack of experience, or information on designing training programmes that develop the skills required in emerging and competitive financial markets. The impediments as indicated in Box 9.7 may range from management's lack of understanding of the financial benefits of training, to the trainer's inability to update the training material and make the programme continuingly relevant.

To overcome these impediments, management may decide that, although the official trainer is the catalyst, training in the bank is everyone's job. Through professional training methods, and training programmes based on a proper 'needs analysis', the bank has a chance to harmonize its short-term and long-term objectives with the expectations of staff wanting to develop their knowledge, skills and abilities, and contribute to their personal career growth and the efficiency of the bank's operations. Banks with clearly defined objectives, and with management and staff professionally equipped to achieve these objectives will be the ones to prosper under competitive market conditions. They will achieve the results that their stockholders, board, and customers expect and deserve.

9.8   SUMMARY

This chapter has emphasized the need for banks in developing financial markets to have a broad view of human resource management. This view underscores the importance of having the right individuals in the right jobs, and ensuring that staffing constraints on the achievement of a bank's goals and objectives are minimized. In addition, the chapter has recognized the various human resource challenges facing bank management in these markets and has suggested a set of general and specific approaches to them.

The general approach would be for management to identify the goals and objectives, know the difference between the bank's human resource needs and skills available to meet these needs, and embody such information in a human resource plan that should be effectively implemented. The specifc approach would be to introduce a system of performance appraisal based on performance standards and measurement, establish a corporate culture that would enhance work performance through appropriate rewards and incentive programmes, restructure the training function to meet the need for skills in the various functional areas, and facilitate management and staff adaptation to the required changes in technology. The effective implementation of these approaches would foster competitive advantage.

10 Regulatory and Supervisory Structures

Safe, sound and strong banks provide the underpinnings of a growing economy. In market economies, commercial banks play a critical role in gathering funds from the public and in channelling these funds to their most productive uses. Funds allocation decisions are made not in accordance with an economy-wide plan or credit directives from the government or the central bank, but instead, by a vast number of credit and investment officers, acting independently of each other and responding to market opportunity – basically market signals.

However, credit allocation decisions may be distorted by such unsound practices as insider and related party transactions, justifying the need for regulatory restrictions. In spite of the potential for these practices, supervisory oversight must not be so restrictive as to inhibit banks to compete effectively. Thus, the regulatory structures that accompany financial market liberalization must be designed to control the risks inherent in credit and investment allocation decisions. Risk control structures are even more pivotal when the basic source of funding of bank credit is considered.

What must be taken into account, in considering the regulatory and supervisory structures for banks operating in developing financial markets, is the elementary point that banks are fiduciary institutions. The public surrenders valuable purchasing power to banks while receiving nothing of concrete value in return. Depositors depend critically on trust. In fact, they merely receive evidence of the bank's indebtedness to them, a promise that this indebtedness will be repaid on a demand or a term basis with or without interest. To be willing to hold balances with banks, depositors must have confidence that they will receive their funds, together with the promised interest on time. When such trust is lacking, the amount of available banking resources will be insufficient to support the capital formation process. An objective of bank regulation and supervision may, therefore, be to ensure that the banks that will be permitted to operate are those that clearly recognize and effectively perform their fiduciary functions by complying with the prudential standards established by the industry, and more particularly by the bank supervisory and regulatory agencies.

This chapter discusses a set of issues relating to bank supervision in developed and developing financial markets. It recognizes the need for effective bank regulation and supervision in situations of transition from a planned to a market economy, and from a repressed to a liberalized financial market. Both situations are concerned with the regulation and supervision of unaccustomed risks in the banking system.

Attention is focused on developed financial markets' regulation and supervision mainly to identify the scope for transferring the practices and experiences of these markets to the developing financial markets. The chapter reviews the techniques used by bank regulators and supervisors to promote safety and soundness and to maintain confidence in the banking system. It classifies these techniques into preventive, protective, and systemic support methods. It identifies two fundamentally different banking system models, and the regulatory and supervisory systems that fit them. It argues a case for adequate supervisory authority – the authority to stop violations of banking laws and regulations and to prevent the undermining of the regulatory and supervisory system's integrity.

Moreover, the chapter emphasizes the need for product and service restrictions on bank powers, loans to insiders, loan size, ownership, and guaranteed liabilities and the authority to impose such restrictions. Effective supervision of banks and their related entities in foreign markets depends on the availability of information on a consolidated basis and the ability of the supervisors to interpret the key indicators derived from consolidated and other regulatory reports. The chapter, therefore, identifies and reviews the supervisory implications of a set of key performance indicators and discusses a selection of regulatory and supervisors issues related to consolidated information. Finally, the chapter has identified a few regulatory and supervisory concerns about shell branches, parallel-owned banks and parent banks established in offshore and underregulated financial centers.

10.1   TECHNIQUES OF BANK REGULATION AND SUPERVISION

Besides taking deposits and extending credit, banks carry out a number of other activities in the areas of payments settlement, custody of assets and management of investments. And there are features in their balance sheets that can be sources of regulatory and supervisory concern. Examples of these features are: (1) mismatches of assets and liabilities; (2) low capitalization; and (3) high-risk loan and investments portfolios. These potential sources of concern, together with their close interaction with and influence over several aspects of economic activity, explain the reasons for banks to be subject to official regulation and supervision, even in liberalized financial markets. The essential objectives of regulatory and supervisory policy are to promote bank safety and soundness and to maintain confidence in the banking system as a whole. A variety of approaches or techniques have been used to address these concerns. The techniques have often been classified into three major groups.

The first group relates to preventive regulations that seek to contain the risks incurred by banks, or increase their ability to carry those risks. These techniques include: (1) market entry requirements, such as licensing and chartering, the establishment of management standards and the setting of minima for capital subscriptions; (2) capital adequacy rules, that in addition to the already mentioned minimum requirements, provide for the establishment and maintenance of appropriate relationships between capital and total assets, risk assets, or liabilities; (3) balance sheet control criteria that seek to regulate certain types of lending, concentrations, and currency denomination of banking transactions; and (4) inspection that can be conducted through a variety of methods such as periodic reporting requirements, on-site examinations, informal consultation, and moral suasion.

The second group refers to depositors' protection through deposit insurance schemes. Although these schemes tend to vary across countries, they uniformly seek to instill confidence in the banking system. It must be noted that deposit insurance schemes, particularly the overextended ones remove market discipline that constrains the increased riskiness of weak banks. Normally, in the absence of deposit insurance, depositors will shift funds away from undercapitalized, unprofitable, and risky banks, thus forcing them to decrease their risk. However, with deposit insurance and no or little risk of loss, depositors will be willing to supply funds to weaker banks engaged in activities producing inadequate returns and excessive risk. With so little to lose, weak undercapitalized banks may have a perverse incentive to take excessive risk – the moral hazard problem – thus exposing the insurance funds and eventually the taxpayers to losses. Moral hazard risk arises in these, as in any other insurance schemes, making it desirable to have as clear as possible a definition of the boundaries of these schemes (for example, maximum insured amounts, territorial frontiers, or whether or not to cover deposits in foreign offices and subsidiaries, and deductible amounts).

Finally, the third group addresses the ultimate systemic support that monetary authorities may extend to banks in difficulty. This support is embodied in the lender of last resort role of the central banks, typically envisaged to be used only in emergency situations and at a relatively high price. Here again the specific characteristics of this function may vary among countries. But the aim of preventing the problems of an individual bank from affecting the system at large is common to all.

Besides facilitating the establishment of banks with the ability to operate effectively under competitive market conditions, regulators and supervisors are responsible for promoting systemic stability particularly in markets where banks are undercapitalized, and are included in a group of independent financial institutions, with common owners and with no consolidated information available to the supervisors. The promotion of stability will enhance financial intermediation, improve savings performance and contribute to efficiency in resource allocation and use, all of which are critical to elicit supply responses in the economy. These responses, in turn, will foster support for reduced restrictions and government direction, and increased market discipline. Nevertheless, the adoption of some preventative regulatory measures can be a critical complement to systemic stability. The creation of standards for soundness and viability of long established and new banks is a matter of priority for developing financial markets.[1]

10.2   BASIC MODELS OF REGULATION AND SUPERVISION

Two fundamentally different banking system models may be considered by bank regulators and supervisors in developing financial markets. At one extreme is a system that offers no special protection to depositors, creditors, or the private payment system. Under this system all bank customers are exposed to losses, banks are not subject to any special regulatory structure, and are treated like firms in other industries. At the other extreme is a system that offers protection to some depositors, creditors, and the private or inter-bank payment system. There are advantages and disadvantages in both models.

There are at least two advantages of the model that allows for no special protection to any banking clients and the private payment system. The first advantage is the market discipline applicable to bank management. Banks may be unable to attract any funding unless they are adequately capitalized and are following prudent lending and investing standards. The second advantage relates to minimizing taxpayers' losses. Taxpayers are not exposed to losses in the event of bank insolvencies. Losses are shared by depositors and creditors and are not funded by an insurance scheme or taxpayers.

Balanced against these advantages are disadvantages in terms of systemic and other vulnerabilities. For example, (1) in the event of an insolvency, small and unsophisticated depositors may lose their savings; (2) banks are vulnerable to deposit runs; and (3) the inter-bank payment system, where banks exchange payment claims on each other, is exposed to major disruptions should a participating bank fail. These disadvantages cannot be overemphasized. The first example alludes to the need for a safety net for depositors who do not have the information or knowledge to determine if a bank is well managed and is avoiding excessive risk; the second refers to the potential for liquidity evaporation in the banking system; and the third relates to the disruptive impact on the financial system and the economy of a payment system failure.

In the case of the second model that allows for the protection of some depositors and creditors, as well as the private payment system, the disadvantages of the first model are avoided. Unsophisticated depositors and creditors are given some protection, the banking system is less vulnerable to deposit-runs that feed on themselves, and the payment system is protected. However, this model creates distortions in the decision making process. In fact, instituting a safety net weakens market discipline as depositors fail to seek out the sound, well-managed and well-capitalized banks, and hold their balances with the most conveniently located banks or with the ones offering higher interest rates.

Thus, rather than depositing in banks that allocate their savings to sound and profitable borrowers and issuers, depositors will be attracted to the banks that pursue excessively risky lending and investing practices and to those diverting resources to managers, directors and their affiliates. Added to the problems of resource misallocation, is the tendency for banks with safety nets to have less capital – providing a smaller cushion of protection for taxpayers. Surely, banks do not need as much capital to attract deposits when their deposits are insured.

Regulators and supervisors in developing financial markets may follow those in developed financial markets where there has been the tendency to adopt the second model. Thus, a challenge for bank regulatory and supervisory agencies is to create a system that limits vulnerability to excessive risk-taking, insider transactions, and resource misallocation while granting the protection of a safety net. In addition, because of financial market integration, the regulatory and supervisory systems created in the developing financial markets will have to be coordinated with those existing in the developed financial markets if inefficiencies and inequalities associated with different regulatory standards are to be avoided. However, for any coordination effort to succeed, regulators in developing financial markets must at least identify the principal elements of the developed financial markets' regulatory framework and adapt these elements as far as the circumstances of their own markets will permit. The end result may well be a regulatory and supervisory system that addresses the several regulatory and supervisory areas identified in Box 10.1.

The regulatory and supervisory framework governing banks in developing financial markets may have major weaknesses. These weaknesses may be corrected if legislative reform expands regulatory and supervisory authority and if measures not requiring legislative reform are implemented promptly and effectively. Legislative reform efforts may be focused on: (1) establishing the legal basis for substantial strengthening of bank regulation and supervision, including the establishment of prudential standards

Box 10.1   Areas of regulation and supervision in developed financial markets

- *Legal reserve requirements*: banks are required to hold reserves at central banks in most developed financial markets. Legal reserves are not normally a regulatory burden for these banks.
- *Liquidity supervision and regulation*: banks hold liquid reserves in cash, accounts at the central bank, and short-term marketable securities. This liquidity allows banks to sustain unusual deposit outflows. These short-term assets also balance against banks' short-term liabilities, thus mitigating the effect of interest rate changes on portfolio values.
- *Reporting requirements and supervision*: supervision of the safety and soundness of banks is based on on-site examinations, independent audits and periodic written, and oral reports.
- *Capital standards*: risk-based capital requirements are in effect. Some countries impose additional minimum capital requirements that are not risk-based.
- *Limits to bank services*: in some markets, banks or affiliated organizations can offer a full range of financial services, while in others they have restrictions on securities and insurance underwriting activities. Ownership structure (for example, ownership concentration, and cross-ownership among banks and other financial and non-financial firms) is also affected by banking regulations.
- *Deposit guarantee programmes*: these programmes exist in different forms (for example, types and limits of coverage, sponsorship by government or private sector, funding by assessments, or tax revenue and so on). There is a policy that some banks are too big to fail. The policy implications for future costs to the government, public and banks can be severe.
- *Compliance regulation*: the compliance programmes place the responsibility on banks to safeguard their clients' deposit and credit transactions, protect employees, and promote public service activities.

for banks operating in these markets; (2) providing for supervision of related financial entities on a consolidated basis; (3) increasing minimum capital requirements and introducing risk-based capital adequacy standards; and (4) enhancing the authority of bank supervisors to address banking powers, clarify the criteria and procedures for bank liquidation, and define the respective roles of the finance ministry, insurance fund and other agencies in the regulatory and supervisory structure.

One of three basic regulatory and supervisory frameworks may be adapted to the circumstances of developing financial markets. These are: (1) the segmented structure in the US and Japan; (2) the universal structure in most European countries: and (3) some middle ground between the two, such as the Canadian subsidiaries structure.[2] As countries modernize their regulatory and supervisory system, the structural distinctions in (1) and (2) may move towards the middle ground. Segmented structures may become more universal, and universal structures, more segmented. Regulatory and supervisory models for developing financial markets may, therefore, reflect, as appropriate, the models of developed financial markets. They must be dynamic as well.

The US financial structure separates banking from other financial functions, including insurance and securities activities. Technically, Japanese banks operate under a framework similar to that of the US, but in practice, Japanese banks operate within a network of securities, insurance, and commercial companies through extensive cross-ownership arrangements. In contrast to the segmented approach, the universal banking structure allows financial institutions to conduct a full range of commercial, investment banking, and insurance activities, on an integrated basis. Banks in most major European countries operate in a universal banking framework. In Germany and France, for example, banks are permitted to provide all financial services, including securities and insurance, on an integrated basis. In the UK, banks are permitted to provide a wide range of financial services through conglomerate organizations. Universal banking is the model applied in the European Community. Finally, some countries' regulations take the middle road between segmentation and complete integration of financial services. In Canada, for example, banks may have wholly-owned securities subsidiaries but cannot engage directly in securities and insurance activities. In Italy, commercial banks may operate in multifunctional financial services groups, but some activities are restricted or limited.

Bank regulations in developing financial markets have placed varying degrees of restrictions on the operations banks can perform and services they can provide. In most of these markets, activities other than short-term lending are restricted in order to minimize the risk to banks' portfolios presented by these other operations. Mexico, in accordance with its long tradition of close association between banks and industrial groups, has a universal banking system in which banks underwrite, issue and trade in corporate securities. In Argentina, Bolivia, Chile, and Uruguay, banks can supply limited related services such as credit cards, trade financing and trust management. Furthermore, banks in these countries can lend at any length of maturity, conduct foreign exchange transactions and trade public securities.[3]

10.3   ADEQUATE SUPERVISORY AUTHORITY

It is widely accepted that supervisors must have authority to stop violations of banking laws and regulations promptly or else the integrity of the regulatory and supervisory structure will be undermined. Supervisors also need to have adequate scope for discretion because regulations cannot be expected to address every problem. Inevitably situations that are not fully addressed by regulations will arise and pose a threat to taxpayers, depositors, and creditors. In these circumstances, the supervisor will need the authority to correct the problem.

In most financial markets, bank regulatory and supervisory responsibilities are shared in varying degrees between the finance ministries and central banks. In developed financial markets the tendency has been for the central banks to have supervisory, and for the finance ministries to have regulatory, responsibilities. In developing financial markets, the finance ministries tend to dominate both responsibilities, thus curtailing the authority of bank supervisors to implement prompt corrective action when considered necessary. For example: (1) bank supervisors may be permitted to perform bank examinations, but prevented from taking corrective actions, unless approved by the finance minister; and (2) the legislature may enact laws that fail to vest rule-making authority on the supervisor or provide a simple administrative procedure for making or approving regulations. Before implementation, all regulations may have to receive the approval of the legislature.

In some Latin American financial markets, for instance, the Superintendency of Banks has effectively been under the control of the finance ministry and has focused on monitoring formal compliance with banking regulations rather than analysing the solvency of financial institutions. Bank interventions required the approval of the finance minister, thus making the intervention process vulnerable to political pressures, and prolonged delays. Such delays, in turn, could permit bank management to maintain their positions and continue improper banking practices for an extended period. The supervisory roles of superintendency, central bank, and deposit insurance agency in dealing with bank illiquidity or insolvency have been ill-defined. The superintendency may have no authority to require capital increase, sale, merger or dissolution of financial institutions.

Until recently, Latin American and Caribbean financial markets provided impressive examples of inadequate supervisory authority and regulatory standards. In some of these markets prudential standards for capital adequacy, asset quality, or related party transactions have not been formulated, external audits were ineffective because regulatory and accounting standards were inadequate, and the superintendency has not been sufficiently equipped to perform the prudential responsibilities in an effective manner. And, as in the case of the US savings and loan crisis, these deficiencies have sometimes been reflected in costly banking crises of 1990s.[4] However, regulatory and supervisory reforms are being rapidly and effectively implemented in most of these markets. These reforms have been influenced, in part, by the experiences of developed financial markets. Box 10.2 summarizes the responsibility for bank regulation and supervision in a selection of developed financial markets. The US regulatory system is excluded because its complexity and uniqueness do not make it easily transferrable to the circumstances of developing financial markets.[5]

An important component of supervisory structure is the ability to supervise banks and their domestic and foreign financial affiliates on a consolidated basis. Such supervision assists in determining evasion of regulations relating to reserve requirements, capital adequacy, and limits on related party transactions. The absence of consolidated supervision, creates incentives for financial groups to divert problem loans or losses to those institutions where supervision and reporting requirements are weak or non-existent and to channel deposits into institutions that are not subject to reserve requirements. Furthermore, the organization structure of financial groups permits evasion of limits on loan concentration and lending to related parties. The absence of authority to supervise banks on a consolidated basis provides opportunities for regulatory arbitrage which when exploited will eventually weaken the groups themselves and the financial sector as a whole.[6]

In several developing financial markets banks typically form part of a larger financial group. Although the regulatory framework may be based on the principle of specialized banking, in practice there is, more often

Box 10.2   Responsibility for regulation and supervision

- *Japan*: Finance Ministry has responsibility for bank licensing, regulation and supervision. Bank supervision, including direct examination responsibility, is shared with the Bank of Japan, which has entered into broad supervisory agreements with individual banks as a condition of access to bank credit services and payment facilities.
- *Germany*: bank regulation and supervision are the responsibilities of the Federal Banking Supervisory Office (FBSO), an agency of the Finance Ministry. For certain regulatory changes the concurrence of the Bundesbank is required. Banks regularly report to the Bundesbank which analyses these reports and shares its findings with the FBSO. The FBSO and the Bundesbank have authority to undertake bank examinations but both normally rely on independent auditors to perform this function.
- *Canada*: bank regulatory policy is determined by the Finance Ministry. Bank regulation and supervision are the responsibility of an independent agency, the Office of the Superintendent of Financial Institutions, whose head is appointed by the Finance Minister.
- *Switzerland*: bank regulation and supervision are the duty of the Federal Banking Commission, which is independent of the Government and the Swiss National Bank, but administratively comes under the Finance Ministry.
- *United Kingdom*: although the legislative framework for supervision is established by the Treasury, bank regulation and supervision are the responsibility of the Bank of England, whose Governor is appointed by the Prime Minister.
- *France*: policy for overall bank regulation is established by the Committee for Bank Regulation chaired by the Finance Minister, with the Governor of the Bank of France as Vice-Chair. Bank supervision is the primary responsibility of the Banking Commission, chaired by the Governor, and a high ranking Finance Ministry Official as Vice-Chair. The Governor is nominated by the Finance Minister.
- *Italy*: bank supervision is the responsibility of the Bank of Italy. Policy decisions of the Government are made by the cabinet-level Inter-Ministerial Credit and Savings Committee, chaired by the Minister of Treasury.

---

than not, a universal banking system. The financial group may be a composite of legally independent financial entities, under common ownership, providing their clients with a full range of financial services. Financial groups may consist of commercial banks, mortgage banks, finance, insurance and leasing companies, brokerages, and liquid asset funds, and offshore affiliates. In addition, mainly through their commercial banks, financial groups may offer trust fund operations and operate money desks to channel wholesale funds directly from investors to borrowers.

Mexico has addressed the issue of regulating and supervising financial groups in a law enacted in 1991. This law allows for the formation of three kinds of financial group: (1) financial groups led by a bank without a brokerage house or securities firm; (2) financial groups led by a brokerage house without a bank; and (3) financial groups consisting of both a bank and brokerage house and led by a holding company. Holding companies must own at least 51 per cent of the shares of the firms in the group and may not have liabilities of their own. The advantages of forming a financial group include name recognition for the whole array of services offered under one umbrella, economies of scale in the distribution of services through a single branch, and other operating synergies resulting from the concentration of computer, advertising, and other corporate services.[7]

Initially, some financial group members were established to circumvent interest rate controls. They were, however, retained after interest rate liberalization as a means to avoid reserve requirements and to capture short-term deposits used to finance activities elsewhere within the group. Short-term deposits were often used to fund long-term fixed rate assets, thus creating substantial maturity mismatches and vulnerability to interest rate changes. Although the commercial banking members of the group, were sometimes required to bridge the maturity gap in their affiliated companies assets and liabilities, there was no single regulatory agency with the authority to supervise these groups on a consolidated basis. Consolidated supervision forces the analysis of the financial institutions' accounts on a group level, taking full consideration of the inter-relationships between banks and other financial entities in the same group.

The information that provides the basis for consolidated supervision is not simply the summation of balance sheet data of the individual group members. A summation of data from the balance sheet published by each financial institution in the group on the same date may be deficient because: (1) intragroup operations are not netted out; and (2) the data may be incomplete because of the absence of a published balance sheet for each group member. It should also be noted that the methodology of full consolidation of the various group components with intragroup operations netted out, corrects the above deficiencies. Thus, consistent with the principle of consolidation, supervisors should be given the authority to require banking and financial entities in a group to report their exposure to each other on a net basis.

A bank's balance sheet structure may differ substantially from that of the financial group, when the accounts are prepared on a consolidated basis. For example, holding of cash and other liquid assets may appear to be quite large when only the bank's balance sheet is considered, but if these assets represent intragroup deposits with the bank, they may be sharply lower when the accounts of the group are consolidated. The same may be true for capital. In addition, the relative magnitudes of 'other assets' and 'private deposit liabilities' may change substantially when the accounts are consolidated. These differences may be less marked when published accounts of the group members are simply added, suggesting that the summation method should not substitute for a thorough consolidation. In the absence of consolidation, the structure of a commercial bank's balance sheet can be a very misleading indicator of the true condition of the bank or the financial group as a whole. While consolidated supervision is necessary, it is not sufficient to ensure effective supervision of financial groups in developing financial markets. The authority to supervise on a consolidated basis must be combined with efficient supervisory staff and adequate resources for effective prudential oversight. Even with consolidated supervision, all supervisory authorities should retain the right to continue monitoring the market risk of individual entities on a non-consolidated basis to ensure that significant imbalances within a group does not escape supervision. Moreover: (1) prudential norms covering such areas as capital adequacy, loan classification, provisioning, and lending to related parties must be established; (2) banks' offshore operations must be monitored; and (3) external audits must be based on adequate accounting standards and regulations.

Bank regulators and supervisors in developing financial markets should support the concept of consolidated supervision on the grounds that problems in one affiliate could have a contagion effect on the group as a whole. Moreover, consolidated supervision reduces the scope for risk to escape measurement by being held in unsupervised locations. It also ensures that banking groups have group capital to support their risks, thus preventing excessive gearing up on the same capital base.[8]

For banks with offshore affiliates, the practice of passing positions between related entities in different time zones may be a matter of supervisory concern. A bank can reduce positions at the close of business by engaging in a transaction with an affiliate in a later time zone (that is, 'passing' its position). This practice may be a perfectly legitimate device to enable banks to manage their positions continuously or to reduce intragroup imbalances. If all positions, irrespective of location, were measured at the same moment in time, no problem would arise. However, reporting is likely to take place on the basis of accounts drawn up at the end of a business day and it is possible that positions passed continuously over time zones will escape reporting all together. Supervisors should, therefore, be especially vigilant in ensuring that banks do not pass positions on reporting dates to affiliates whose positions escape measurement because of time zone differences.

10.4 PRODUCT AND SERVICE RESTRICTIONS

Regulations are necessary for free markets to operate efficiently. However, regulations must be transparent, and their enforcement must be prompt, impartial, and effective. The existence of regulations, no doubt, implies restrictions on market freedom. But these restrictions are not the ones of repressed financial markets with their fixed interest rates, wide positive spreads between interest income and interest expense, and credit allocations to priority sectors. The restrictions, in developing financial markets, are mainly about reducing risks, and establishing product, service, and quantitative limits on banks. While there may be differences in the detail, the areas of regulatory restrictions are generally similar. These areas are mainly restrictions on: (1) bank powers; (2) loans to insiders; (3) loan size; (4) ownership; and (5) guaranteed liabilities.

In restricting bank powers, regulators may focus on reducing the riskiness of banks' portfolios by limiting the kinds of assets and activities that are permissible. For example, limitations may be placed on direct ownership of real estate by banks, given the high-level of risk and low liquidity of such investments. Because of volatility of equity prices in developing financial markets, banks may be restricted in holding equity positions in enterprises, or prevented from underwriting certain securities. As the holding or underwriting of securities can pose unacceptable levels of price risk, bank powers to conduct these activities funded by public deposits should be restricted.

There has been a long history of bank losses and insolvencies resulting from abuses by insiders, namely, bank managers, directors, and owners. These abuses typically take the form of insider loans that other banks, because of the favourable rates relative to the credit risk, will find unacceptable. To limit the potential for insider abuse, restrictions must be focused on the bank's total exposure to insiders and their related interests. It is not uncommon for management and staff of banks in developing financial markets to have business interests that are funded by the banks in which they are employed.

In some markets, non-financial firms are not allowed to own commercial banks. This restriction aims at preventing these firms from accessing high-risk bank loans, funded, in some cases, by insured deposits. If bank ownership by non-financial institutions is permitted, tighter restrictions on transactions between the banks and their owners should be imposed to curtail the potential for insider abuse. At least transactions must be on conditions similar to those offered to non-owner borrowers. In other words, all transactions with owners, and other insiders must be at 'arms length'. An objective of loan size restrictions is to reduce concentration risk through proper diversification. Diversification can be improved by limiting the size of individual loans relative to the bank's capital. Limits may be differentiated on the basis of secured and unsecured loans, the type of collateral held, and the credit standing of the borrower. For example, loans to government entities, or loans collateralized by investment grade securities, or bank deposits may be less restricted than loans for venture capital, or other speculative purposes. Loan limits for individual borrowers may be computed on an aggregate basis to reflect all on- and off-balance sheet exposures of the bank and its related entities. Concentration limits may also be placed on loans to particular sector or region of the economy.

Deposit insurance payments to depositors, in the event of a bank failure, may be funded by assessments on bank deposits and supplemented by tax revenues. To reduce taxpayers' exposure to losses due to the settlement of guaranteed liabilities, limitations may be placed on the size and the type of deposits covered by the safety net. Safety net protection may be extended only to individuals who are least able to judge the soundness of the banks. In addition to limiting potential taxpayer losses, guaranteed liability restrictions introduce market discipline on the part of those not protected by the safety net. As unprotected depositors and creditors will be more inclined to search for sound banks, banks that depend on such depositors and creditors will be pressured to pursue prudent policies and practices.

However, balanced against the advantages of limiting depositors' safety net protection are certain disadvantages related to a bank's liquidity and the inter-bank payment system. Banks dependent on unprotected funds are vulnerable to deposit-runs. Concerns about the liquidity of such banks can prompt a simultaneous effort by exposed customers, with possible spill over effects into other banks with uninsured depositors. Liquidity problems of a major bank can disrupt the entire inter-bank payment system.

In formulating banking activity or ownership restrictions, regulators may seek the input of the industry's representatives, without sacrificing the ultimate objectives of effective regulations and supervision. These objectives may be to promote a safe and sound banking system, efficient competition, and consumer protection. Industry input may be focused on ensuring that regulations are not burdensome and do not unnecessarily restrict management's ability to maximize return on equity. Thus, regulatory and industry synergies should produce regulations that reduce systemic risk, protect the deposit insurance, and permit banks to be competitive, profitable and viable.

Understanding the approach to business strategy determination will assist bank regulators to appreciate the critical role of management in the formulation of regulations and supervisory practices. Like other businesses, banks evaluate numerous factors including markets, competitors, customers, operating capabilities, and corporate culture to determine their strengths and weaknesses. Based on the results, each bank decides the best way to serve its customers. In making this decision, management will draw a 'road map' indicating where they want their business to go in the future, while allowing for the regulatory restrictions to be encountered on the way. Management participation will be centred on restraining or removing restrictions on opportunities envisioned in their strategic plan.

Of course, the product and service restrictions imposed by the regulatory and supervisory framework may result in business strategies that are less than optimal. In the regulatory formulation process, bank management may reasonably argue that their banks: (1) are less efficient than they could be because they are compelled to use regulatory creativity to extend their activities; (2) cannot use their operational and distribution systems to their full capacity; (3) are unable to serve their customers as efficiently as they are capable of doing; and (4) are limited in the extent to which they can diversify their risks. These are powerful arguments that must be considered by the regulators. Disregarding them may increase the very risks that regulators may want to minimize.

10.5 SUPERVISORY INFORMATION

Apart from information derived from on-site examination, at least two sets of off-site surveillance information are necessary for effective supervision of banks in developing financial markets. These are: (1) information from which bank performance indicators can be derived; and (2) information that facilitates supervision of banks' offshore offices and subsidiaries. Performance indicators are essentially ratios derived from a bank's balance sheet and income statements. The principal indicators of supervisory interest are: profitability, asset quality, and efficiency.[9] Information on banks' offshore activities should provide a necessary supervisory perspective of their operations on a consolidated basis.[10]

Pre-tax return on equity (ROE) is the usual profitability indicator. Supervisors should be aware that the biggest problem with evaluating performance by looking at a bank's ROE in any particular year arises from the timing differences between the recognition of income, and expenses, and the risk in the bank's accounts. Broadly, income and expenses are taken through the profit and loss account annually over the life of the loan but credit risk is only recognized when the recovery of the loan is in serious doubt. Because borrowers are more likely to encounter difficulties in a recession, changes in the bad debt charge would cause reported profits to have a cyclical pattern.

Although an increase in income, whether resulting from a loan expansion or increased net interest margin, can be considered a positive development, a bank supervisor who does not have a detailed knowledge of the bank's portfolio will not be in a position to evaluate the extent to which such an increase will cover any change in the level of risk that management has decided to take. This evaluation will be possible only when the risk is recognized through the bad debt charge in subsequent years, or through on-site examinations. Equally, banks with rapidly growing loan portfolios are more likely to have higher ROE because problems are less likely to emerge shortly after a loan has been approved while banks will recognize the extra income on their expanding loan portfolios.

Loan provisioning is not a precise science and banks will differ in how conservative they are when making assumption about, say the value of security or collateral. As a result, different banks will have different levels of provision in their balance sheet for the same amount of risk. One consequence is that banks that make relatively large provisions will reduce the equity element of the ROE equation and thus improve their ROE in subsequent years, as long as the provision remains on their balance sheets.

The ratio of bad debt charge to loans is an asset quality indicator. However, it is difficult to draw authoritative conclusions from this ratio in the absence of detailed knowledge of the bank's portfolios. While a high ratio indicates a deteriorating asset quality, a low one may disguise management's reluctance to provide against problem loans indicating deeper asset quality problems. Similarly, a high ratio of provisions to loans may indicate a poor quality portfolio, or more positively, a conservative approach to provisioning. In either event, comparisons are distorted by the differences in the speed at which non-performing loans are written off. This speed, no doubt, will be influenced by differing tax treatment.

A high provision to non-performing loan ratio may be a better indicator of adequate provisioning than the ratio of bad debt charge to loans, although the timing of write-offs, and definitional problems regarding non-performing loans, especially in the case of overdrafts, can cause some difficulties. Moreover, banks may argue that their provisioning needs should not be determined by such broad-brush ratios but by the distinct needs of their own portfolios. In particular, the ratio will indicate if non-performing loans are well secured, in which case low provisions will suggest that recoveries are expected to be high.

The most commonly used indicator of a bank's efficiency is the cost to income ratio. This ratio does have its strengths (for example, it is easy to calculate, and readily understood). Furthermore, the failure of a bank to hold down costs would result in a deterioration (that is, a rise) in this ratio relative to its peers. However, its broad-brush nature means that differences between banks, or even changes from one year to the next for the same bank, may be caused by factors other that cost efficiency. For example, the ratio could alter for reasons related to income as well as to costs. Income may increase because of an increase in the level of trading profits, loans outstanding, and risk assumed. More generally, given that profits can be broadly defined as income less costs, the amount of additional information obtained from expressing the difference as a ratio is necessarily somewhat limited.

Bank supervisors in developing financial markets must also be aware that it can be misleading to compare the cost to income ratios of different types of bank or, by extension, of diversified banking groups with different business mixes. To take two examples: (1) retail banking involves higher administrative costs than corporate banking; and (2) fee-earning businesses tend to have a relatively high cost to income structure. Thus, a high cost to income ratio is not necessarily an adverse sign itself, particularly if the business is a profitable, high-volume and low-risk one. Technical accounting reasons may also explain the inter-bank differences in cost to income ratios. For example, a bank will tend to have a lower ratio if it has a large life insurance subsidiary whose contribution is included as a one-line entry (that is, income net of costs) in the bank's consolidated profit and loss account.

In order to supervise on a consolidated basis, parent bank supervisors must be able to evaluate all aspects of their banks' operations that bear on safety and soundness, wherever those operations are conducted. This evaluation can be done through a variety of means, including on-site examinations, access to audit reports, or through the review of regulatory information. The regulatory information may be quantitative and qualitative and may be distinguished on the basis of its supervisory usefulness. For instance a distinction can be drawn between: (1) preliminary information needed to approve an authorization to conduct business; (2) regular information required to perform ongoing supervision; and (3) exceptional information requirements in a 'watch' or crisis situation. In addition, parent bank supervisors must distinguish between what information is essential or desirable, and what is material or inconsequential.

The quantitative information must be reported on a regular basis and should include data needed to calculate the bank's capital adequacy ratios, large exposures or legal lending limits, as well as its funding and deposit concentrations. Supervisors should expect the parent banks they supervise to have this information and to make it freely available to them. While banking regulations may stipulate the type of information that should be available for effective consolidated supervision, the supervisors should still be responsible for verifying the accuracy of the quantitative information they receive.

Supervisors also need certain qualitative information for effective consolidated supervision. The principal reasons for such information are to assure the supervisors that: (1) the banking group has a risk management system that adequately covers its offshore and onshore activities; (2) the internal controls and internal audit procedures for controlling the group's offshore operations are of a sufficiently rigorous quality; (3) changes in ownership and control of partly owned subsidiaries are monitored; (4) the reporting process by which the supervisor receives information is reliable; (5) the quality of management is adequate; (6) the quality of assets and the levels of concentrations are known and are within appropriate parameters; (7) the liquidity of the institutions is being monitored and there is no excessive reliance on a single third-party source, or a small number of funding sources; and (8) there is compliance with laws and regulations.

In the past, parent bank supervisors' access to information on the operations of their banks' foreign offices and subsidiaries was impeded by secrecy requirements designed to preserve the confidentiality of customers' transactions and deposit balances. Although there are legitimate reasons for protecting customers' privacy, it is almost axiomatic to state that secrecy laws should neither impede the ability of supervisors to ensure safety and soundness of banks with international operations, nor be used to protect confidential relationships banks may have with customers engaged in criminal activities. However, it must be emphasized that what may be criminal in one regulatory or supervisory jurisdiction may be legal or customary in another. In fact, a requirement for consolidated supervision may well be the existence of universally accepted laws and regulations, accounting standards, and supervisory practices for all banks with cross-border operations. A critical issue in this regard is how and when will this requirement be established and effectively implemented.[11]

As secrecy laws may curtail the availability of information required for effective supervision on a consolidated basis, parent bank supervisors may have to establish information sharing agreements, with supervisors in offshore jurisdictions or host-country regulators and supervisors, to facilitate the availability of safety and soundness information while protecting the privacy of customers. Under normal circumstances, bank supervisors do not need to know the identity of individual depositors. Really, their interest is in aggregate liability changes primarily to monitor a bank's overall liquidity. What typically they need to know is whether there are deposit concentrations and if so, the amount involved. Accordingly, aggregate information on deposits above a threshold that is significant in relation to the banks' deposit base, balance sheet, or capital base, along with some information on the geographic source of these deposits, would usually be required.

However, in certain well-defined circumstances depositors' names and account information may be needed. A supervisor may want to verify whether or not a given depositor is among a bank's large depositors, in order to: (1) monitor deposit concentrations or the funding risk of the deposit being withdrawn; or (2) track all transactions made by, or on behalf of, a single client, which may include a group of related companies. If a supervisory problem is anticipated and this problem is clearly defined in terms of preserving the bank's safety and soundness, parent bank supervisors may need to have access to individual depositors' names and deposit account information.

To protect the privacy of bank customers, it is important that the information obtained by supervisors is subject to strict conditionality. The conditions may include: (1) a clear specification of the purpose for which the information is sought, and of the matter being monitored or investigated; (2) a restriction on the use of the information received (for example, this information should be restricted solely to officials engaged in prudential supervision and not passed on to third parties without the prior consent of the supervisor providing the information); (3) assurance that all possible steps will be taken to preserve the confidentiality of information received by the supervisor in the absence of explicit consent of the customer; and (4) an undertaking that before taking supervisory or other action, the supervisor receiving the information will undertake to consult with the one supplying it.

Several channels through which parent bank supervisors can receive information on their banks' offshore offices and subsidiaries are available. Indeed, effective consolidated supervision relies on a clear hierarchy of information flows from the foreign banking activity to the parent bank supervisor. For example, information may flow from: (1) the subsidiary or branch to the head office or parent bank; (2) the parent bank or head office to the parent bank or head office supervisor; (3) the foreign subsidiary or branch to its foreign supervisor; and (4) from the foreign supervisor to the parent bank supervisor. Supervisors will determine what channel they will use for prompt and effective results.

Apart from the surveillance information that directly addresses the condition of banks' foreign operations, bank supervisors in developing financial markets must obtain surveillance information that addresses a set of issues that could impact the foreign operations of banks under their jurisdiction. The information obtained must enable the supervisors to: (1) monitor any economic and political developments that may influence stability in the financial centers concerned; (2) keep abreast of the regulatory framework, payment and settlement systems, and other matters bearing on systemic stability, including major fraud and corruption; (3) track particular markets to which the parent banks and their affiliated entities are exposed, whether directly or indirectly; and (4) remain informed about the activities and global strategies of the major banks, the particular risk they face in the foreign markets and the key individuals who control them.

10.6   SUPERVISION OF SHELL BRANCHES AND OTHER ENTITIES

A shell branch is normally a booking office licensed in one regulatory and supervisory jurisdiction managed or controlled from another such jurisdiction, which may be located in a developed or a developing financial market. The jurisdiction responsible for regulating and supervising the bank establishing the shell branch is defined as the 'home' jurisdiction, the one in which the branch is licensed is termed the 'host' jurisdiction. In cases where the regulatory or supervisory jurisdiction cannot be identified, the branch may not be effectively supervised.

In addressing the need for strengthened supervision of banks and their offshore affiliates on a consolidated basis, a Basle committee has specified a set of minimum standards. These standards are: (1) all international banks should be supervised by a home country authority with the capability of supervising on a consolidated basis; (2) the creation of a cross-border banking establishment should receive prior consent of both the host and home country authorities; (3) home country authorities should possess the right to gather information from their cross-border establishments; and

(4) if the host country authority determines that any of these standards is not being met, it could impose restrictive measures or prohibit the establishment of banking offices. These standards are applicable to all home and host country relationships, including the supervision of shell branches.[12]

It is now commonplace among bank regulators and supervisors that the supervision of shell branches, or any branch for that matter, is an important part of the consolidated supervision exercised by the home country supervisor and that no offshore unit should escape supervision. The host supervisor is expected to ensure that the branch to be licensed will be effectively supervised. In the event that any host supervisor receives an application to license a new shell branch that will be managed in another jurisdiction, that supervisor will be expected to notify both the home supervisor and the supervisor in the jurisdiction where the shell branch will be managed. Before approving the shell branch, the host supervisor should be aware of how the home country supervisor would ensure the effective supervision of the branch.

Indeed, all supervisors involved in the creation of shell branches (for example, the home supervisor, the host supervisor or licensing authority, and the authority from whose jurisdiction the branch is managed and controlled) should ensure that each of their fellow supervisors is consulted on the entity or office to be established. Home supervisors should not authorize their banks to establish or acquire offices in any host jurisdiction without satisfying themselves in advance that such offices will be subject to appropriate supervision. If any authority believes that a supervisory gap exists, it should discuss the matter with the other relevant supervisors with a view of ensuring that the operations of shell branches are brought under effective oversight. Ultimately, it is the responsibility of the home supervisor to ascertain the closure of any such gap.

A parallel-owned bank is one that is established in one jurisdiction, has the same ownership as a bank in another jurisdiction, but is not a subsidiary of the other. Such 'sister' institutions may not be subject to consolidated supervision but at the same time a relationship may exist with other entities in the group. For example, it may be that funds are switched from one to the other if a problem arises. Bank regulators and supervisors in home and host jurisdictions should require the operations of parallel owned banks to be subject to consolidated supervision, even if a change in the group's structure is required.

Another situation that requires regulatory and supervisory attention arises in the case of parent banks incorporated in under-regulated financial centers. The need for attention arises if these banks are undertaking cross-border operations without effective supervision in their country of incorporation. The need becomes even more compelling if the parent bank is an unsupervised holding company, or a bank that does not have a single parent. There is a clear potential for abuse by stand-alone banks incorporated in under-regulated financial centers and for unlawful or unauthorized banking activity in other jurisdictions. Home supervisors that license banking entities have a responsibility to monitor the entities' operations on a worldwide basis. No entity should be allowed to use the word 'bank' in its name if it is not conducting banking activities and being supervised as a bank.

Supervisors in host jurisdictions should be extremely cautious about approving the establishment of cross-border operations by banks incorporated in under-regulated financial centers, and even more cautious about accepting other financial institutions conducting banking activities from those centers. Similarly, supervisors, even if they act predominantly as hosts, need to guard against reputational risk resulting from a range of unauthorized or inadequately supervised activities by banks and near-banks incorporated in their jurisdictions.

10.7   SUMMARY

This chapter has identified the principal objectives of bank regulation and supervision in developing financial markets as the promotion of safety and soundness of individual banks and the maintenance of confidence in the banking system as a whole. It has therefore specified and reviewed the supervisory approaches available to achieve these objectives. In addition, the chapter has argued that the nature of the banking system would influence the appropriateness of the regulatory and supervisory approaches adopted.

If the banking system provided no protection for depositors, creditors, or the payment system, market discipline would substitute for regulation and supervision. On the other hand, if the system offered such protection, bank regulators and supervisors would have a enormous responsibility of limiting risk taking without imposing unnecessary constraint on management's ability to maximize their banks' profitability and efficiency.

To fulfill this responsibility, bank supervisors must have adequate supervisory authority, competent staff and ample resources. They must also obtain prompt and reliable information on banks' offshore and on-shore activities, and on entities comprising financial groups headed by or conducting business transactions with the banks being supervised. To reduce gaps in the regulatory and supervisory process, and to improve supervisory effectiveness in the changing world of international banking, bank supervision must be conducted on a consolidated basis without endangering the individual client's privacy rights while ensuring the safety and soundness of the individual banks wherever they are located. Moreover, bank supervisors should consider establishing partnerships with: (1) bank management to appreciate the impact of regulatory and supervisory restrictions on banks' ability to service the legitimate needs of their customers efficiently and profitably; and (2) supervisors in other jurisdictions where their banks are licensed, chartered and managed.

With financial market integration, and with banks establishing offices in offshore and other international centers, the surveillance responsibilities of bank supervisors in developing financial markets have expanded. In fulfilling these responsibilities supervisors would have to keep themselves informed of developments in these centres' regulatory framework, payment systems and other matters bearing on systemic stability, including major criminal activities to which their banks might be exposed.

11 Capital in Bank Regulation and Supervision

In developed financial markets, minimum capital standards have been one of the most important tools to control risk and reduce exposure caused by safety net protection. A major element of strengthened regulation and supervision of banks in developing financial markets will be the creation and enforcement of rules relating to capital adequacy. Bank regulators and supervisors in developed financial markets have recognized that capital adequacy is important to assess the strength of individual banks, as well as to evaluate the safety and soundness of the entire banking system. Bank supervisors may also use capital adequacy to determine the propriety of bank reorganization through mergers and acquisitions, and expansion through branches and subsidiaries.

Regulators and supervisors believe that adequate capital: (1) assures public confidence in the stability of individual banks and the banking system; (2) supports the volume, and type of banking activities conducted; (3) provides for the possibility of inherent losses; (4) assures the appropriate distribution of risks between bank owners, depositors, creditors and taxpayers; and (5) enables an uninterrupted supply of bank credit under changing economic conditions. To support this belief, bank regulators and supervisors must assess whether a bank's capital is sufficient to permit it to operate as a viable institution. This assessment, which may be influenced by a wide range of quantitative and qualitative factors, must be continuous and comprehensive and must be based on accurate and up-to-date measurement of capital.

This chapter reviews the objectives and advantages of adequately capitalized banks in developing financial markets, provides some perspectives on the quantitative and qualitative factors for evaluating capital adequacy, and discusses regulatory and market-determined capital ratios. The chapter recognizes that the issues of capital adequacy and prompt corrective action or closure of capital impaired banks are closely related. It, therefore, discusses the requirements for implementing prompt corrective action, analyses the supervisory policy of early closure of these banks, and provides a framework for capital-based supervision in developing financial markets.

11.1   ADVANTAGES OF CAPITAL ADEQUACY

In competitive financial markets, capital protects the banks' equity owners, debt holders, and taxpayers against unexpected losses. Capital must be exhausted before operating losses erode debt holders' principal. Adequate capital reduces the probability of bankruptcy and thus protects equity owners. Bank deposit insurance programmes, if they exist, are normally funded mainly by deposit assessments. However, in the event of a systemic or large bank failure, the insurance fund may have to be supplemented by tax revenues. The higher the capital, the greater is the buffer between the banks' insured liabilities, and the insurance funds and taxpayers. Thus, the safety net provided by deposit insurance increases the importance of capital. Taxpayers are therefore potential losers when banks with insured liabilities fail.[1] It is important to emphasize that losses by taxpayers are not the only costs imposed on the society by capital deficient and problem banks. There are the social costs of misallocated credit funded by insured deposits and extended by these banks.[2]

Bank supervisors in developing financial markets may fail to implement strong measures against capital deficient and problem banks. The failure to take appropriate action, including the closure of these banks, can create price distortions and ultimately resource misallocation. Interest rates on credit to unprofitable and higher-risk activities may be lower, while interest rates on credit to profitable and lower-risk activities may be higher than they should be. Moreover, as inadequately capitalized and unprofitable banks pay higher rates to attract more deposits, competitive incentives become increasingly distorted as adequately capitalized and profitable banks are compelled to increase their deposit rates. Adequate capital can assist in reducing market distortions, and in imposing market discipline on bank management in developing financial markets.

Substantial advantages can be derived from adequately capitalized banks. At least, there are five such advantages, ranging from reducing the chance of failure to increasing competitive advantage. More specifically, adequate capital: (1) lowers the probability of bank failure; (2) reduces the incentive to take excessive risk, and more particularly, the incentive provided by the existence of deposit insurance to generate unsound assets; (3) provides a buffer between the insurance fund, if one is established, and taxpayers; (4) lowers the prospect for credit scarcity; and (5) enhances long-term competitiveness. The implications of these advantages are summarized in Box 11.1.

While adequate capital is essential to ensure the safety and soundness of banks operating in developing financial markets as in any other markets, it

Box 11.1   Advantages of capital adequacy

- *Lowers the probability of bank failure*: there is a direct relationship between the size of the bank's capital and its ability to withstand unexpected losses without becoming insolvent. Adequate capital makes banks safer and decreases the likelihood of failure, by giving bank management and bank supervisors sufficient time to resolve problems. Adequate capital also helps to ensure that existing shareholders retain control, even if unsuspected shocks deplete the bank's profits.
- *Reduces risk taking incentives*: inadequate capital, combined with deposit insurance, tends to create a 'moral hazard' problem. Owners with little of their own wealth at stake and with practically unlimited supply of funds, have an incentive to take risk. This incentive is explained by the fact that gains from excessive risk-taking accrue to the owners, while losses in excess of capital are shared with the bank's debt holders, the insurance funds, and taxpayers. A larger capital cushion implies that equity owners must lose more of their own wealth before losses are imposed on debt holders or taxpayers. Owners with significant amounts of their own wealth will, therefore, have an incentive to control the amount of their bank's risk-taking.
- *Provides a buffer between insurance fund and taxpayers*: every amount of loss absorbed by capital is equivalent to the amount of unexpended resources by the insurance fund and taxpayers. Capital, therefore, ensures that bank owners suffer losses before the insurance fund and taxpayers are involved.
- *Lowers the prospect for a credit shortage*: in an economic downturn, inadequately capitalized banks with operating losses tend to restrict credit to maintain regulatory capital standards. Adequately capitalized banks with operating losses tend to maintain credit supply under similar economic circumstances.
- *Increases long-term competitiveness*: since capital helps to ensure a bank's long-term viability by reducing the probability of failure, it helps the bank to develop and maintain long-term client relationships. Capital also assists in providing the time (by absorbing losses) and the financial resources to respond to changes in economic circumstances.

---

is not enough to protect taxpayers and debt holders from the risk of bank failures. Strong supervision and 'market discipline' exerted by equity owners with substantial amounts of their own wealth invested in the banks must be added to the mix of measures against bank failure and excessive risk-taking. Moreover, adequate capital must be measured in terms of asset size and risks, including the risk of on- and off-balance sheet activities. Capital must also be clearly defined.[3]

In responding to the pressure to improve capital ratios, management may attempt to improve retained earnings by increasing the bank's high-risk assets and reducing their low-yielding liquid ones. The consequences of these adjustments can be a decline in the banking industry's liquidity and stability. One way of meeting higher capital requirements without sacrificing liquidity is to issue new equity. But the ability to raise equity will depend on investors' expectations about the movement of prices in bank stocks, and particularly in the case of developing financial markets, the existence of an equity market. If an equity market does not exist, or if investors expect the prices of bank stocks to decline, capital deficient banks may be compelled to increase their capital by increasing their retained earnings and consequently their risk-taking activities. The objective of higher capital ratios may therefore result in weaker banks in developing financial markets.

A phase-in period to raise capital by way of equity offerings, retained earnings, and other means may be required to reduce risk-taking and ensure the safety and soundness of these banks. The need for such a period is reinforced by the argument that new offerings of common equity may decrease the per share value of a bank's common stock if interest on debt is tax deductible, and dividends on equity are not. Any preferential tax treatment of interest over dividends will tend to increase a bank's tax liability by substituting equity for debt. This increased liability will, in turn, lower the discounted value of a bank's future after-tax earnings, and consequently the price of the bank stocks.[4] A period that allows for the stable growth of retained earnings and any favourable adjustment in the tax treatment of dividends will facilitate the resolution of the tax issues.

There are other reasons to expect the per share value of a bank's stock to fall with new offerings of common equity. One of these reasons relates to the increased availability and quality of information to the bank's existing and prospective equity owners under competitive in contrast to repressed financial market conditions. There is a hypothesis that new equity offerings may reveal information that management has kept confidential about the bank's performance or investment opportunities. Such information can be good news if investment opportunities are better than expected, or bad news, if management believes that banks' stock prices are too high because earnings do not reflect adequate loan loss reserves, or asset quality problems. The conventional wisdom is that equity offerings are considered to be bad news for those banks that have tended to misrepresent their earnings performance, and hence prices will fall for reasons unrelated to leverage changes.

Another reason to expect the per share value of a bank's common stock to fall with new offerings of common equity may be found in the relationship between higher capital ratios and the value of the safety net put option, which is an asset for banks with deposit insurance. The value of this asset accrues to the bank's shareholders and varies directly with the size of the insurance subsidy and indirectly with the bank's capital ratio. A higher capital ratio will lower the value of the put option. Increased capital may reduce the price of bank stocks by decreasing the implicit government subsidy that a bank with insured deposits enjoy.

In the long run, the effect of increased capital ratios on a bank's stock prices may be positive. Increased capital is likely to be viewed as strengthening the bank's competitiveness and viability. In the short-run, a lower probability of failure as a result of capital adequacy will reduce the expected costs of bankruptcy and uninsured debt. Such costs reductions may offset any negative effects of increased capital on stock prices and the overall cost of capital.[5]

11.2   CAPITAL RATIOS AND RISK-BASED CAPITAL GUIDELINES

Branches of foreign banks, indigenous banks created by the nationalization of these branches or from the establishment of *de novo* banks owned by the government or private investors, were the principal commercial banking institutions in repressed financial markets. Normally, the indigenous banks maintained low capital levels indicated by capital to total asset ratios between 2 per cent to 3 per cent.[6] But because of the support they received from their central banks and their government owners, indigenous banks had a low probability of failure. In repressed financial markets, where the risks were minimal compared with those of developing financial markets, and where banks were owned by the government or by holding companies with owners connected to the government, low capital ratios did not weaken public confidence in the banking system. Depositors perceived that the indigenous banks in repressed financial markets could not fail and the branches of foreign bank were under the impenetrable safety net provided by the parent.

Because of the increased and unaccustomed risks of developing financial markets, the removal of the government support after a bank's privatization, and the fact that banks in these markets tended to be small, supervisors have emphasized capital adequacy as the new and important regulatory tool. As asset size expands, capital ratios will tend to fall and the incident of failure, particularly among the smaller banks, to increase. Some bank owners may respond by increasing their banks' capital ratios beyond the regulatory minimum, believing that, in the circumstances of higher asset levels, asset concentration, and volatile financial market conditions, their banks will need a large capital cushion to ensure their long-term viability.

Bank regulators and supervisors in developed financial markets have been emphasizing capital-based supervision with risk-based capital being the cornerstone of the regulatory and supervisory system.[7] The related regulatory and supervisory guidelines may be relevant for banks in developing financial markets because financial market integration, and the increased freedom of entry and exit have compelled the need for common capital standards for banks operating in both developed and developing financial markets. The relevance of these guidelines may be determined by understanding their objectives which are to: (1) include on- and off-balance sheet risks in evaluating capital adequacy; (2) reduce the disincentive to hold liquid low-risk assets; (3) promote coordination between supervisory authorities; and (4) decrease competitive inequalities resulting from the inter-country differences in capital standards.

Risk-based capital guidelines assign a bank's on- and off-balance sheet items to one of four risk categories to a bank's on- and off-balance sheet items. Each category is given a risk weight equal to 0 per cent, 20 per cent, 50 per cent or 100 per cent depending on the perceived credit risk of a given asset class. Off-balance sheet items are also given risk weights which are applied after these items are adjusted by a conversion factor. Table 11.1 provides hypothetical on- and off-balance sheet items used to illustrate the computation of risk-based capital ratios. Total weighted

Table 11.1   Asset and off-balance sheet components ($ million)

Assets	
Commercial loans	500
Mortgages	200
Loan loss reserves	(50)
Bank placements	100
Treasury bills	50
Total assets	<u>840</u>
Off-balance sheet items	
Unused loan commitments	100
Standby letters of credit	50
Total off-balance sheet items	<u>150</u>
Capital accounts	
Common equity and surplus	100
Loan loss reserves	10
Total capital accounts	<u>110</u>

Table 11.2   Risk-adjusted asset computation ($ million)

	Nominal amounts	Conversion factors	Risk weights	Risk-weighted asset equivalents
Assets				
Commercial loans	500	–	100%	500
Mortgages	200	–	50%	100
Bank placements	100	–	20%	20
Treasury bills	50	–	0%	0
Off-balance sheet items				
Unused loan commitment	100	50%	100%	50
Standby letters of credit	50	100%	100%	50
Total risk-weighted assets	–	–	–	720

assets, including off-balance sheet items, are computed based on risk weights for the on- and off-balance sheet items, and on the conversion factors and risk weights for the off-balance sheet items as shown in Table 11.2. The risk-weighted assets and off-balance sheet items serve as the denominator for computing the risk-based core capital and total capital ratios indicated in Table 11.3. In other words, the denominator used in the computation is total risk-weighted assets, not total assets as used in the leverage capital ratio computation. Core capital is represented by tangible common equity or Tier 1 capital. Tier 2 capital items, such as loan loss reserves, perpetual cumulative stock, long-term debt, and other qualifying forms of capital, are added to Tier 1 capital to obtain total capital.

The disqualified allowance shown in Table 11.3 is due to the fact that risk-based capital standards limit the amount of loan loss reserves that can be included in the total capital computation to 1.25 per cent of total risk-weighted assets. Since risk-weighted assets total $720 million, the amount of qualified loan loss reserves will be $9 million (that is, 1.25 per cent of

Table 11.3   Risk-based capital ratio computation ($ million)

Capital accounts	Core capital	Total capital
Common equity	100	100
Loan loss reserves	–	10
Less: Disqualified allowance	–	1
Total	100	109
Risk weighted assets		720
Capital ratios	13.9%	15.1%

$720 million). Given loan loss reserves of $10 million, the disqualified amount will be $1 million (that is, $10–$9 million).

The current minimum risk-based capital ratio standards are 4 per cent for core capital, and 8 per cent for total capital. Tables 11.1, 11.2 and 11.3 illustrate a bank that exceeds both capital standards.

The creation of risk-based capital standards has been recognized as an improvement in the traditional capital standards that excluded off-balance sheet activities, and asset risk profiles in the capital ratio computations, and allowed for the inclusion of a complex mix of items in the definition of capital accounts. However, risk-based capital standards have several weaknesses. Among these weaknesses are: (1) the focus on credit risk and the downplay of interest rate, liquidity and exchange rate risks; and (2) the failure to differentiate between credit risk within the same asset class (for example, all commercial loans to private sector customers have the same risk weight despite the fact that credit risk between individual customers will certainly be different).

In spite of these weaknesses, risk-based capital guidelines represent a significant step in the measurement of capital adequacy and can serve as a useful innovation in the regulation and supervision of banks in developing financial markets. The guidelines: (1) strengthen the quality of capital by increasing the emphasis on common equity and by restricting the amount of loan loss reserves that can be counted as capital; (2) recognize the relative degree of credit risk associated with various asset classes by setting different capital requirements for some asset classes that have less credit risk than others; (3) require banks to hold capital against their off-balance sheet activities in a systematic manner; and (4) help in making the definition of capital and the minimum standards internationally uniform.[8]

Bank regulators in developing financial markets may institute a minimum leverage ratio, based on total capital as a percentage of total assets, to supplement the risk-based capital standards. Bank management may, therefore, be required to maintain capital to satisfy risk-based capital standards as well as the minimum leverage ratio. The minimum leverage ratio may be necessary because the risk-based capital guidelines, which have been designed solely to measure credit risk, can create the possibility for significant leverage. For example, assets that have no credit risk receive a zero percent risk weight, and therefore, require no capital. However, banks should have a least a base level of capital as protection against other banking risks not covered by the risk-based capital standards (for example, interest, liquidity, operational and concentration risks). A minimum leverage ratio based on total assets can establish a base level of capital for all banks.

It has been suggested that market-based capital ratios should substitute for the risk-based and leverage ratios being used by bank supervisors. Market-based capital is defined as the market capitalization of a bank and is calculated as the number of shares outstanding times the price per share. Depending on market price variations, the market value of the bank's capital may be higher or lower than its book value. Equation 11.1 provides a formula for computing the market capital ratio.

$$MCR = \frac{MC}{TA + MC - BE} \qquad (11.1)$$

where:

$$
\begin{array}{rcl}
MCR & = & \text{market capital ratio} \\
MC & = & \text{market capital} \\
BE & = & \text{book equity} \\
TA & = & \text{total assets.}
\end{array}
$$

Advocates of the market approach have expressed concerns about the reliability of accounting measures traditionally used to evaluate the financial condition of banks and other entities. Under US Generally Accepted Accounting Principles (GAAP), asset and liability items are carried on a bank's balance at their historical costs, with subsequent changes in market values not being recognized unless the items are sold or settled. This approach has been criticized as leading to discrepancies between accounting and economic measures of income and capital, thus impeding any accurate evaluation of a bank's true condition.

Under the market approach, sometimes alluded to as market value accounting, assets and liabilities are carried on the balance sheet at their estimated fair market values. Supporters of this approach argue that it: (1) provides economically more meaningful measures of capital, thus facilitating the identification of problem banks; (2) makes the bank's actual performance and financial condition transparent to investors and supervisors, thus enhancing management accountability; (3) is comprehensively risk inclusive and risk transparent; and (4) is consistent with any asset liability management objective. A particular aim of the market approach is to discourage transactions, such as trading gains, which are motivated by accounting rather than by economic considerations.

Despite these advantages, the market approach to capital adequacy determination has a number of problems that argue against its implementation. An important requirement for the effective implementation of this approach is the existence of active trading markets in a bank's assets and liabilities. Because active trading markets do not exist for most of these items, fair market values will have to be estimated using, for example, some form of discounted cash flow analysis.

The subjectivity inherent in any estimating procedure will reduce the comparability of fair market value estimates across banks and increase the difficulty in verifying valuations through audits and supervisory examinations. Such subjectivity tends to make financial statements more prone to manipulation, thus increasing uncertainty about the true conditions of banks in developing financial markets, whose viability will become less dependent on government support, and more reliant on market discipline or public confidence. Although specific standards can be developed to provide the basis for appropriate accounting and auditing practices in this area, because of a limited availability of skills in these markets, the development of such standards is likely to take considerable time.

The market capital approach may be of limited usefulness where most banks are privately owned and have no market quotes, stock markets are underdeveloped or non-existent, and market prices are too volatile to be usable. In some developing financial markets, banks may be wholly-owned subsidiaries of publicly traded holding companies. Only the stocks of the holding company are traded, not those of its subsidiaries. Stock markets may be in their embryonic stage, extremely shallow, volatile, and structurally inadequate. Thus, market participants may not be adequately sophisticated to comprehend fully the complex issues of banking under competitive conditions, and the price signals the stock markets emit may be unreliable indicators of risk or value. Surely, developed stock markets, with analysts devoting substantial amount of time, and effort to understand and convey the risk and return prospects of publicly traded companies, provide more reliable estimates of risk and value.

An alternative to the comprehensive market approach is to apply market value accounting only to those assets that have secondary market values, such as marketable securities, and residential mortgages. However, recording some balance sheet items at market and others at historical costs will, for example, reflect incorrect sensitivity gaps and provide incorrect information for minimizing interest rate risk. Because this partial approach will result in volatility and distortion in reported income and capital, and provide misleading indicators of a bank's true financial condition, it may not be adopted by bank supervisors in developing financial markets.

Perhaps an alternative may be to require banks to estimate the fair market value of their assets and liabilities and to disclose these estimate as supplements to their financial statements and regulatory reports. The advantages of the disclosure approach are its cost effectiveness and flexibility. The disclosure approach will be less costly to implement than the comprehensive market approach. In addition, the former approach will provide flexibility and time for accounting bodies and users of financial reports, including the regulators and supervisors themselves, to assess the reliability and cost of market value information. Thus, the disclosure approach may well be the precursor of the more comprehensive market approach.

11.3   CAPITAL ADEQUACY EVALUATION

While capital ratios are important quantitative measures, there are qualitative risk factors that must be included in determining the capital adequacy of individual banks. Regulators and supervisors in developing financial markets must recognize that banks are exposed to varying degrees and types of risk, and therefore any comprehensive capital adequacy evaluation will have to be made on a case-by-case basis emphasizing both quantitative and qualitative factors. Among the qualitative factors are the quality of management, earnings performance, asset quality, risk diversification, ownership, operational and internal control procedures and strategic planning.

The qualitative factors will facilitate bank supervisors' evaluation of the appropriate minimum capital ratio for each bank. In general, the notion of an appropriate minimum capital ratio is essentially concerned with determining the maximum level of systemic risk that society is willing to tolerate. On a bank-by-bank basis, this notion may be interpreted as ascertaining the maximum level of risk bank supervisors will accept, taking into account the qualitative factors indicated in Box 11.2 and the probability of failure based on both qualitative and qualitative factors.

However, this probability of failure approach has not received general acceptance by bank supervisors because of its underling analytical and statistical complexity, uncertainty and limitations. In the final analysis, bank supervisors in developing financial markets must have some flexibility in establishing capital adequacy standards considering the complexity of the task as well as the fact that the banks in their jurisdiction may also be operating in foreign financial markets with different regulatory standards.

In evaluating capital adequacy, bank supervisors may attempt to ascertain management's compliance with the quantitative standards, and to evaluate the qualitative factors. More specifically, the bank examination

Box 11.2   Qualitative factors affecting capital adequacy

- *Management quality*: sound management exists if there is evidence of effective implementation and monitoring of policies and procedures, internal controls, and audit. The absence of such evidence suggests that inept or dishonest management will ultimately result in a deterioration of the bank's capital.
- *Funds management*: funds management includes monitoring and control of the bank's liquidity and interest rate sensitivity. There must be procedures to minimize liquidity risk, or mismatches that may affect earnings and ultimately capital levels.
- *Earnings and retention*: high earnings enable banks to expand, remain competitive, and increase available capital. The bank's dividend policy is also important. Excessive dividends can weaken the capital position.
- *Asset quality*: lower quality assets have a greater potential for loss and should be reflected in a stronger capital base. Supervisors must ensure that banks have established asset classification systems and that loan loss reserves are based on these systems.
- *Risk diversification*: a greater degree of asset and liability concentrations increases the need for capital. Supervisors must review on- and off-balance sheet items for concentrations in industries, product lines, customer types, funding sources, and non-bank activities.
- *Ownership*: owners' influence on their bank's operations varies directly with the degree of ownership concentration and predisposition. A financially distressed, self-serving, and concentrated ownership will erode capital adequacy over a period of time; conservative ownership may be unwilling or unprepared to cope with the competitive environment of developing financial markets.
- *Operating procedures and controls*: inefficient or lax operations are costly. System, procedure and control deficiencies expose a bank to loss through fraud, defalcation, or employee error. Such losses can impact the bank's capital levels.
- *Planning*: a dynamic planning process is essential for banks operating under competitive market conditions. Planning assists banks to identify potential changes in their environment or operations, and to adjust to these changes in a manner to maintain capital adequacy. Bank supervisors must evaluate the effectiveness of a bank's planning process.

process should: (1) determine the adequacy of policies and practices as they relate to capital accounts and dividends; (2) ascertain compliance with established capital adequacy guidelines; (3) evaluate the suitability and consistency of present and planned levels of capital and dividend policy relative to the bank's existing conditions; (4) determine the scope and adequacy of the audit and internal control functions; (5) assess management compliance with laws and regulations; and (6) initiate corrective action when policies, practices, procedures or internal controls are deficient, or when violations of laws and regulations are apparent.

11.4   TIMELY CORRECTIVE ACTION

Supervision is an important tool for controlling the perverse incentives facing undercapitalized banks. Banks have increasingly less to lose from following aggressive, high-risk investment strategies in an attempt to return to profitability, as they approach the condition of insolvency. Stringent rather than permissive supervisory action must be applied to banks that demonstrate such strategic predisposition. However, the ability of supervisors to take effective and early corrective action against under-capitalized banks will depend on, at least, the following three factors: (1) the supervisors' competence in identifying potential banking problems before they threaten the banks' solvency; (2) the adequacy of the super-visors' authority to implement corrective action or to avert further deterio-ration, once the potential problems have been identified; and (3) the willingness of supervisors to impose appropriate and timely corrective measures given the fact that they have identified the problems and are vested with the authority to imposed such measures.

Proposals to strengthen the supervision of undercapitalized banks may be expressed in terms of a range of capital ratios, indicating safety levels above which no supervisory concerns will exist, and a 'trigger' level below which increasingly severe supervisory action will be taken depend-ing on the size of the deviation below this level. Supervisory action based on the safety and trigger levels of capital adequacy assumes that reported capital levels correctly reflect a bank's solvency condition. In some in-stances, this assumption may not be true for banks in developing financial markets. For example, because of misguided optimism about loan recov-ery or deliberate misrepresentation, a bank's loan losses may be under-stated and capital levels overstated. The accuracy of reported capital will depend on: (1) the bank supervisors' ability to detect misrepresentation of the bank's asset quality and ensure that appropriate reserves or charge-offs are made; and (2) the frequency of on-site examinations. The super-visory process may fail to detect the misstatement of capital because of the infrequency of on-site examinations, and the inability of the off-site surveillance to detect regulatory reporting deficiencies.

Experience in developed financial markets has indicated that: (1) trou-bled banks tended to report declining capital ratios just prior to their failure; (2) banks that failed are inclined to be undercapitalized prior to their failures; (3) some of the failed banks have misrepresented their capital condition in their regulatory reports; and (4) the frequency of on-site examinations facilitates the early detection of undercapitalized and potential problem banks.[9]

The available regulatory and supervisory options will influence the actions that may be taken against undercapitalized banks. Supervisors should be empowered to issue cease-and-desist orders, enter into agreements with management, prohibit affiliate relationships that endanger safety and soundness, and impose fines and penalties. Providing supervisors with the authority to impose conditions on banking operations using any of these measures can reinforce market discipline and increase the incentives for banks to maintain adequate capital. The conditions imposed on bank operations may include: (1) suspension of dividends, or other in appropriate fund transfers; (2) restrictions on growth including prohibitions on acquisitions and the exercise of non-traditional powers; and (3) forced divesture of affiliates or removal of management. The authority to impose such action will end when capital is restored to acceptable levels.

Special regulatory and supervisory concerns may exist if undercapitalized banks are funded by large deposits reflecting funding concentration risk. To minimize this risk, supervisors must have the authority to prohibit undercapitalized banks from accepting, renewing, or rolling-over large deposit, unless the supervisors themselves determine the concentration will not create safety and soundness problems for the banks. Surely, any restriction on the ability of undercapitalized banks to take deposits can impair their growth and earnings potential. However, growth must be controlled to minimize concentration risk particularly in the case of undercapitalized banks with asset quality problems.

An argument against increased supervisory authority is that the aggressive exercise of such authority will reduce the banks' franchise value, and the costs of failure that may have to be borne by their uninsured depositors, and creditors. This argument is based on the premise that: (1) bank management decisions based on market considerations will produce results superior to those based the supervisors' judgement or guidelines; and (2) forced removal of management, divestiture of affiliates, arbitrary restrictions on growth, or on specific activities have the potential to reduce the banks' capacity to maintain their best customers under competitive market conditions.

Supporters of the idea of effective regulatory authority and prompt corrective action have argued that decisions made by management of undercapitalized banks could be impaired by improper incentives to grow and take risk, and the threat of supervisory sanctions could persuade bank management not only to maintain adequate capital but also to minimize risk-taking. Nevertheless, the question whether imposing restrictions on a bank's operations should be mandatory or be based only at the supervisors' discretion is a valid one. Again, supporters of mandatory restrictions have suggested that, if supervisors were given the discretion, they might delay exercising their authority when the circumstances demand quick and effective action. However, if supervisors are not competent to initiate timely and appropriate action against undercapitalized banks operating under competitive market conditions, then a cautious approach to regulatory action may be preferred.

A compromise position in the debate on the issue of mandatory or discretionary restrictions may be the creation of a regulatory and supervisory structure where undercapitalized banks can expect some well-defined and pre-specified treatment. Supervisors may be allowed to deviate from this treatment provided they justify their action to a higher authority accountable to the public. Such a structure may enhance supervisory accountability and reduce the social cost of inappropriate supervisory forbearance. In the final analysis, the effectiveness of this structure will depend on the supervisors' ability to identify the undercapitalized banks and their problems, and to initiate appropriate action in a timely manner. This ability in turn, will depend on the: (1) frequency of on-site bank examinations; (2) competence of the examiners themselves; (3) integrity of financial and other regulatory reports submitted by management; and (4) quality of the supervisors' off-site surveillance practices.

It must be emphasized that accurate financial reports are important not only for prompt and effective supervision but also for competent management. Management must have accurate, timely, and reliable financial information to be able to plan and measure performance to achieve and sustain growth in portfolios and earnings under volatile and competitive market conditions. Financial information helps to measure the inherent risks in lending and in funding asset portfolios. It also forms the basis for early and informed decision making by management and supervisors. To the extent that regulatory reports may be misleading, financial information used by management may also be misleading. However, management, having accurately determined their banks' deteriorating financial condition may decide that this condition should not be communicated to their supervisors in their regulatory reports.

A requirement for prompt corrective action against undercapitalized and troubled banks is the willingness of supervisors to use their authority to initiate such action. It has been argued that bank supervisors could be captured by the industry under their jurisdiction, meaning that they are predisposed to serve and promote the interest of the industry they are responsible to regulate or supervise.

There are several reasons for this argument ranging from the location of the required competence in the industry to the supervisors' personal stake in protecting the banks under their charge. For example, because of the technical knowledge required to regulate and supervise banks operating in developing financial markets with their high-risk levels, the regulatory and supervisory agencies may be staffed mainly by individuals recruited from the industry. Moreover, bank supervisors in developing financial markets will be confronted as never before with the responsibility to examine and evaluate sophisticated and new financial products about which they may not have the training to understand, and with banking assets that are intrinsically difficult to value. The training needed to fulfill their responsibility, may be available only in programmes that are sponsored for bank personnel.

Consequently, their common training and experience may cause bank supervisors and management to have similar positions on certain issues. In addition, the likelihood of eventual employment with the industry may induce the regulators or supervisors to maintain a close and partial relationship with the management of banks they are required to regulate and supervise. Finally, regulators and supervisors may envision their job security and status as connected with the continued existence and profitability of the banks under their jurisdiction. They may, therefore, develop the position that the banks they regulate and supervise are their constituents that they should defend.

Political influence can also determine the inclination of bank supervisors to implement prompt and effective action against undercapitalized banks. The influence of the government on the supervisors' willingness to act may be exerted through: (1) political appointees serving as management personnel of the regulatory and supervisory agencies; (2) government oversight of these agencies; and (3) informal contacts between agency management and senior government officials. It is certainly proper and necessary for regulatory and supervisory agencies to be politically accountable for their action. However, in the relationship between regulators, supervisors, and government officials, it is important to ensure that improper political pressures are minimized and do not impede effective regulatory and supervisory action.

Bank regulators and supervisors in developing financial markets must be aware that undercapitalized banks cannot be selected for prompt corrective action until they are identified as such. They must also recognized the foundation of effective supervision is the availability of information obtained mainly from reported financial data and examination findings that provide early signals of deterioration. However, both information sources may give misleading signals of a bank's condition, perhaps until shortly prior to its failure. The reliability of information obtained from these sources is therefore critical for timely and effective supervisory action.

11.5   CORRECTIVE MEASURES

In an effort to rescue undercapitalized banks, bank supervisors may: (1) encourage a recapitalization or a merger; (2) prevent inappropriate fund transfers out of the bank or the taking of undue risk by management attempting to return to profitability; (3) restrict growth by, among other things, prohibiting the acquisition and the exercise of non-traditional powers, and (4) force divesture of affiliates or remove management. Dividends restrictions, improper funds transfers and reorganization are among the more complex measures that bank supervisors in developing financial markets may be required to implement.

The position has often been taken that until owners comply with regulatory capital requirements they should be prevented from taking out any capital from their banks. This position is supported by the fact that: (1) dividends paid by an undercapitalized bank will increase the costs carried by the bank's creditors and depositors in the event of a bank failure; and (2) if the bank is deposit insured, the cost to the insurance fund and taxpayers will also be increased.

Thus, the issue to be addressed by bank regulators and supervisors in developing financial markets is concerned with determining whether depositors, creditors, the insurance fund, taxpayers or the shareholders, or some combination of these, should carry the cost of a failed bank and the amount of this cost, if any, they must bear.

An argument against restricting dividend payment is that undercapitalized banks will be constrained from raising capital from new investors who know that dividend payments by capital impaired banks will be eliminated. It should be noted, however, that the decision to invest in capital deficient banks, although dividend payments are restricted, may depend on the investor's expectations of the probability of failure of these banks. For banks considered to have more than a minimal probability of failure, capital may be available but at a considerably high cost to them. This high capital cost is no doubt consistent with the regulatory or supervisory strategy of shifting the burden of a bank failure to the shareowners and away from depositors and creditors, although the implementation of any closure or reorganization policy should be based on impersonal and market-determined events. Subjective factors, such as social and political pressures, will limit this approach. The use of these subjective factors creates the potential for conflict between bank management and supervisors particularly with regard to asset valuation and appropriate charge-off of problem assets. In fact, the conflict potential can be high where loans are not readily marketable; and reliable information about the financial condition and repayment ability of borrowers is unavailable. Banks may participate in other banks loans, or purchase these loans if they can evaluate the credit risk of the borrowers. To the extent that asset valuation cannot be objectively ascertained, management will be justified in appealing or disagreeing with the supervisors' evaluation of their banks' capital adequacy, thus delaying the implementation of corrective action.

In spite of the potential for conflict, corrective action must be taken when deemed necessary. To reduce the scope for abuse of supervisory authority, at least a framework specifying the supervisory action, if any, that will be taken at certain capital levels should be established. The full participation of industry representatives must be obtained in the development of this framework. It can be expected that banks with high capital levels will be subject to minimum supervisory action and those below the minimum capital requirements will be subject to intervention. The framework may have a range (numeric or otherwise) indicating banks with strong capital positions and those with weak ones (for example, the range may be '1–5' with '1' being strong, '2' satisfactory, '3' fair, '4' marginal, and '5' unsatisfactory). Rewards and supervisory remedies would depend on each bank's position within the range.

Banks rated strong will realize the most regulatory freedom. To achieve a strong rating, banks would have to maintain risk-based capital significantly above the minimum capital requirements. While the exact amount will be established by regulations, it is important that banks be rewarded if they maintain additional levels of equity and other forms of capital such as retained earnings and subordinated debt. The most important reward for banks with a strong capital rating will be the ability to engage in a broad range of new financial activities either directly or through a financial services holding company. Other regulatory rewards may include expedited procedures for opening new branches; and acquiring new banking and non-banking affiliates.

Banks rated satisfactory will be the ones that comply with their minimum capital requirements, but do not have the additional equity capital to be rated strong. In most cases these banks will not receive any of the regulatory rewards obtained by banks rated strong, although they will be permitted to conduct any new activities if they satisfy certain regulatory conditions. For example, they may be required to: (1) demonstrate substantial progress in meeting the strong rating requirements; and (2) possess the financial and managerial resources necessary to conduct the new activities. However, banks rated satisfactory will not be subject to any of the corrective actions that apply to banks with lower capital position ratings.

Banks rated '3', '4' and '5' will be the ones that fail to meet their minimum capital requirements by progressively larger amounts. These banks will be subject to various levels of supervisory stringency. For example banks rated '3' or fair and '4' or marginal may be subject to dividend restrictions, growth constraints, and other supervisory actions. Banks rated '5' or unsatisfactory, with no apparent prospect of recovery, will be promptly placed into conservatorship for subsequent sale or liquidation.

Banks rated fair will be ones with capital below any of the minimum capital requirements, but not sufficiently deficient to require drastic supervisory action. Corrective measures for these banks may include: (1) the filing of an acceptable capital plan to restore the banks to a strong or satisfactory rating; (2) a prohibition on expansion by acquisition or branching unless such expansion will improve their capital condition; (3) the restrictions on dividends and asset growth and on risky activities by the banks and their affiliates that threaten their safety and soundness; and (4) the removal of management.

Banks rated marginal will have capital substantially below any minimum capital standard as defined by the regulator, and will be one step away from mandatory conservatorship. Supervisory action will include: (1) a prohibition on dividends; (2) the filing of an acceptable capital plan that will restore them to a satisfactory rating or facilitate their sale; a (3) restriction on growth and other actions applied to banks rated fair.

Finally, banks rated unsatisfactory will be those with capital below a 'critical level'. The supervisory action will be early resolution through conservatorship or receivership, with their subsequent sale or liquidation unless they were recapitalized into a higher rating. During the conservatorship, bank operations may be reduced in anticipation of either a sale or eventual liquidation. The objectives of this reduction are to: (1) penalize the bank's management and owners for excessive risk-taking; (2) limit the potential for depositors', creditors' and taxpayers' losses; and (3) protect against any systemic risk.

It must be emphasized that an important factor for the success of prompt corrective action is whether or not bank owners and management are convinced that pre-announced measures will in fact be effectively implemented if capital declines. If such conviction exists, the probability that owners and management will act prudently will be high. There is, however, a risk that the inflexibility of this framework may force prompt corrective action in situations where supervisory forbearance may be appropriate. An effective capital-based regulatory system may, therefore, be one that combines rules with discretion and provides guidelines on how and when discretion will be exercised. Bank supervisors may therefore be authorized to grant relief from the requirements of the rules if in their opinion such exceptions are in the public interest.

11.6 SUMMARY

This chapter has attempted to capture the important features of capital-based supervision of banks in developing financial markets. In the process, it has found that adequate capital provided a number of benefits, including the maintenance of public confidence in a bank's ability to cope effectively with the risk inherent in competitive markets. It has emphasized that capital funds provided a measure of a bank's strength, and constituted a base for expansion, a cushion for loss absorption, and a basis for the maintenance of solvency. The chapter has recognized the potential for conflict between bank management wanting to reduce capital in order to increase return on capital, and bank regulators and supervisors wanting to increase capital to improve safety and soundness of individual banks and the banking system. No doubt, a compromise in this conflict would be to discover the balance between the need to maintain the capital required as protection against risk, and the use of capital to increase shareholders' return through appropriate leverage. The chapter, therefore, provided a framework of regulatory requirements for banks with different capital levels, and indicated the rewards and penalties for compliance or non-compliance with these requirements. It has suggested that management or industry input would be critical in the formulation stage of this framework, while, for the sake of its credibility, prompt and effective action would be necessary after its establishment.

The chapter has suggested that the rewards of capital-based supervision would be greater regulatory and supervisory freedom for well-capitalized banks to expand and engage in the product and service innovations of the developing financial markets. These rewards should provide an incentive for banks to maintain their capital as well as to increase it. In addition, the corrective measures or sanctions of capital-based supervision should be designed to help correct supervisory problems before they grow into larger ones. Inevitably some capital deficient banks would have to be closed, and must be done promptly and efficiently to minimize the cost to depositors, creditors, the insurance funds if the bank has insured liabilities, and to the taxpayers.

12 Control Systems and Asset Quality Evaluation

Among the most important responsibilities for bank management in developing financial markets are to establish and maintain efficient accounting and other records, and internal control systems that ensure the protection of the bank's assets; and to originate and maintain assets of the highest quality. The maintenance of adequate record keeping and internal control systems should be one of the regulatory requirement for establishing and operating banks in these markets. Such records and controls are required to enable management to prepare and present correct accounts to shareholders and the public, and reports to the regulators and supervisors.

No bank should be regarded as conducting its business in a prudent manner unless it maintains or, as the case may be, will maintain adequate accounting and other records of its business, and adequate control systems for its business and records. As bank frauds are generally associated with false accounting, weak internal controls, and inadequate supervisory surveillance, supervisors must be vigilant in ensuring the adequacy of these systems.

Furthermore, in order to manage effectively under competitive market conditions, management must not be distracted by accounting, documentation and other system deficiencies but must be dedicated to providing the services needed by customers. Among these services are the various types of commercial, including accounts receivable financing, installment and real estate loans provided not only by the banks but also by their non-bank competitors. In response to the competition from non-bank sources, banks may attempt to modify many existing services and expand into new ones. In spite of such expansion, however, commercial and other lending will continue to constitute the principal assets, and supervisors will continue to emphasize asset quality evaluation, including the adequacy of credit administration, documentation, and control systems.

This chapter addresses issues relating to the establishment and maintenance of adequate accounting and other record keeping and internal control systems, reviews the principal aspects of effective internal control, and discusses a set of pertinent points to be considered by bank supervisors in evaluating bank's internal control systems. In addition, it discusses the general approaches to asset quality evaluation, using as examples the evaluation of commercial, accounts receivable, consumer and real estate loans.

12.1   ACCOUNTING AND OTHER RECORD SYSTEMS

It is the responsibility of bank supervisors to determine whether the regulatory requirements relating to accounting and internal control systems, for authorizing a new banking operation or the continuation of an existing one, are satisfied. Bank supervisors may not consider it appropriate to detail the manner in which a particular bank should maintain its accounting and other records and internal control systems. Rather, supervisors may establish the scope and nature of the financial information that the accounting and other records must be designed to capture, contain, and provide for management, and may emphasize the scope and nature of the internal control systems and the purpose for which they are established by management. The scope and nature of the accounting and other records required for a bank to conduct its business in a prudent manner should: (1) be commensurate with the bank's needs and particular circumstances, and (2) have regard to the manner in which the bank's business is structured, organized and managed, to its size, and the nature, volume and complexity of its transactions and commitments.

As access to these records is important, they should be located where they will best assist management to conduct the bank's daily business in a prudent manner, and the supervisor to evaluate if the bank is prudentially managed and operated. If, for instance, the accounting and other records of the bank's foreign branches or subsidiaries are kept in the foreign jurisdiction, head office management should establish arrangements that allow it easy access to these records. Such access will facilitate the availability of information required by the bank supervisors.[1]

It is the responsibility of the board and management to decide what information is required and who should receive it. The system should have the capability to provide appropriate management information to: (1) the individuals responsible for exercising managerial functions or for maintaining accounting and other records; (2) executives who, either alone or jointly, are under the immediate authority of the board and are responsible for the conduct of the bank's operations and business; and (3) the board itself.

The accounting and other record systems should provide information to assist the board and management to monitor, assess, and control the performance of the bank's business, and the risk to which it is exposed. Such information should be prepared separately for the bank and its affiliates and on a consolidated basis. The frequency with which information is prepared, its level of detail, and the amount of narrative analysis and explanation will depend on the level of management to which it is addressed.

Some types of information will be needed on a more frequent basis than others, and it may be appropriate for some information to be presented on a basis of exception reports that reflect, for instance, non-compliance with agreed limits. The information prepared would be influenced by management, external audit, and regulatory and supervisory requirements. While supervisors may be disinclined to establish a comprehensive list of accounting and other records a bank should maintain, they should at least attempt to provide general guidelines with which the bank should comply. Among other things, these guidelines should address the scope, details, and record maintenance requirements as indicated in Box 12.1.

For bank supervisors, the management information delivered by the system will be considered appropriate if it shows: (1) the correct condition of the bank; (2) the operational results of the business on a cumulative basis and by discrete periods; (3) comparison with budgets and previous periods; and (5) the bank's exposure to each type of risk compared with the relevant limits set by management. It will also be considered appropriate if the system provides analyses of the bank's assets and liabilities, and its off-balance sheet positions showing how they have been valued, as well as its income and expenses indicating how they relate to different asset and liability categories and off-balance sheet positions.

12.2 INTERNAL CONTROL SYSTEMS

The scope and nature of effective control systems should take into account of a number of factors including the: (1) bank's size; (2) diversity of its operations; (3) volume and size of its transactions; (4) degree of risk associated with each operational area; (5) amount of control by senior management over day-to-day operations; (6) degree of centralization; and (7) extent of reliance on information technology.

Bank supervisors may not consider it appropriate to impose a comprehensive list of internal control requirements that would be generally applicable, or a detailed list of specific procedures to be followed, where appropriate, by all banks operating in their jurisdictions. Nonetheless, bank supervisors would expect management to design a system that provides reasonable assurance that the bank's income accrues to its benefit, its expenses are properly authorized and disbursed, its assets are adequately

Box 12.1   General accounting and other record requirements

Accounting and other records should meet the following requirements:

- Capture and record on a timely basis and in an orderly manner every transaction or commitment that the bank enters into with sufficient information to explain its nature and purpose; any asset or liability, actual or contingent, that respectively arises or may arise from it; any income or expense, current or deferred, that arises from the transaction or commitment.
- Provide details, as appropriate, for each transaction or commitment showing the parties including, in the case of a loan, advance or other credit exposure, whether and if so, to whom its is sub-participated; the amount and currency; the contract, roll-over, value and settlement or repayment dates; the contractual interest rates of an interest rate transaction or commitment; the contractual exchange rate of a foreign exchange transaction or commitment; the contractual commission or fee payable or receivable together with any other related payment or receipt; the nature and current estimated value of any security for a loan or other exposure; the physical location and documentary evidence of such security; and in the case of any borrowing, whether it is subordinated and, if secured, the nature and book value of any asset upon which it is secured.
- Be maintained in such a manner that financial and business information can be extracted promptly to enable management to monitor the quality of and safeguard the bank's assets, including those held as custodian; identify, quantify, control and manage its exposure by related counterparties across all products; identify, quantify, control and manage its exposures to liquidity risk, and foreign exchange and other market risks across all products; monitor the performance of all aspects of its business on an up-to-date basis; and make timely and informed decisions.
- Contain details of exposure limits authorized by management that are appropriate to the type, nature and volume of the business undertaken. Where relevant these limits should include counterparty, industry sector, country, settlement, liquidity, interest rate mismatch and securities position limits; provide information which can be summarized in such a way as to enable actual exposures to be readily, accurately and regularly measured against these limits.
- Contain details of the factors considered, the analysis undertaken and the approval or rejection by management of a loan, advance or other credit exposure.
- Provide, on a memorandum basis, details of every transaction entered into in the name of and behalf of another party on an agency or fiduciary basis where it is agreed that the bank itself is not legally or contractually bound by the transaction.

safeguarded and liabilities recorded, and its compliance with statutory requirements relating to prudential reporting and other conditions is satisfactory. Box 12.2 specifies the assurances a bank's internal control systems should provide.

Box 12.2   Internal control system requirements

A bank's internal control system should provide the assurance that:

- The bank's business is planned and conducted in an orderly and prudent manner in compliance with established policies and procedures.
- Transactions and commitments are entered into in accordance with management's general and specific authority.
- Management is competent to protect the assets and control the liabilities of the bank; to implement measures to minimize the risk of loss from irregularities, fraud and errors; and to identify them when they occur.
- The bank's accounting and other records provide complete, accurate and timely information.
- Management is able to monitor, on a regular basis, the adequacy of the bank's capital. earnings, and asset quality.
- Management can identify, assess and quantify when necessary, the risk of loss in the conduct of business so that the risk can be monitored and controlled on a regular and timely basis; and appropriate provisions can be made for classified assets, and for any other on-or off-balance sheet exposures.
- Management can prepare, on a timely basis, complete and accurate reports in compliance with regulatory and supervisory reporting requirements.

The scope and nature of the specific control procedures required for the bank to conduct its operations in a prudent manner should fit the bank's needs, and should be influenced by the way its business is structured, organized, and managed, and by the complexity of its transactions and commitments. Although bank supervisors will be disinclined to prescribed detailed control requirements that are generally applicable, they would, no doubt, identify special areas for control focus. Among these areas are: (1) organizational structure; (2) monitoring procedures; (3) segregation of duties; (4) authorization and approval; (5) completeness and accuracy; (6) safeguarding of assets; and (7) personnel. Box 12.3 outlines the focus of control procedures for these areas.

The effective management of risk, the designing and pricing of new products and services, and the offering of a mix of services efficiently and promptly will require banks in developing financial markets to improve their information technology and hold more information in electronic form. The information held in this form within a bank's information system is a valuable asset to be protected against unauthorized access and disclosure. The control objective indicated in Box 12.3 apply equally to operations undertaken in both manual and electronic environments, although there are additional risks associated with the electronic environment.

Bank supervisors will expect management to understand the extent to which a bank relies upon electronic information to assess the value of that

Box 12.3   Specific internal control procedures

- *Organizational structure*: banks should have documented the high control levels in their organization, defining and allocating responsibilities, identifying lines of reporting for all aspects of their operations, including the key controls and giving outline job descriptions for key personnel. The delegation of authority and responsibility should be clearly stated.
- *Monitoring procedures*: banks should have procedures to ensure the availability of relevant and accurate management information covering their financial performance, condition, and their risks. Such information should be provided to the appropriate management levels on a regular and timely basis. Procedures should also be established to ensure compliance with policies, including any limits on delegated authority, and with regulatory and supervisory requirements.
- *Segregation of duties*: an important control arrangement is the separation of those responsibilities or duties that would, if combined, enable one individual to record and process a complete transaction. Segregation of duties reduces the risk of manipulation or error and increases the element of checking. Functions that should be separated include those of authorization, execution, valuation, reconciliation, custody and recording. In the case of computer-based accounting system, systems development and daily operations should be separated.
- *Authorization and approval*: all transactions should require authorization or approval by an appropriate individual and the levels of responsibility should be clearly stated.
- *Completeness and accuracy*: banks should have controls to ensure that all transactions to be recorded and processed have been authorized, and are correctly recorded and accurately processed. Such controls include checking the accuracy of the accounts, and valuations; checking of totals, reconciliations, control accounts and trial balances, and accounting for documents.
- *Safeguarding assets*: banks should have controls designed to ensure that access to assets or information is limited to authorized personnel. This includes both direct access, and indirect access through documentation to the underlying assets. These controls are of particular importance in the case of valuable, portable or exchangeable assets, and assets held as custodian.
- *Personnel*: banks should have procedures to ensure that personnel have capabilities that fit their responsibilities. The proper functioning of any system depends on the competence and integrity of those operating it. The qualifications, recruitment, and training, as well as the innate personal characteristics of the personnel involved, are important features to be considered in setting up any control system.

information and to establish appropriate control systems. Supervisors recognize that an appropriate system will be one that combines manual and automated controls, the balance of which will vary between banks, and will reflect the need for each bank to address its particular risks associated

Box 12.4   Information technology risks

- *Fraud and theft*: access to information systems can create opportunities for the manipulation of data in order to create or conceal significant financial loss. Additionally, information can be stolen, even without the physical removal or awareness of the fact, that may lead to loss of competitive advantage. Such unauthorized activity can be committed by persons with or without legitimate access rights.
- *Errors*: although they most frequently occur during the manual inputting of data and the development or amendment of software, errors can be introduced at every stage in the cycle of an information system.
- *Interruption*: the components of electronic systems are vulnerable to interruption and failure; without adequate contingency arrangements, such interruption can lead to serious operational difficulty and financial loss.
- *Misinformation*: problems may emerge in systems that have been poorly specified and inaccurately developed. These problems may become immediately evident, but can also continue undetected for a period during which they can undermine the veracity of supposedly sound information. This undetection is a particular risk in systems where audit trails are poor and the processing of individual transactions difficult to follow.

with the introduction and use of information technology. There are, of course, several such risks as indicated in Box 12.4.

In addition, management should be aware of its responsibility to promote and maintain a climate of security awareness and vigilance throughout the bank. In particular, management should consider: (1) its security education and training designed to make all relevant staff aware of the need for, and their role in supporting its security practice, and the importance of protecting the bank's assets; and (2) its security policy, standards, procedures and responsibilities, designed to ensure that arrangements are adequate and appropriate.

Internal audit is another area of a bank's internal control system. It provides independent assurance over the integrity and effectiveness of both the accounting, other records and internal control systems. Internal audit may the assigned the following control functions: (1) review of accounting and other records and the internal control environment; (2) review of the appropriateness, scope, efficiency and effectiveness of the internal control systems; (3) detailed testing of transactions and balances, and the operation of individual internal controls to ensure that specific objectives have been met; and (4) review of the implementation of management policies; and special investigations.

It is important to ensure that the internal audit function is appropriately structured and resourced to enable it to provide the independent appraisal of the bank's internal controls. There should be clearly defined terms of reference and the functions's independence should be assured by an oblig-ation to report regularly to an audit committee, or in its absence, an execu-tive specified by the board, with the right of access to the audit committee, where one is established.[2]

The internal audit function should not have authority or responsibility for the activities it audits. Internal audit should have unrestricted access to all of the bank's activities, records, property and personnel to the extent necessary for the effective completion of its work. This function should be staffed with individuals who are appropriately qualified either by holding professional qualifications of by having the required experience.

12.3   ASSET PORTFOLIO EVALUATION

Bank supervisors may have several objectives when evaluating a bank's asset portfolio. These objectives may range from the determination of the credit officers' compliance with established policy to the initiation of cor-rective measures when required. At least seven supervisory objectives for asset quality evaluation can be identified. These are to: (1) ascertain if the bank's policy, procedures, practices and internal controls with respect to asset portfolio management are adequate; (2) determine if bank officers are operating in conformance with established guidelines; (3) verify the scope and adequacy of the internal control and audit functions; (4) evalu-ate the overall quality of the asset portfolio and how that quality relates to the soundness of the bank; (5) prepare information on the bank's function in a concise and reportable format; (6) determine compliance with laws and regulations; and (7) initiate corrective measures when the bank's policy, procedures, practices or internal controls are deficient or when violations of laws or regulations are determined.

The supervisory programme may focus on a detailed review of individ-ual assets and their documentation to identify problems in the bank's asset portfolio. However, while such a detailed review of each asset and related documentation will identify problems in this portfolio, it may not be needed each time the lending function is evaluated by the supervisors. Instead, the programme may require a sampling of the asset portfolio, and evaluation results that are consistent with such specific supervisory object-ives as: (1) quantifying the asset quality; (2) evaluating the adequacy of credit administration practices, and credit review system; (3) determining compliance with laws, and regulations; and (4) monitoring the implemen-tation of effective corrective action.

An asset quality evaluation may be triggered by a number of general and specific factors. The general factors may be the macroeconomic changes (for example, changes in inflation, exchange, or interest rates, and cyclical downturn in the economy) that affect the borrowers' repayment ability. The specific factors may be: (1) an observed deterioration in asset quality based on such ratio indicators as bad debt charge to loans, loan loss provisions to total loans, or to non-performing loans; (2) the supervisors' lack of confidence in the bank's credit administration process including the control systems; and (3) changes in the credit personnel or philosophy, or an unacceptable internal loan review system.

An important underpinning of any supervisory programme is the bank supervisor's ability to anticipate safety and soundness problems. A basic requirement of anticipatory supervision is a thorough knowledge of the bank's policy, procedures and controls. As far as the credit function is concerned, anticipatory supervision will require bank supervisors to evaluate bank management's ability, and the internal control systems to identify potential asset quality problem in a timely manner so as to pre-empt its realization. For example, bank management must be able to anticipate the loans that will be non-performing in an economic downturn, or if inflation, interest or exchange rates exceed certain levels. The internal control systems must be able to identify loans with documentation deficiency and repayment problems.

It is not unusual for serious lending and internal control deficiencies to be concealed when economic conditions are booming and for credit quality problems to surface when the economy is in a downturn. Bank supervisors must, therefore, review the bank's credit control responsibilities to determine if they are clearly delineated. For the supervisor, the bank's credit control function should encompass policy development and implementation, credit approval, collateral documentation, credit monitoring, collection practices including supervision of workout loans, and management information system.

The review of the bank's credit control systems will be based on the review of individual loans in the bank's portfolio. Such individual loan reviews are necessary for banks with or without asset quality problems. For banks with asset quality problems, the review will determine the cessation of poor lending practice and other corrective measures to improve asset quality. For bank without asset quality problems, the review will determine the existence of any poor lending practices and the potential for asset quality problems. The objectives of individual credit reviews may be to: (1) determine the reliability of a bank's own credit evaluation analysis or its problem loan identification capability; and (2) test compliance with laws and regulations particularly relating to insider activities. The effectiveness of any supervisory approach to asset quality evaluation lies in the timely follow-up on identified weaknesses. At each supervisory event, management should be required to commit to and provide time-frames for corrective action. In some instances, it may be necessary to formalize management's commitments in an administrative action document such as a commitment letter, memorandum of understanding, formal agreement, or cease and desist order. Reviews designed to determine the adequacy and effectiveness of management corrective action should be performed. The scope of this type of review will be influenced by the nature of the deficiencies and the proposed corrective action.

Bank management may venture into new product or growth areas that may create supervisory concerns. For example, management may want to enter into asset-based lending, or extend credit to securities dealers collateralized by the dealers' inventory of high-risk securities.

Supervisors may require bank management to finance business inventory or accounts receivable with carefully structured loans collateralized by receivables of a higher value than the loans, and to desist from the loose financing arrangement inherent in the traditional overdraft system common in many developing financial markets. In the event that such a switch in inventory financing arrangement is stipulated, bank management will have to establish a system of effective control of the inventory or accounts receivable pledged. The system of control may range from a blanket assignment of inventory, to financing under warehouse receipt.[3] To address these concerns, bank supervisors may have to conduct target reviews or reviews that are activity specific.

Because a principal objective of asset quality reviews is to test the adequacy of the bank's policy and internal control systems to prevent a set of specific problems, bank supervisors must identify these problems and decide if they are being addressed in an adequate manner by existing policy, practices, or procedures. Examples of specific problems that should receive supervisory attention are the bank's ability to identify problem credits, past due loans, and credit documentation deficiencies. However, such identification will be facilitated if the bank's policy defines a problem credit, state when a credit is past due, and specify the documentation required for each type of credit. Violations of laws and regulations, credit concentrations, evidence of self-dealing credit transactions, and collateral documentation, are other specific problem areas that must be addressed by bank policy and control systems, and would be reviewed by the supervisors in evaluating the quality of the bank's asset portfolio.

The position has been taken that bank supervisors must emphasize the correlation between these specific problem areas with the overall system of policy, practices, procedures and internal controls instituted by the bank to prevent such problems.[4] The purpose of this correlation is to determine the causes of existing problems and weak situations that represent a potential for future problems. By focusing attention on credit policy, practices, procedures and internal controls, bank supervisors in developing financial markets will enhance their ability to detect situations that have the potential for future deterioration and that may affect the bank's safety and soundness. In the final analysis, an asset quality evaluation report will indicate the supervisor's decision on the: (1) quality of the entire asset portfolio; (2) quality of management review; and (3) scope and adequacy of policy, practices, procedures and internal controls.

12.4 CREDIT POLICY REVIEW

Bank supervisors in developing financial markets should place considerable emphasis on the existence of formal policy and guidelines. Generally, supervisors take the position that before a bank grants credit, its objectives, policy, guidelines, and practices must be clearly established. Before evaluating the bank's credit function, the supervisors will review these objectives, policy, guidelines and practices to determine if they are reasonable and adequate to ensure a sound and effectively controlled asset portfolio. In the absence of written policy and guidelines, the supervisors, without doubt, will decide that there is a major deficiency in the credit area and that the board has failed to discharge its duties and responsibilities. While some banks may have formal credit policies, others may resist them because of the perception that a formal credit policy may be too constraining on credit extension activities. Furthermore, in the absence of effective internal control systems and penalties for non-compliance with policy and guidelines, the mere existence of formal policy does not guarantee management conformance with them.[5]

The establishment of formal credit policy provides the foundation for sound asset portfolio management. In general, bank supervisors will focus on the board's approval of this policy, and on its implementation and amplification by management. Generally, the board has a responsibility to depositors and shareholders. However, in some privately-owned banks, where the shareholders, board, and management are identical, the responsibility is mainly to the depositors. The nature of this responsibility is to: (1) extend credit on a sound and collectible basis; (2) invest the bank funds profitably, and for the protection of depositors, as well as for the benefit of shareholders; and (3) serve the legitimate credit needs of the community where the bank is located.

In reviewing a bank's credit policy, supervisors should emphasize a set of specific issues relating to: (1) the scope and allocation of the bank's credit facilities; (2) the manner in which credits are made, serviced and collected; and (3) the processing of credit not covered by the policy. Supervisors will expect the credit policy to contain a general outline of the scope and allocation of the bank's credit facilities and the manner in which credits are extended, serviced and collected. Moreover, in the context of developing financial markets with their new product and market opportunities, they may want the policy to be broad in nature and not too restrictive. The formulation and enforcement of inflexible rules, stifle initiative, hamper profitability, and prevent the bank from responding efficiently to changing market conditions. For the bank supervisor, a satisfactory credit policy should provide for the presentation, to the board or a committee of the board, those credit requests that management believes are worthy of consideration, but are outside the scope of the formal policy or guidelines. Flexibility must exist to facilitate a speedy reaction and early adaptation to changing conditions in the bank's asset mix and its primary market area.

Despite this need for flexibility, the established credit policy must be consistent with the financial and other capabilities of the bank, and must not be discriminatory in the sense that it allows for preferential treatment of insiders and their related interests. Supervisors will expect that management, when formalizing the credit policy, will consider the bank's available financial resources, credit personnel, facilities and growth potential. Management will also be expected to specify in the policy, provisions that clearly identify: (1) who will receive credit, and of what type and price must the credit be granted; and (2) who will grant the credit, in what amount, and what organization structure will be used to ensure compliance with guidelines and procedures.

As the delegation of credit approval authority expands within the bank due to the increasing and complex demand for credit, bank management will be required to establish efficient control systems for monitoring compliance with policy and guidelines. In this regard, the supervisor will evaluate the bank's internal control and reporting systems. Satisfactory systems must inform the board and senior management of how the credit policy and guidelines are being implemented and report to them on: (1) the performance of officers with delegated authority; (2) the condition of the overall asset portfolio, and (3) the contribution of the individual officers to this condition.

Supervisors may look for the existence of certain policy components to determine if the credit policy contributes to the bank's safety and soundness. A selection of these components is listed in Box 12.5. In general, all

Box 12.5   Supervisory prospective on credit policy

- *Geographic limits*: the bank's primary service area must be specified and credit officers and directors must be aware of the geographic limitations for credit extension purposes. This area should be distinguished from any secondary service area so that emphasis may be properly placed.
- *Category distribution*: limitations based on aggregate percentage of total credit of different types may be specified. Such a policy should allow for deviations approved by the board or a board committee to permit the distribution of credit in relationship to changing market conditions.
- *Credit types*: the credit policy should state the types of credit to be granted and the condition for extending each credit type. The credit types should be based on consideration of the lending officers' expertise, the banks' deposit structure, and anticipated credit demands. Credits that have resulted in an abnormal loss to the bank should be controlled or avoided within the framework of the stated policy. Term credits should be limited to a given percentage of the banks stable funds.
- *Maximum maturities*: credits should be granted with realistic repayment terms related to the anticipated source of repayment, the purpose of the credit and the useful life of the collateral. For term credit, the policy should state the maximum repayment term.
- *Pricing*: rates on the various credit types must be sufficient to cover the funding and servicing costs, including general overheads, and probable losses, while providing for a reasonable margin of profit. Periodic price reviews should be done to enable adjustments that reflect changes in costs or other competitive factors.
- *Maximum ratio of credit amount to appraised value of acquisition costs*: credit policy should outline where the responsibility for appraisals lies and define the formal, standard appraisal procedures.
- *Financial information*: sound and safe credit extension depends on complete and accurate information on the borrower's credit standing. One possible exception is when the credit is predicated on readily marketable collateral. Financial information should be required throughout the term of the credit.
- *Aggregate credit limits*: as a guide in limiting the total amount of credit outstanding, relationships to other balance sheet items should be established. Controls over the credit portfolio may be expressed in terms of deposits, capital, or total assets. In setting such limits, management will consider such factors as credit demand, deposit volatility, and credit risk.
- *Credit concentration*: the credit policy should emphasize diversification within the portfolio and a balance between maximum yield and minimum risk.
- *Credit authority*: the credit policy should establish limits for lending officers, and credit committees. Compliance reporting procedures and the frequency of credit committees' meeting should be defined.

the components included in the supervisors' policy review framework may not be applicable to every bank. The generally applicable components will be those that directly limit credit risk and contribute to asset quality enhancement and credit recovery in cases of problem credit situations. These components are mainly those related to lending limits, credit concentration, credit documentation including financial information on the borrower, and collection and charge-offs of problem assets.

Supervisors will be particularly interested in reviewing the policy limits on the amount of credit extended to finance the acquisition of securities by the bank's customers or by related or non-related securities dealers. There may or may not be legal restrictions on the maximum ratio of credit to the market value of the securities pledged. In the absence of such restrictions, supervisors will expect the bank's credit policy to be explicit about margin requirements for all types of securities acceptable as collateral; and that these requirements to be related to the marketability of the security, and establish the frequency for periodic pricing of the collateral.

As banks extend credit to unaccustomed areas, lose their prime borrowers to non-bank competitors, and retain only the marginal borrowers, their credit risk increases and the volume of problem credit grows. Supervisors will want the credit policy to define delinquent obligations of all types and to dictate the appropriate reports to be submitted to the board or a board appointed committee to review these obligations. In evaluating the implementation of the bank's collection and charge-off policy, the supervisor will review the reports to determine if they include sufficient detail to allow for risk factors, loss potential, and alternative courses of action.

12.5   CAUSES OF ASSET QUALITY PROBLEMS

In general, the preconditions for asset quality problems are: (1) failure of the board to establish sound credit policy; (2) failure of management to establish adequate written procedures; and (3) failure of both the board and management to monitor and administer the credit function within established policy and guidelines. But there are also specific sources and causes for asset quality problems and these will receive the special attention of bank supervisors. Examples of these sources and causes are shown in Box 12.6. However, the two principal but related causes of credit problems for banks in developing financial markets will be competition for borrowers and poor selection of risks.

Bank supervisors are aware that competition among banks for size and market influence can result in the compromise of credit principles and the

Box 12.6   Sources and causes of problem credits

- *Self-dealing*: self-dealing explains a significant number of serious problem bank situations. It manifests itself in the form of an overextension of credit on an unsound basis to directors or shareholders or their interests.
- *Anxiety for income*: the bank's credit portfolio is usually the most important revenue generating asset. Management may be inclined to permit the earnings factor to outweigh that of soundness with the result that credits that carry undue risks or unsatisfactory repayment terms are granted. Unsound loans usually cost more than the revenue they produce.
- *Compromise of credit principles*: management may grant credits that have undue risk or unsatisfactory terms with full knowledge of the violation of sound credit principles. The reasons for compromising such principles may be timidity in dealing with individuals with influential connections, friendships, or personal conflicts of interest, self-dealing, anxiety for income, and competitive pressures.
- *Incomplete credit information*: complete credit information is the only acceptable and reasonably accurate method for determining a borrower's financial capacity. The lack of supporting credit information (for example, purposes of the borrowing, intended plan, source of repayment, progress reports) is an important cause of problem credits.
- *Failure to obtain or enforce repayment agreements*: this failure constitutes an important cause of problem loans. Credits extended in the absence of a clear repayment agreement violate a fundamental banking principle. The bank may have a repayment agreement but fails to collect the principal payments promptly.
- *Complacency*: complacency may be demonstrated by the lack of adequate monitoring or control of established or familiar borrowers; dependence on oral information provided by borrowers in place of reliable financial data; and optimistic interpretation of known credit weaknesses based on past survival from recurrent hazards and distress.
- *Follow-up deficiency*: many credits that were initially sound may deteriorate in quality because of ineffective monitoring and follow-up action by credit officers. This deficiency may be explained by the lack of knowledge of the borrower's business over the term of the credit.
- *Technical competence*: the technical ability to analyse financial statements, and to obtain and evaluate other credit information, is a requirement for all able and experienced bankers. When this ability is absent, unwarranted credit losses are certain to occur.
- *Overlending*: credit beyond the capacity of the borrower to repay is unsound. Nowhere is technical competence more at a premium than in determining a sound borrower's safe maximum credit level.

---

acquisition of unsound loans and other assets, and that the ultimate cost of unsound credits will outweigh the temporary gains of asset growth and market share. Nonetheless, management may be prepared to compromise sound credit principles by failing to observe the bank's underwriting and risk-selection standards. This compromise may be reflected in credit extended to new ventures, and for real estate transactions, as well as those with misplaced expectations and purpose, and the ability to place the bank in a risky dual position. Box 12.7 identifies a set of general credit types that bank supervisors may consider poor management selection risks.

Banks may minimize their credit risk by strengthening their internal credit review system. This system may allow for junior officers' lending being evaluated by a senior credit officer, or an independent department staffed by credit analysts inspecting the quality of a sample of loans to enable early detection and management notification of problem credits. Although supervisors have tended to develop asset classification procedures that are independent of any internal evaluation performed by bank management, there is some merit in including management's internal credit review in the supervisory procedures. Management's internal

Box 12.7   Credit types categorized as poor selection risks

- *New ventures*: credit to finance a new business venture to which the bank advances an excessive proportion of the required capital relative to the equity investment of the owners.
- *Misplaced expectations*: credit based more on the expectation of successfully completing a business transaction than on existing net worth.
- *Speculation*: credits for speculative purchase of securities or commodities.
- *Collateral deficiency*: collateral credits carried without adequate margins of security.
- *Real estate transactions*: credits for real estate transactions against narrow equity ownerships.
- *Misplaced purpose*: credits extended because of other benefits, such as the control of large deposit balances in the bank and not because of cash flows, sound net worth or collateral.
- *Dual position credits*: loans based on the non-marketable stocks of a corporation in conjunction with credit extended directly to that corporation. The bank is placed in a dual position. It may be forced to finance the corporation beyond warranted limits to avoid a loss on the credit collateralized by the corporation's stock.
- *Collateral liquidation value*: supervisors will evaluate the bank's internal credit review system to determine its effectiveness in detecting problem credit situations and notifying management for appropriate corrective action. Credits predicated on collateral of problematic liquidation value. Bank supervisors acknowledge that a moderate amount of such credits, when recognized by bank management as subject to inherent weakness, may cause few problems. Should they become the rule, however, the bank will have serious problems.

evaluations may provide information on credits that should be selected for supervisory review.

An effective internal credit review system will combine independent review with the identification of credits extended by individual officers. Because of frequent contact with borrowers, the credit officers will be able to identify potential problems before they can be discovered by the bank supervisors. It is also a system that ensures that credit officers do not become complacent and monitor the credit throughout its term with continuing rigor. In addition, the system must discourage the officers from withholding any credit from the review process. Through the use of statistical sampling, bank supervisors may determine whether the internal credit review system adequately identifies problem credits.

12.6   EVALUATING SPECIFIC CREDIT TYPES AND ACTIVITIES

In an effort to increase income without increasing assets and capital, banks in developing financial markets may expand their off-balance sheet activities, including the origination, sale and servicing of various types of credit. Asset origination and sales not only provide attractive servicing fees but also provide a benefit from reinvesting the proceeds of the asset sales. Improper management and inadequate control of these activities by the originating bank can cause certain supervisory concerns. For example, if the sale proceeds are used to originate additional loans to be serviced, the bank may find itself responsible for servicing more credits than it is capable of doing or than is considered prudent by the supervisor based on management limitations. Surely, any failure to service the loans in an efficient manner may lead to legal and financial liabilities with adverse consequences for the bank's capital. Bank supervisors will, therefore, evaluate the bank's servicing activities to ensure that: (1) these activities are conducted in a safe and sound manner; and (2) servicing fees or other income derived from the activities are amortized over the term of the credits.

Supervisors are also directly interested in evaluating the different types of credit whether they are retained in the bank's balance sheet or sold to other banks as loan participation or to special purpose vehicles for securitization purposes. The principal credit types are commercial, accounts receivable, installment, and real estate loans. Although these loans are characteristically different, the supervisory evaluation objectives already identified are applicable to all of them.

Commercial loans are usually loans which are not maintained by either the real estate of consumer or installment loan departments of the bank.

Commercial or business loans normally account for a substantial proportion of a bank's assets. These loans may be secured or unsecured and may have short- or long-term maturities. They include working capital advances, term loans, agricultural credits, and loans to individuals for business purposes. The evaluation of a bank's commercial loan quality, will be based on the supervisor's review of its internal controls, policy, practices and procedures for making and servicing these loans, and a concise documentation of the findings. Supervisors will want to determine: (1) if the board has adopted a written commercial loan policy that establishes procedures for reviewing and controlling commercial loan applications, defines qualified borrowers; and establishes minimum documentation standards; and (2) whether the commercial loan policy is reviewed at least annually to determine if such policy is compatible with changing market conditions. Supervisors will also review the system for preparing, posting and reviewing of the loan, interest, and collateral records to evaluate the adequacy of its internal control, and compliance performance.

Accounts receivable or inventory financing is a specialized area of commercial lending in which the borrowers assign to the lender, their interests in the accounts receivable or inventory as collateral. Many borrowers unsuited for unsecured credit may satisfy their financing needs through accounts receivable financing. Typically accounts receivable borrowers may be those with: (1) businesses that are growing rapidly and need continuing financing in amounts too large to justify unsecured credit; (2) working capital that is inadequate for the volume of sales and type of operation; and (3) previous unsecured borrowings that are no longer warranted because of various credit factors. Supervisors may evaluate this type of credit by assessing the accounts receivable collateral, the borrowers's financial condition and debt servicing ability, and the bank's internal controls, policies, practices and procedures.

Although the accounts receivable loans are collateralized, it is important to analyse the borrower's financial statements. Even if the collateral is of satisfactory quality, and in excess of the loan value, supervisors will want financial information that demonstrates the borrower's capacity for full repayment without collateral liquidation. In addition, in order to evaluate the bank's control of accounts receivable financing, bank supervisors may want to determine management's ability to recognize a borrowers' financial problems, if any, as they develop, and to initiate orderly liquidation if necessary.

Banks face substantial risks from accounts receivable financing. The methods for managing such risk should be of interest to bank supervisors. One method is to enter into an agreement that allows the liquidation of the credit line as soon as a repayment problem is evident. Of course, the credit line may theoretically be fully liquidated by discontinuing further credit and collecting on the assigned receivables. In reality, such action could cause the closing of the borrowers business, and result in a probable deterioration of the collateral value. Furthermore, lender liability suits may be filed by the borrower against the bank for abrupt cancellation of the credit line or sudden liquidation. Consequently, the bank may notify the borrower of a contemplated liquidation. This notification will give the borrower enough time to seek other financing sources, and permit the liquidation of the credit line in an orderly manner without losses and other adverse consequences. Unless the bank has initiated an orderly liquidation, bank supervisors will criticize the accounts receivable financing of any business with a declining financial condition and anticipated deteriorating collateral value.

Accounts receivable financing, if it is properly structured, will be a substantial improvement on the traditional overdraft financing arrangement practiced in many developing financial markets. Overdraft financing may not be purpose specific and may have no easily identifiable collateral. The collateral may be a second of third mortgage on the company's fixed assets which at best may be overvalued and not easily marketable. There is a specific purpose and identifiable and marketable collateral for accounts receivable financing. In addition, there must also an accounts receivable loan agreement that establishes the conditions governing the handling of the accounts and the remedy available in the event of a default. Among the major conditions are: (1) a percentage advance against acceptable receivables; (2) use of only acceptable receivables; and (3) a maximum dollar amount due from any one account debtor.

The percentage advance on acceptable receivables may depend on the gross profit margin from the sale of merchandise and the credit quality of the borrower's customers. If, for example, a borrower has a gross profit margin of 30 per cent, the maximum advance might be 70 per cent with the actual advance being less if the borrower's customers are not of the highest credit rating. Acceptable receivables will have to be defined in the bank's credit policy and may include only those accounts that are current, or not more than a specified number of days past due. The entire amount of receivables may be unacceptable if a policy specified percentage (for example, 10 per cent) is 90 days or more delinquent. The maximum dollar amount recognizes the possibility of unforeseen and undisclosed credit failure, or a return of merchandise by the borrower's customers. A policy specified benchmark may be not more than 20 per cent of the receivable assigned should be from any one customer.

Whether or not the bank has perfected its security interest in the accounts receivable consistent with the uniform commercial code (UCC) that may exist is an important factor in the evaluation of accounts receivable financing. The UCC of most developed financial markets applies to any transaction that is intended to create a security interest in accounts receivable. However, to create a valid and enforceable security interest, the bank and the borrower must enter into a written security agreement; and take all other steps consistent with the requirements of the UCC. Together with the UCC compliance factor, there are other factors, as indicated in Box 12.8, that would influence supervisors' evaluation of the bank's account receivable financing.

Normally, a bank's installment loan portfolio consists of a large number of small loans, each amortizing over a specific period of time. Although most of these loans are for consumer purchases, installment loans for business equipment purchases are not uncommon. There are also indirect loans for the purchase of consumer goods. These are loans granted to dealers for

Box 12.8   Supervisory evaluation factors for accounts receivable credits

---

- *Turnover of the receivables pledged and borrowers' credit limit*: if the turnover of the receivables is decreasing, the quality of the receivables may be deteriorating and the balance on the credit line may be endangered.
- *Aging of accounts receivable*: the bank should obtain a monthly aging of the accounts receivable pledged. The bank supervisor should note the percentage delinquency of the accounts in relation to the total accounts pledged, concentrations, and accounts with past due balances.
- *Concentration of debtor accounts*: the bank may be vulnerable to loss if a large percentage of the dollar amount of receivables assigned is concentrated in a few accounts. A list of concentration should be prepared periodically showing the largest accounts.
- *Ineligible receivables*: the bank supervisor should be aware of receivables that may expose the bank to unwarranted risk. An example of such receivables is a financing facility to affiliated companies. Although such receivables may be valid, the temptation for the borrower to create fraudulent invoices could be significant.
- *Financial strength of debtor accounts*: the bank should maintain credit information and trade reports on large debtor accounts in the borrower's credit file. The bank supervisor should ascertain whether the debtor accounts are significant to the borrower's business and are well rated and financially strong.
- *Returns and offsets*: the borrower should provide the bank reports on returns and offsets. The bank supervisor must analyse these reports. A large and increasing volume of returns and offsets can adversely affect the bank's collateral position.

on-lending purposes. The basic functional areas of the installment loan process are: acquisition, servicing, payment processing and collection. The acquisition area originates the loan, which includes direct contact with the customer or the dealer, the gathering and review of credit information, and the decision to approve or reject the loan. Servicing includes disbursing loan proceeds, processing loan forms, preparing payment records, controlling notes, collateral and documentation, and preparing reports on delinquencies, extensions, renewals, and irregular payments. The payment area handles the collection, processing, and posting of all payments received by the bank. The collection area provides the follow-up, adjustment, and other related activities involved with delinquent loans.

These functional areas will be reviewed by the supervisor in evaluating the quality of the bank's installment loan portfolio and in determining the causes for any operational or other deficiencies in the process. Among these causes may be the lack of competence of staff involved in the process or the absence of clear duty and responsibility specifications for the staff. Thus, in the initial stage of evaluation, the supervisor must determine the organization of duties and responsibilities within the installment loan department. This determination will help to insure a smoother flow of information between the supervisor and the bank personnel and a comprehensive evaluation of the various functional areas.

The emphasis of the supervisor's evaluation, however, will be on the overall policy, acquisition procedures, and control systems relating to installment loans. Moreover, the review will not be limited to identifying current portfolio problems, but will include potential future problems resulting from permissive lending policy, unfavourable trends, potentially dangerous concentrations, and lending to insiders and their related interests. Specific indicators in the lending process may signal policy, procedure and control weaknesses. Examples of these indicators are listed in Box 12.9.

Box 12.9   Installment loan policy weakness indicators

- Granting the borrower continuous extensions or refinancing to correct chronic delinquencies.
- Financing the full purchase price. The borrower should have some equity in the consumer product being acquired.
- Financing contracts with balloon payments that materially lengthen the indicated maturity.
- Weak collection effort in the early stages of delinquency.

Real estate loans are loans primarily secured by real property. The inherent risk in these loans will depend on the loan amount, the interest rate, and other special terms. A consideration of the value of the real property over the anticipated life of the loan is of major importance. Supervisors will therefore expect the bank's lending policy and procedures to include an appraisal programme together with limits on: (1) the maximum amount that may be granted on a given loan; (2) the maximum aggregate amount that may be granted on a given category of real estate loans; (3) the maximum aggregate amount that may be loaned on all real estate loans; and (4) the need for amortization on certain loans and the amount of annual amortization required.[6]

Supervisors will no doubt review the qualification and independence of the appraisers, as well as the procedures and control systems to reviewing the reasonableness of all newly received appraisal reports. But the appraisal report is only one factor to consider when granting real estate loans. Some bank may incur significant loan losses, and may own a large amount of real estate for placing too much reliance on the appraisal. The bank's real estate loan policy should ensure that loans are granted with the reasonable probability that the borrower will be able and willing to meet the payment terms. Any loan that fails to meet that standard would be considered unsound by the supervisor regardless of the collateral value or the favourable ratio of collateral value to the outstanding loan.

Although a bank's collateral may be represented by a first mortgage on the real property, the mere reality of having such a mortgage does not preclude the loan from being evaluated unsound by the supervisor. A first mortgage loan may be unsound because of several reasons, principal of which are if: (1) its liquidation depends on the sale of the underlying real estate; (2) the amount of the loan is large relative to the fair market value of the property; (3) the ability of the borrower to pay is questionable; and (4) the loan has remained dormant a long time, indicating that its transfer to another borrower through the sale of the property will become necessary.

In the final analysis, the supervisors' evaluation of the quality of a bank's real estate loans portfolio will focus on a set of specific factors. These are: (1) the risk of a particular loan; (2) policy decisions on the relationship of real estate loans to the bank's asset or deposit structure; (3) legality of specific loans; and (4) adequacy of appraisal policy. The most convincing proof of the quality and soundness of a real estate loan is a favourable payment history. Conversely a long dormant real estate mortgage loan is never desirable, no matter how adequately protected by the value of the underlying collateral. The regular payment history of real estate mortgage loans is essential to their continued soundness and desirability.

12.7 SUMMARY

This chapter has focused on the role of effective accounting and other records and control systems in ensuring the safety of banking operations, and on the approaches and expectations of bank supervisors in evaluating the ability of these systems to protect the bank's assets, particularly its loans, and control its liabilities in the competitive and high-risk environment of developing financial markets. The chapter has, therefore, reviewed the management and supervisory requirements for these systems, and has stressed the need to maintain accounting and other records in a manner to facilitate the identification, and control of the bank's credit, and other risks. Among the requirements emphasized is the need for the board and bank supervisors to be assured that management is adequately competent to implement the measures appropriate to minimize the risk of loss from irregularities, fraud and errors.

The chapter has recognized the importance of strong asset quality for the safety and soundness of banks operating in developing financial markets. It has, therefore, argued that the accounting and other records and control systems must provide bank supervisors the information they would need to evaluate the bank's asset quality, to determine management's compliance with laws and regulations, and to monitor the implementation of corrective action recommended by the supervisors. In addition, the chapter has underscored the point, which might not be fully appreciated by the board and management of some banks, that an important underpinning of any supervisory programme is the supervisors' ability to anticipate safety and soundness problems, and that a basic requirement of anticipatory supervision is a thorough knowledge of the bank's policy, procedures and controls. Thus, bank supervision would be facilitated if policy, procedures and controls are established and available for their review and evaluation.

13 Conclusion

Throughout this text, several comments were made about the responsibilities of the board of directors in overseeing the management of banks operating in developing financial markets. One of the more general comments related to the expanded responsibilities of directors resulting from the increasing complexity of banking in these markets. The competitive forces, and unaccustomed risks associated with financial liberalization, have placed tremendous pressures on bank management. Some banks have failed to establish risk management systems to identify, monitor and control the risks inherent in these markets; and if even the systems were established the directors might not have the information or competence to monitor and enforce compliance with the systems' prudential requirements.

This chapter highlights most of the issues covered in the text and presents them in the context of their influence on the directors in the performance of their responsibilities. It argues that banks are different from other corporations and, to be effective, directors must understand not only this difference, but also the fundamental nature of the banking business, and the condition and performance of their banks. This understanding is significantly influenced by the nature of the information and analysis presented to the board by management, auditors and bank supervisors.

13.1 DIRECTORS' RISK AWARENESS

Banks, like other corporations issue stock, pay dividends, and are overseen by a board.[1] Both banks and corporations get their initial capital from their shareholders, but after this initial capitalization, bank's are funded mainly by deposits gathered from the public. Consequently, bank depositors assume the role of bank creditors and become linked to the bank's fortunes. This relationship contrasts with most other firms where customers simply pay for goods and services and never become the firms' creditors. Bank management and directors must act in such a manner as to maintain public trust that ultimately protects the integrity of the insurance fund, if one has been established.

In some developing financial markets these deposits are insured by the government or a government supported entity. Thus, the principal difference between banks and other corporations is that banks are funded mainly by private deposits insured by a public entity, and other corporations are not. Insured deposit funding of banking activities creates systemic risk which may be minimized by the way in which the board monitors and controls the risks inherent in the activities of their individual banks.

Banks provide a number of important functions for the economy that involve the use of liquid bank deposits. One basic function is to provide a safe place for small unsophisticated depositors to store liquid assets. Another important function is to provide a safe payments system for demand and other transactions accounts. A third important function is the intermediation of liquid deposits of savers into specialized, illiquid loans, particularly for borrowers with no access to the securities markets. No doubt, as developing financial markets evolved, the relative volume of this type of intermediation will decrease as non-bank competition intensifies, and borrowers increase their direct access to the securities market. Nevertheless, bank intermediation will continue to be crucial to the economies of developing countries, deploying resources in productive investments that might not otherwise be made.

Each of the banking functions involves the use of liquid bank deposits, or extremely short-term liabilities that are often withdrawable on demand. At the same time, bank assets are concentrated in highly illiquid loans, that cannot be sold quickly without a loss in value. Directors should be made aware of the fact that the combination of these two factors makes banks inherently susceptible to deposit runs, or panic withdrawals.

Thus, a positive public perception is extremely important to the viability of banks in developing financial markets. Any deterioration in a bank's financial condition can create a depositor run. The public has entrusted its primary assets to banks, and bank owners and directors must be reminded of the fact that funds used for lending belong neither to them nor the bank's officers and staff but to the depositors and other creditors.

Runs are a destructive form of market failure in which unfettered market forces are unable to achieve the most efficient use of resources. A sustained withdrawal of funds itself creates losses because a bank must sell illiquid assets at forced-sale prices to meet the demands for liquidity. Sooner or later, a run will itself cause a bank to fail, regardless of the bank's actual condition at the time the run began. As a result, a depositor has an incentive to run on the belief that others will run, regardless of the bank's actual condition. Those at the beginning of the withdrawal line lose nothing; those at the end risk losing everything.

Compounding this problem is the difficulty of determining in any precise manner a bank's risk profile, because banks invest in illiquid assets requiring individualized credit judgements. Even bank management with access to information, and directors who, incidentally, may not be adequately informed about the bank's risk exposures, are often wrong about the condition of a troubled bank, implying that it will be much more difficult for the depositors to assess this condition. Market volatility, increased competition, insider activities, and management operating with no formal and board approved credit, liquidity or other policies, combine to heighten any uncertainty about a bank's condition. This uncertainty, in turn, helps to create incentives for runs at the first sign of a troubled situation.[2] Nevertheless, there is a risk larger than the risk of a deposit run on an individual bank that should capture the awareness of directors. This risk is systemic risk or the probability that the problem of one bank will spread to other banks or other parts of the economy. Systemic risk is often discussed in terms of contagious runs; correspondent banking problems, and payments system difficulties.

Contagious runs occur when a run on one bank generates a run on another unrelated bank. For example, a depositor may assume that a problem in one bank of a certain type (for example, a bank that is domestic owned and managed, in contrast to a bank that is foreign owned and managed) is likely to affect all banks of that type. Given the uncertainty in evaluating banking risk, the fear that other depositors will panic, and the low cost of withdrawing funds, systemwide panic is highly probable if deposit insurance does not exist. Moreover, depositor losses can create asset quality and liquidity problems for other banks if depositors who lose funds in one bank can no longer make good on their loan payments to another bank. Resulting loan losses can cause additional bank failures.

The failure of a large bank with a correspondent banking system can create systemic failures. The size of deposits with the correspondent that fails may be larger than the insured deposit limit. If the uninsured depositors of a correspondent bank are not protected, the failure of that correspondent bank can weaken or cause the failure of the banks that deposit with it.[3] Bank directors, therefore have an additional responsibility in ensuring the safety and soundness of large banks with a correspondent banking network. Finally, depositor losses could spread to other banks through the payments system. Default in payments to one bank can in turn create defaults on other payment obligations, with the process spreading through a chain reaction.

Directors will be assisted in performing their responsibilities if they have some idea of how banks work and what are their specific duties as directors. Each board may have directors with different competence and characteristics. For instance, a board may have directors who are political,

Box 13.1   Specific duties of the board

- Hire and fire executive managers.
- Approve the strategic plans and budgets.
- Monitor operating performance and advise and guide management.
- Approve large credit extensions, investment or exception to the bank's credit and investment policies.
- Approve asset sales, and compensation programs.
- Avoid self-serving practices and preferential transactions with insiders
- Establish an audit committee to review financial statements and maintain internal controls.
- Establish formal policies on finance, credit, and personnel.

---

aggressive or abusive. The board may also be a nominal one, with one director dominating the proceedings and decisions, and the other directors being uninformed and passive. Passive boards have tended to encourage management indiscretion and bank failures.[4] Undoubtedly, the composition, role, responsibility and accountability of the board will influence the bank's behaviour and condition.

A selection of specific duties of the board is listed in Box 13.1. Directors need to know that banking is a highly leveraged, low margin, high volume business. Because loans are a bank's principal assets and deposits are the primary liability, banks are exposed to a high degree of credit and interest rate risks.

13.2   THE BANKING BUSINESS

One of the responsibilities of directors is to ensure that the bank maintains adequate capital. Core capital, consisting of stockholders' equity and loan loss reserves, is an important indicator of a bank's financial strength. Generally, banks with high ratios of capital to assets are better prepared to withstand the competitive and instability forces of developing financial markets and support their asset growth than banks that are capital deficient. In comparison to other corporations, capital represents a small part of a bank's total assets. Banks are highly leveraged entities.

This highly leveraged condition brings both problems and opportunities. Several large loan losses or imprudent investment decisions can diminish a bank's capital base and investor's returns, a seemingly insignificant profit on the bank's assets can result in a favourable return for the shareholder. For example, assume that if only eight cents of one dollar belongs to the bank investor, and the bank earns one cent return on that dollar, the investor's return will be 12.5 per cent. Obviously, the situation is reversed if the bank loses one cent return on that dollar.

Generally, banks operating under competitive market conditions are considered strong earners if their return on average assets is equal or greater than 1 per cent. Directors may want to know the reasons for their banks not being able to make much more than 1 per cent on each dollar of assets. Being a low margin business, banking carries costs that tend to offset the yields received on loans and securities. To understand the relationship between costs and yields, it would be useful to analyse the composition and nature of a bank's income and expenses.

Generally, loans represent a bank's principal earning asset, and they generate the largest share of income. With this asset distribution and income generation propensity of loans, banks should invest all their available funds in loans. In reality, well managed banks do not have all their funds in loans. To meet unanticipated deposit withdrawals, banks hold a certain proportion of their assets that are easily converted to cash (for example, securities). Loans provide higher yields than securities, but securities and other short-term investments are needed for liquidity. Bank management cannot seek to maximize profits without considering the continuing flow of deposits to fund future loans. A deposit run will ensue if depositors perceive the bank as having a liquidity problem. Determining an appropriate level of liquidity is, therefore, unavoidable.

On the liability side of the balance sheet are the bank's sources of funds. Interest expense on deposits is a bank's single largest cost. Because of competitive pressures from non-bank entities, a bank's share of low cost demand deposit and savings accounts will contract. High interest bearing short-term deposits may represent the major proportion of a bank's deposit mix. Obviously, if banks are required to increase the rates paid for deposits, the rates charged on loans must increase or interest margins will suffer. Although this strategy appears to be a simple solution for maintaining favourable profit margins, increased loan rates are often associated with higher credit risk and loan loss provisions. These risks and reserves, in turn, erode profit margins. High overhead expenses also weaken a bank's ability to be profitable. Overhead expenses include salaries and benefits of employees, rent or debt payments on the bank building, furniture and equipment, data processing systems and assessments for deposit insurance, if any.[5]

As banking involves varied degrees of risk, losses are inevitable, particularly loan losses. In anticipation of problem loans, directors may require their bank to expense funds on a routine basis to build loan loss reserves.

The level of reserves, determined as a percentage of total loans, will vary with the bank's asset quality. Well managed banks with no perceived asset quality problems will have lower reserve levels than banks with asset quality problems or banks with high levels of loan concentration or risky loans.

Because loan loss reserves can be one of the larger expense items, management may be reluctant to make adequate provisions. When management is under pressure to limit losses or enhance profits, the loan loss provision is an easy target to cut. Directors should know that underprovisioning for the sake of demonstrating profitability may have serious earnings impact at a later period. If, for example, loan quality begins to deteriorate, an even greater shock to earnings can occur if the bank supervisors insist that sizeable increases to the loan loss reserve are necessary. Bank directors should, therefore, ensure that adequate loan loss reserves are maintained.

Directors must also understand the nature of risks to which their banks are exposed. In developing financial markets, credit risk is a principal risk. This risk relates to the quality of the loan portfolio and the likelihood that a borrower will be able to repay the loan in accordance with the agreed terms. Banks may lose their prime borrowers to other banks and non-bank entities, and borrowers' repayment ability may be impaired by the volatility of interest and exchange rates. To minimize credit risk, bank management must screen loan applicants to determine their creditworthiness. Inadequate analysis of a borrower's repayment ability will lead to unsatisfactory loan quality, loan losses, and the erosion of the bank's capital. As loans are normally funded by deposits and not by the investment of the bank's shareholders, directors must ensure the existence of adequate underwriting standards and procedures, and strict management compliance with them.

Interest rate risk is the other risk that directors must understand. This risk is normally associated with the variation of earnings caused by variation in interest rates. In other words, interest rate risk is normally translated in terms of the sensitivity of the bank's assets and liabilities to interest rate changes. A bank that is asset sensitive has more assets than liabilities that will be repriced as interest rate changes, and vice versa for a bank that is liability sensitive. For an asset-sensitive bank, rising interest rates will benefit the bank's earnings because a larger volume of assets than liabilities will be repriced at the higher rate. If the bank is liability sensitive, it will be favourably affected by falling interest rates.

By providing clear guidelines to management and establishing a system that monitors compliance with these guidelines, directors can ensure that interest rate changes do not expose their banks to unacceptable levels of risk. These guidelines should define the acceptable level of risk in terms of the potential effect of interest rate changes on net interest income or earnings.

13.3 DIRECTORS' ROLE

Directors have a fiduciary duty that requires them to act: (1) within charged authority and powers; (2) with due care and diligence; and (3) with loyalty and in good faith in all matters regarding the bank. In addition to the duties require of a director as specified in Box 13.1, a firm commitment to the bank is crucial. Board meetings will be required to establish or revise policies and objectives, to supervise loan and investment decisions, to review strategic plans, and to monitor bank management. Directors may be required to evaluate loan collateral, research investments, and develop new banking business. If for any reason the bank's condition is rated less than satisfactory by bank supervisors, additional time and work may be required to ensure that corrective measures are appropriate and effectively implemented. Directors must be prepared to resign if they cannot perform their duties.

The directors' role entails a high degree of trust. Directors receive and have access to confidential information on companies and individuals. Moreover, some information on the bank itself is confidential and may be accessible only by bank regulators and supervisors, directors, and management. Directors should, therefore, refrain from using confidential information in a manner that would breach the trust required of them.

Regular attendance to board and committee meetings is important to a director's role. Generally, less than 75 per cent attendance at board meetings will render a director ineffective because regular attendance facilitates an improved understanding of the issues facing the bank. Directors should also note that their responsibilities as directors does not end because of but remains in spite of their absence from board meetings. Through committees, the board is dependent on the representative director to monitor management and contribute to the bank's operations. Failure to attend committee meetings could imply that management is not adequately supervised resulting in unsound loan and investment decisions. Although the board can delegate its authority to a committee, it must monitor the committee's activities because the board is ultimately responsible for all committee actions.

Although some directors may believe that approval of issues must be unanimous, unanimity is not necessary for effective policy making or monitoring. However, a director may not agree with management or with a board majority on all issues. The minutes of the board should reflect all discussion both for and against a measure, and all votes should be registered. Participation must be based on knowledge, judgement and overall willingness to learn.

One of the most important roles of a director is the development of policies for the various functional areas, and activities of the bank. Although policies are normally formulated by management, directors should have significant input in this formulation. Policies should be developed in writing, reviewed and revised by the board at least annually, and properly communicated to management and staff. Although banks operate under several policies, the policies that are of primary importance are those that address the areas of credit, investment, and asset-liability management.

A sound credit policy is important for the daily operations of a bank. A credit policy that does not establish clear standards for installment lending will not be adequate for a retail-oriented bank; just as a credit policy that fails to establish clear standards for commercial lending will be inadequate for a wholesale-oriented one. A few of the important credit policy areas on which directors should focus and carefully delineate are the types of loan desired, collateral standards, credit criteria, and size and mix of the desired loan portfolio. Failure to delineate prudent underwriting standards is the initial cause of unsatisfactory asset quality; and failure to follow these standards is the principal cause of later problems.

The investment policy should require the holding of investments that satisfy specified liquidity and investment quality standards. The bank's investment policy will be constrained by laws and regulations that define the investments that the bank can hold. Within these constrains, directors, must recognize that long-term investments that offer a current high yield may cause problems if interest rates rise and liquidity is needed in the future. Investment quality is also important in protecting the bank against losses. Quality, size, mix and maturities of the investment portfolio should be specified in the bank's investment policy.

Finally, asset-liability management is vital to the future earnings performance of the bank and must be evaluated and fully understood by the board and senior management. On the basis of this understanding, an asset-liability management policy should be formulated by management and established by the board. Banks in developing financial markets have experienced financial distressed due to maturity and pricing mismatches between their assets and liabilities. Many of these banks have matched short-term deposits against long-term fixed rate assets. Although these assets may be of good quality, they are slow to reprice, offer thin margin, and are illiquid in times of rising interest rates (that is, the borrowers have no incentive to prepay). It can take a long time to correct poorly priced assets and liabilities.

It must be emphasized that once policies are established they must be followed. It is the ultimate responsibility of the board to ensure that management, staff and the directors themselves comply with established policies. Policies not observed are useless at best. Directors must not only be familiar with the policies but must evaluate reports prepared by the internal and external auditors, and bank supervisors indicating the state of policy compliance. Generally, policy exceptions should require board approval.

13.4   RISK MONITORING AND CONTROL SYSTEMS

Risk monitoring reports prepared by management for the board must be accurate and timely. Banks may fail because of management's omission, intentional or otherwise, to provide the board with accurate and meaningful information. Although it is difficult to prevent or detect the intentional misrepresentation of facts, by establishing a standard set of information requirement for its review the board would be alerted of any management deviations from these requirements. Omissions or any change in the information required should be explained by management. The board will therefore have to specify the standard set of information that management must submit to each board meeting. This information set should include information related to the bank's condition, earnings, asset quality, liquidity and capital adequacy as indicated in Box 13.2. Correct earnings and liquidity information is critical for the board's evaluation of the safety and soundness of the bank.

Earnings information should not only be correct, it should be accompanied by an analysis indicating the adequacy of the reported earnings. The criteria for determining this adequacy are many. They include, for instance, the sufficiency of earnings to: (1) pay the contractual interest rate on deposits and a rate that encourages customers to continue depositing with the bank; (2) provide shareholders with a return on their investment sufficient to encourage them to provide the equity cushion needed to protect depositors against the impact of adverse economic conditions or management incompetence; (3) cover the bank's operating expenses, in-

Box 13.2   Directors' information package

- *Statement of the bank's condition*: this statement should detail the assets and liabilities of the bank as of the most recent month end of business. Unusual other assets and liabilities should be detailed.
- *Income and expense statement*: a detailed income and expenses statement as of the recent month end and year-to-date should be provided. Actual performance compared to monthly and annual budget projections should be noted and variances explained.
- *Watch list*: watch list loan information should include all past due and non-accrual loans, not just those loans past due for 30 days. Progress on sales of other real estate and repossessions should also be noted.
- *Loan approvals and denials*: information on the credit, collateral, character, and capacity of each borrower must be provided for board evaluation. Management endorsement must also be provided. Any time a director has a possible conflict of interest relating to a loan, the directors should abstain from voting on the loan.
- *Investments*: information on securities bought and sold should be provided. The information should include the quality and maturity of the portfolio.
- *Liquidity*: liquidity ratios should be reported.
- *Capital*: information on capital adequacy should be provided. This information should be in relation to regulatory and supervisory guidelines, and the bank's condition and assets. Directors should monitor, assess and plan the bank's capital adequacy.
- *Policy exceptions*: information on all policy exceptions should be provided to the board.
- *Peer group comparison*: information ranking the bank's condition and income performance with its peers should be provided.

---

cluding paying suppliers and compensating staff sufficiently to allow the bank to attract competent personnel; (4) reconstitute the bank's equity base to offset any impairment in the value of its asset base resulting from the failure of some borrowers to repay their loans; (5) generate the equity needed to maintain the proportionate size of the equity cushion in view of growth in inflation and in the bank itself; and (6) provide investors with long-term growth in their stock value.

It must be emphasized that to compete effectively, a bank must provide high quality services at a low cost. If a bank fails to compete on cost control and service quality it will not survive under competitive market conditions. It is, therefore, important for directors to understand the bank's relative performance compared to the market or over a period of time. This understanding is more important than an analysis of individual financial statements. The principal objectives of the analysis for the board are to determine the sources, quality, and substainability of the bank's earnings, and the adequacy of its liquidity and capital. The earnings analysis will allow the board to assess management efficiency, and thus the ability of the bank to compete successfully.[6]

A basic requirement for public confidence in any bank, and the banking system as well, is that depositors should believe that they have access to their funds whenever they need them. The board should be provided information on the maturity profile of the bank's assets and liabilities. This information is represented by a spreading of the bank's major asset and liability categories over time based on their anticipated remaining time of maturity. This process requires substantial additional data collection, but provides much more useful information on a bank's liquidity profile over time and thus on any future liquidity problems.

The board's control of the bank's affairs is based on correct information provided by management as well as by the bank's auditors. Control is also exerted through the processes of management succession, budgeting and planning. The board should require an annual audit of the bank's financial condition and a review of its internal accounting and other records and control systems. In most instances, minimum audit requirements are specified by regulations, and compliance with these requirements will be reviewed by bank supervisors in their evaluation of the bank's accounting and control systems.

If any major irregularities are discovered in the bank's financial condition or control systems, the board is obligated to have the irregularity pursued. The annual audit should be conducted by a competent independent third party with instructions that all findings should be directed to the board. To be independent, the auditors must have no insider ties to the bank, particularly no borrowing relationship. In addition to the external audit, internal audits should be conducted and the audit findings should be directed to the board. The internal auditor should be independent from the daily lending and operations functions of the bank.

The board should ensure establishment of a formal succession plan for key management positions. Management succession is important to the survival of any organization, but it is even more critical for banks in developing financial markets because of the complexity of banking, and the shortage of management skills in these markets. Regardless of the size of the bank, qualified and capable individuals must be identified to assume management responsibilities in cases of emergencies.

The board should require management to prepare a detailed annual budget that serves as a benchmark for evaluating the bank's performance. The annual budget should be supported by a formal strategic plan indicating the bank long-range goals and the measures to achieve them. The plan must be detailed, realistic and clearly understandable. The past experiences of directors in formulating budgets and plans should be fully utilized in the process.

13.5 INSIDER TRANSACTIONS AND CONFLICTS OF INTEREST

Effective supervision and control of banks in developing financial markets require the establishment of laws and regulations that limit transactions between the bank and its directors together with their related interests. Limitations on insider transactions reduce the potential for fraud and mismanagement that eventually result in banking failures.[7]

The regulations should permit loans to directors and management on the condition that such transactions are subject to considerable disclosure and prudence in handling. The regulations should also outline the procedures for granting, and the limitations on such loans. Significant limitations must be imposed on transactions with affiliates of the bank and related interests of the directors. Directors have the responsibility to understand these regulations and comply with them. In the absence of such regulations, the board should establish policies and procedures to limit insider transactions and these must be applied, without exception to the staff and the directors themselves.

Conflict of interest is another area of concern for the board and could impact the bank's safety and soundness. Conflicts of interest can be financial or personal, direct or indirect. If a director is an attorney, appraiser, or real estate agent and would receive a fee for services rendered on a recommended loan, the director should abstain from voting on the loan. Loans for relatives or business partners of directors would also require the related directors to abstain from voting. Conflicts of interest may not be limited to loans, if a director is providing any services to the bank, that director should disclose his or her interest and abstain from voting on the matter. No director can know every law or regulation that affects his or her responsibilities. However, directors should be familiar with the laws and regulations that affect them personally. Regulations on insider transactions and conflicts of interest are probably the most important ones.

13.6 SUMMARY

This chapter has outlined the requirements that directors should satisfy to perform their duties and responsibilities as effectively as possible. For example, it has suggested that at all times directors must act in a manner to maintain public confidence. No doubt, such action would depend on the directors understanding of the nature of banking and their access to correct and timely information and analysis. Directors need to understand that banking is a highly leveraged, low margin and high volume business, and to obtain information that clearly identifies, describes and quantify the risks to which their banks are exposed. Moreover, they must establish formal policies and guidelines that enable management to control these risk exposures. Finally, the chapter has emphasized that directors must project to the public their awareness of the fact that most of the funds used for lending belong neither to them nor to the bank's officers and staff but to the depositors and creditors. They must, therefore, comply with all policy and statutory requirements relating to insider transactions and conflicts of interests, and ensure that management and staff do likewise.

Notes and References

1 Introduction

1. World Bank (1993).
2. Goldstein and Folkerts-Landau (1993).
3. Morris, Dorfman, Ortiz, and Franco (1990).
4. Comptroller of the Currency (1990).
5. International Monetary Fund, Annex I (May, 1993).
6. Kennickell and Shack-Marquez (1992).
7. Takeda and Turner (1992).
8. Weisbrod, Lee and Rojas-Suarez (1992).
9. Morris, Dorfman, Ortiz and Franco (1990).
10. Siu (1979).
11. Collyns (1993).
12. Latin American countries have separate, not necessarily autonomous, Superintendency of Banks in the following countries: Bolivia, Chile, Colombia, Ecuador, El Salvador, Guatemala, and Peru; the central bank is responsible for bank supervision in the following countries: Argentina, Brazil, Costa Rica, Honduras, Paraguay and Uruguay. See Morris, Dorfman, Ortiz and Franco (1990).

2 Strategic Management

1. Bascom (1994).
2. Wheelen and Hunger (1989).
3. Siu (1979).
4. Wallich (1991).
5. Drucker (1974).
6. McNaughton (1992).
7. Walter (1988).
8. Morris, Dorfman, Ortiz, and Franco (1990).
9. McNaughton (1992).
10. Drucker (1974).
11. Kane (1985).
12. McNaughton (1992).

3 Interest Rate Competition, Structure and Forecasting

1. Some euromarket participants have envisioned the following sovereign risk scenario. The government of a country where eurocurrency deposits and loans are made, in a fit of nationalism or in a desperate attempt to grasp at a way out of foreign exchange difficulties, intervenes in the branches of

279

foreign banks operating in its territory; it seizes the assets of eurobanks but refuses to honor their liabilities. See Giddy (1983).

2. Muksian (1984).
3. Currently these bonds are called 'Brady' bonds, named after a US Secretary of the Treasury, Nicholas Brady, who was instrumental in fostering the issuance of these bonds to replace non-performing foreign debt of developing countries. The bonds are collateralized in part by US Treasury securities.
4. Among these issues were a $200 million eurobond for Bancomex, a large Mexican commercial bank; a $100 million to $150 million eurobond for Bancoldex, a Colombian development bank; and a $100 million for Banco Mercantil, a Brazilian commercial bank. Issuers from Asian countries have borrowed in the euromarkets, by way of bond issues and loans, for project finance purposes. See Thomson Corp (1994).
5. Van Horne (1978) and Conrad (1959).
6. *The Economist* (4–10 February, 1995).
7. Adams (1991).
8. Liebling (1982).
9. Box and Jenkins (1970).
10. Pindyck and Rubinfeld (1976).
11. The reliability and availability of official data for estimating forecasting models needs special comment. Ideally official data should be timely, accurate, comprehensive and objective. Data released by the governents of some countries do not always satisfy these conditions. A common problem is that, many developing countries do not provide an advance calendar of publication dates of official statistics. There are exceptions, however. Hong Kong and Taiwan, for instance, indicate in advance when official statistics will be released. But most governments are vague about publication dates, thus allowing them to delay the release of statistics when the numbers are embarassing.
12. *The Economist* (4–10 March, 1995).

4 Managing Foreign Currency Risks

1. Campfield and O'Brien (1983).
2. The difference between the spot rate of J$33/US$ and the forward rate of J$33.72/US$1.00 is 2.2 per cent. The annual difference in the J$ and US$CD interest rates is 9 per cent equivalent to 2.2 per cent for 90 days.
3. Glen (1993).
4. Scott (1992).
5. For details of the various exchange rate arrangements see Bascom (1994).
6. Campfield and O'Brien (1983).
7. The dollarization phenomenon, that has affected developing countries, particularly those in the early implementation stage of their financial reform policies, has enhanced the tendency for this type of funding activity.
8. Sahay and Vegh (1985).
9. If the rate is better than the original rate the profit on closing will not go to the bank but to the bankrupt company or the receiver appointed by the court.
10. Campfield and O'Brien (1983).

11. Given the overall limit of J\$5 million, a settlement limit of J\$1.5 million and a risk factor of 20 per cent, the J\$700,000 limit for unsettled contracts was obtained as follows: (J\$5 − 1.5) × .20 = J\$700,000.
12. In response to foreign investors' anticipation that the Argentine peso will be devalued and that Argentina would not be able to maintain the convertibility system at the current exchange rate, the Argentine finance minister, Dr Cavallo, has been reported to say 'As a result of our measures, the risk of devaluation has been removed or reduced'. See Vogel Jr (1995). In addition, the central bank gave a clear signal that devaluation was not an option for Argentina. See Fundacion Mediterranea (1995).
13. An important assumption is that there are no risk premiums in the forward market. Risk premium is the incremental amount required to compensate a forward market participant for any uncertainty about the outcome of the contract.
14. Levich (1983).
15. Levich (1983) has argued that news could be modelled in a variety of ways, for example: (1) unanticipated changes in the term structure of interest rates; (2) current account balances; and (3) cyclical income movements. Anyone who can forecast any of these variables better than the market as a whole might outperform the forward rate forecast.
16. Lindert (1986).

5 Term Financing and Compensating Balances

1. In a number of developing countries, stock markets developed many years ago. However, many of these securities markets were dormant until the 1960s. During the past two decades stock markets developed and became active in several developing countries, though they tend to be shallow, illiquid and unsophisticated. See Agtmael (1983).
2. This section relies on Budzeika's work on commercial banks as suppliers of capital funds to business. His findings appear relevant to the current circumstances of most developing financial markets where banks are still the primary source of external financing for firms, and the bond and equity markets, though important are still not the dominant providers of capital funds. See Budzeika (1964).
3. The revolving credit agreement permits the borrower to draw short-term notes on the bank from time to time up to the maximum amount of the commitment, with the privilege of repaying and reborrowing during the life of the agreement. The bank's promise to extend credit is a firm commitment. The line of credit arrangement is similar, differing mainly in the absence of a formal agreement and of a legally binding obligation to extend credit. Both the revolving credit agreement and the credit line differ from the overdraft arrangement. The overdraft arrangement is less formal in terms of maturity, and repayment conditions.
4. Rosenthal and Ocampo (1988).
5. Budzeika (1964).
6. Guttentag and Davis (1964).
7. Hodgman (1961).

8.   Guttentag and Davis (1964).
9.   In the US, finance companies have been important users of link financing, but the technique has been employed by construction and manufacturing firms as well. Some link finance deals are arranged by middlemen who discovered a profitable brokerage opportunity in this activity.
10. Examples of these are a first pay, a medium pay or a slow pay tranche backed by the underlying loans.
11. In developed financial markets, collateralized mortgage obligation (CMO) is a special-purpose vehicle used to purchase mortgage loans and to issue tranches of varying maturity against the loans' cash flows. For maturity matching, a bank may purchase a shorter tranche, while a long-term investor such as a pension fund may purchase a longer tranche.
12. A reserve account or spread account is most often used in bank transactions where, for regulatory reasons, it is important to avoid recourse to the bank. A reserve account is normally funded by the excess finance charge on the assets. The reserve account reimburses any losses incurred by a third party, for example, a bank providing a guarantee against investor losses. In such a situation, the third party does not have recourse to any other assets of the seller or originating bank.
13. Bascom (1992).
14. Snyder (1989).
15. Increasingly in developed financial markets the loan servicing function is being performed by specialized loan servicing companies.
16. The method of interest income recognition may be actuarial, simple interest, or precomputed. The most direct approach is to sell an actuarial portfolio, since the timing of the cash flow requirements between the seller and the investor is the most straightforward. See Reich and Sewright Jr (1989).

6 Managing Credit Risk

1.   McNaughton and Dietz (1992).
2.   McNaughton and Dietz (1992).
3.   Jesser Jr. and Mott (1978); Reed (1963).
4.   Uyemura and Van Deventer (1993).
5.   The American Bankers Association (1973).
6.   Altman (1985).
7.   Beaver (1966).
8.   Libby (1975).
9.   McNaughton and Dietz (1992) have found that in Bangladesh wilful default was common in the 1980s before banking regulators implemented a system to correct this practice. In December 1994 the central bank of Brazil took control of a state-owned commercial bank, Banco Estado do Sao Paulo, mainly because of cash flow problems resulting from the unwillingness of state-owned entities to repay their loans on time.
10. Morris, Dorfman, Ortiz and Franco (1990).
11. Sinkey (1983).
12. Alexander (1978).

7 Credit and Deposit Pricing

1. Paterson (1985).
2. Paterson (1985) has found that to generate a 12 per cent return over costs, the average percentage rate on a $100 1-year loan must be 138 per cent, and on a $500 1-year loan, 40 per cent. In contrast, if costs remained the same, it would only be necessary to charge 15.48 per cent on a 1-year $10,000 loan and 12.87 per cent on a 3-year $10,000 loan to net a 12 per cent return.
3. Loan origination fees may take many forms, for example credit investigation fees, application fees, filing fees, recording fees. These fees may not be rebated in the event of a loan prepayment.
4. Muksian (1984).
5. Paterson (1985).
6. Ando and Modigliani (1963).
7. In the US, the Federal Reserve has periodically surveyed consumers to determine their asset/liability composition and their demand for financial products and services.
8. Santomero (1985).
9. Flynn (1978) and Mason (1979).
10. Santomero (1985).
11. Table 7.3 is based on work by Osius (1992).
12. The earning value of capital refers to the income that could be earned if the bank's capital was used for other purposes. Because capital represents a relatively small proportion of a bank's total funding the earnings value is assumed to be relatively small.
13. McNaughton and Dietz (1992).

8 Managing Asset and Liability Risks

1. Scott (1992).
2. Baker, Jr (1983).
3. Falletti (1992).
4. Uyemura and Van Deventer (1993).
5. Nickerson (1979).
6. The definition of cash flow implies that all revenues for the period have represented inward flows of cash, and that all costs and expenses charged against income for the period in arriving at the figure for cash flow have represented outward flows of cash except for depreciation and other major noncash expenses. This approach assumes the use of cash accounting instead of accrual accounting. Most banks use accrual accounting in determining their income for the period. Accrual accounting means that revenue is accounted for in the period during which it is considered to have been earned, whether or not the payment has been received in cash.
7. Morris, Dorfman, Ortiz, and Franco (1990).
8. The standard deviation of Bank A about the average of $10 is estimated at $1.07, a coefficient of variation of 11 per cent compared to Bank B's standard deviation of $0.53, a coefficient of variation of 5 per cent. The volatility of Bank A's cash flow is, therefore, twice that of Bank B.

9. The discount factor in Table 8.4 was obtained from a standard present value table, the present value numbers were rounded to the nearest thousand.
10. Financial Accounting Standards Board's Statement No. 115 (1 June, 1993).
11. Johnston (1963).
12. In the US banks are prohibited by regulation from providing formal guarantees and instead offer loan commitments as a functional equivalent of a guarantee. Study Group established by the Central Banks of the Group of Ten Countries (1986).

9 Managing Human Resources

1. Small and Lake (1978)
2. The observation has been made that some banks in developing financial markets may be overstaffed by 30–40 per cent, causing their personnel costs to run from 1–2 per cent of assets, including an excess of 0.3–0.8 per cent of assets, which may cut profitability by up to 50 per cent. See Carlson (1992).
3. Carlson refers to the personnel retained or promoted as a result of overstaffing as 'dead wood' which he estimated to represent about 10–20 per cent of the bank's staff. Included in this category of staff are middle-aged or older personnel who might have devoted their entire working careers to the bank, and whose performance might never have been critically evaluated.
4. Workload analysis is generally applicable when the work can be described according to specific work units or outputs, when the work is routine and repetitive, and when one or more work units are assigned to specific jobs.
5. The obstacles to obtaining the required skills for banks in developing financial markets cannot be overstated. These obstacles are explained by the small pool of potential managers and skilled employees in these markets. The inadequate education and intellectual deprivation, in the countries where these markets are located, result in a supply of workers who are ill-equipped to learn the skills necessary to implement new methods of technology or ill-prepared to acquire, despite intensive training, the problem-solving skills needed in business. The hope is in the pockets of potential talents – the educated elite that more often than not have the choice of remaining in their home countries or migrating to foreign counties with more attractive employment opportunities.
6. Copeland and Griggs (1986).
7. Copeland and Griggs (1986) have indicated that South American, European and European-influenced countries tend to have the most centralized decision making. Arab and African countries have strong traditions of consultation in decision making, and because Far Eastern cultures and religions tend to emphasize harmony and perfectibility of humans, group decision making predominates.
8. In Japan, employees tend to be company-oriented, in the US they are job-oriented, and in Latin America they are individual-oriented.
9. Carlson (1992).
10. The approaches to technology adaptation have been summarized as follows: (1) 'first to market' based on a strong R&D programme, technical leadership and risk taking; (2) 'follow the leader' based on strong development re-

sources and ability to react quickly as the market starts its growth phase; (3) 'application engineering' based on product modifications to fit the needs of particular customers in a mature market; and (4) 'me-too' based on superior manufacturing efficiency and cost control. See Ansoff and Stewart (1967).

11. Prasad (1982).
12. Georgia (1978).
13. Sweeney (1978).

10 Regulatory and Supervisory Structure

1. It is clear that no need arose for supervision under the central planning regime not only because economic decisions were all linked to the plan, but also because the concept of risk, essential in the function of supervision, did not arise. In the process of transition toward a market regime, not only do banks become more independent in their decision making but their playing field stretches markedly with the opening and liberalization of the economic system. Therefore, the urgency and importance of an appropriate regulatory and supervisory framework to maintain a measure of order in banking activities and ensure the soundness of the banking sector can hardly be overemphasized. See Guitian (1993).
2. American Bankers Association (1990).
3. Morris, Dorfman, Ortiz and Franco (1990).
4. The direct fiscal cost incurred during 1994 to recapitalize or support weak banks or to pay depositors has been estimated at 13 per cent of Venezuela's GDP or US$8.6 billion. The present value of the US government's cost of the savings and loan clean-up effort has been estimated at about US$215 billion or 4 per cent of GDP in 1990 dollars.
5. The current federal financial regulatory system for US banks is complex, with three agencies having responsibility for regulation and supervision of commercial banking organizations. These are: (1) the Office of the Comptroller of the Currency, an office of the Treasury; (2) the Board of Governors of the Federal Reserve System, or the Federal Reserve; and (3) the Federal Deposit Insurance Corporation or FDIC. There are separate agencies for thrift institutions the Office of Thrift Supervision, an office of the Treasury; and credit unions, the National Credit Union Administration or NCUA.
6. The Venezuela financial crisis in 1994 was caused, in part by the failure of the regulatory agencies to monitor the country's financial institutions on a consolidated basis. During 1994, the authorities were forced to nationalize or close 13 out of 47 banks that were in operation at the beginning of the year, including three of the four largest banks in terms of deposit shares. These 13 banks accounted for about half of total banking system deposits at the end of December 1993. Given the structure of the financial system in Venezuela, whereby commercial banks typically form part of a larger financial group, the authorities were required to take over a wide range of financial enterprises.
7. Alcerreca and Theerathon (1993).

8. Basle Committee on Banking Supervision (1993).
9. A number of financial and accounting ratios are commonly quoted in analyses of bank performance. Although these can be revealing, for example, when comparing different banks, or when trying to identify a trend across a number of years, they must be used with care because of a combination of the nature of banking, accounting conventions, and the complexity of many modern financial institutions. See Chancellor of the Exchequer (1995).
10. Basle Committee on Banking Supervision and the Offshore Group of Banking Supervisors (1996).
11. This issue is being considered by the Basle Committee on Banking Supervision and by regulators and supervisors in developed and developing financial markets.
12. These minimum standards for the supervision of international banking groups and their cross-border establishments were issued by the Basle Committee on Banking Supervision in July 1992 and repeated in the Committee's April 1996 working group report on the supervision of cross-border banking.

11   Capital in Bank Regulation and Supervision

1. Deposit insurance may be viewed as a put option written by the deposit insurance company, with an exercise price equal to the value of the bank's insured liabilities. The value of this option increases directly with the bank's portfolio risk, and inversely with the bank's capital ratio. Thus, as bank's insured deposits and risk assets increase, given an inadequate capital base, the insurance company's exposure expands and so does the risk to taxpayers who serve as the company's lender of last resort. See Kuester and O'Brien (1990).
2. White (1989).
3. The major components of primary capital are common equity and retained earnings, perpetual retained stock, loan loss reserve, and mandatory convertible notes. Risk-based capital standards defines capital in terms of tiers. For instance, Tier One capital is referred to as 'core capital', and Tier Two, 'supplementary capital'. Tiers One and Two are referred to as 'total capital'. Tier One capital is defined as the sum of core capital components less goodwill and other non-qualifying intangibles. Tier One includes the purest and most stable forms of capital – common shareholder's equity (namely common stock, surplus, and retained earnings) non-cumulative perpetual preferred stock, and minority interests in the equity accounts of consolidated subsidiaries. Tier Two capital includes all cumulative perpetual and limited-life preferred stock, hybrid capital instruments, including mandatory convertible securities, term debt, and the allowance for loan and lease losses subject to certain limitations. See Comptroller of the Currency (1995).
4. Berkovec and Liang (1990).
5. The possibility of lower borrowing cost because of increased capital ratio is often referred to as the Modigliani-Miller effect. In brief this effect is based on the argument that because a higher capital ratio lowers the risk of debt

holder loss, the cost of debt falls as the capital ratio rises. See Modigliani and Miller (1958).
6. Banks capital: asset ratios ranged between 2–4 per cent in some repressed financial markets.
7. In July 1988, the central bank governors of the G-10 countries endorsed a system of risk-based capital guidelines for banking organizations under their jurisdiction. These guidelines are referred to as the Basle Accord.
8. Comptroller of the Currency (1995).
9. Brady (1991).

12 Control Systems and Asset Quality Evaluation

1. Banking Supervision Division (1994).
2. The audit committee may have a formal constitution and terms of reference and a minimum of three members; meetings should be attended by the external auditors, the head of internal audit and the officer responsible for finance. The audit committee should have explicit authority to investigate matters within its terms of reference and access to information and external advice. See Banking Supervision Division (1994).
3. Every banker who has handled an inventory loan simply relying on a blanket assignment of inventory has probably visited a failing borrower's premises with hopes of collecting a loan through the sale of the inventory, finding no inventory there and subsequently writing off the loan.
4. Comptroller of the Currency (1995).
5. Branches or subsidiaries of banks from developed financial markets operating in developing financial markets usually have formal credit policy. If these branches or subsidiaries are acquired by investors in the developing financial markets, and managed by local management these polices are maintained though they may not be updated to fit the changing circumstances of the market. Management of banks that were not foreign owned, but were established by local entrepenuers tend to resist any formal structures, or polices that constraint the activities of the owners. Generally the owners and the management are identical. The potential for unsafe credit practices in banks that are owned and managed by the same group can be substantial.
6. Appraisals are professional judgements of the present and/or future value of real property. General approaches to obtain appraised value are the cost approach; market data or direct sales comparison; capitalization of income approach; and discounted cash flow approach. See Comptroller of the Currency (1995).

13 Conclusion

1. The Federal Reserve Bank of Atlanta (1991).
2. Brady (1991).
3. This is an element of the too big to fail argument.

4.   A study has shown that of all bank failures in the US, 60 per cent had weaknesses in their boards, including lack of banking knowledge, as well as uninformed passive board supervision. See McNaughton (1992).

5.   It has been estimated that overhead expenses may be equal to or greater than 3 per cent of average assets. See Federal Reserve Bank of Atlanta (1991).

6.   Barltrop and McNaughton (1992).

7.   In most Latin American countries, banking crises emerged from four important causes: (1) macroeconomic instability, derived in most cases from wrong economic and financial policies pursued by governments; (2) mismanagement; (3) fraud; and (4) banking failures in other countries that affected local banks which were either foreign subsidiaries of branches. See Morris, Dorfman, Ortiz and Franco (1990).

Bibliography

Adams, James Ring (1991) *The Big Fix: Inside the S&L Scandal* (New York: John Wiley & Sons, Inc.).

Agtmael, Antoine W. van (1983) 'Securities Markets in Developing Countries', in Abraham M. George and Ian H. Giddy (eds) *International Financial Handbook* (New York: John Wiley & Sons) Vol. 2, Section 6.10, 3–12.

Alcerreca, Carlos and Pochara Theerathon (1993) *Bank Privatization and Financial Liberalization: The Experience of Mexico* (Miami: The Third International Conference of the International Trade and Finance Association) (20–2 May).

Alexander, Willard (1978) 'Handling Problem Loans', in William H. Baughn and Charles E. Walker (eds) *The Bankers' Handbook* (Homewood: Dow Jones-Irwin) 602–12.

Altman, Edward I. (1985) 'Managing the Commercial Lending Process', in Richard C. Aspinwall & Robert A. Eisenbeis (eds) *Handbook for Banking Strategy* (New York: John Wiley & Sons) 473–518.

American Bankers Association (1973) *A Guide to Developing Commercial Lending Policy* (Washington, DC: Commercial Lending Division).

American Bankers Association (1990) *International Banking Competitiveness: Why it Matters* (Washington, DC: American Bankers Association Economic Advisory Committee) (March).

Ando, Albert and Franco Modigliani (1963) 'The Life-Cycle Hypothesis of Saving', *American Economic Review* Vol. 53, No. 1 (March) 55–84.

Ansoff, I. and J. Stewart (1967) 'Strategies for a Technology Based Business', *Harvard Business Review* Vol. XLV, No. 6, 71–83.

Baker, James V. Jr (1983) *Asset/Liability Management* (Washington, DC: American Bankers Association).

Banking Supervision Division (1994) *Guidance Note on Reporting Accountants' Report on Accounting and Other Records and Internal Control Systems: Notice to Institutions Authorized under the Banking Act 1987* (London: Bank of England) (March).

Barltrop, Chris J. and Diana McNaughton (1992) *Banking Institutions in Developing Markets: Interpreting Financial Statements* (Washington, DC: The World Bank) Vol. 2.

Bascom, Wilbert O. (1992) 'Credit Securitization and Developing Countries' Debt', in Antonio Jorge and Jorge Salazar-Carrillo (eds) *The Latin American Debt* (Houndmills: Macmillan) 100–14.

Bascom, Wilbert O. (1994) *The Economics of Financial Reform in Developing Countries* (Houndmills: Macmillan Press Ltd).

Basle Committee on Banking Supervision (1993) *The Supervisory Treatment of Market Risks: Consultative Proposal* (Basle: Committee on Banking Supervision) (April).

Basle Committee on Banking Supervision and the Offshore Group of Banking Supervisors (1996) *The Supervision of Cross-Border Banking* (Basle: Committee on Banking Supervision) (April).

289

Beaver, W. (1966) 'Financial Ratios as Predictors of Failure', *Journal of Accounting Research: Empirical Research in Accounting* Supplement to Vol. 4, 71–111.

Berkovec, James and Nellie Liang (1990) 'Changes in the Cost of Equity Capital for BHCs and their Effects on Raising Capital', *Working Paper* (Washington, DC: Financial Structure Section, Federal Reserve Board) (July).

Box, G. E. P. and G. M. Jenkins (1970) *Time Series Analysis* (San Francisco: Holden-Day).

Brady, Nicholas F. (1991) *Modernizing the Financial System: Recommendations for Safer, More Competitive Banks* (Washington, DC: The Secretary of the Treasury).

Budzeika, George (1964) 'Commercial Banks as Suppliers of Capital Funds', in *Essays in Money and Credit* (New York: Federal Reserve Bank of New York) 67–71.

Campfield, Thomas M. and John G. O'Brien (1983) 'Foreign Exchange Trading Practices: The Interbank Market', in Abraham M. George and Ian H. Giddy (eds) *International Finance Handbook* (New York: John Wiley & Sons) Vol. 1, 2.4.3–2.4.25.

Carlson, Donald G. (1992) 'Building Human Capital for Banking', in Diana McNaughton (ed.) *Banking Institutions in Developing Markets: Building Strong Management and Responding to Change* (Washington, DC: The World Bank) Vol. 1, 84–116.

Chancellor of the Exchequer (1994) *Banking Act Report for 1994/195* (London: Bank of England).

Chiang, Alpha C. (1974) *Fundamental Methods of Mathematical Economics* (New York: McGraw-Hill Book Company) 2nd Edition.

Chung, Pham (1970) *Money, Banking, and Income* (Scranton: International Textbook Company).

Collyns, Charles (1993) *Private Market Financing for Developing Countries* (Washington, DC: International Monetary Fund).

Comptroller of the Currency (1990) *Comptroller's Handbook for National Bank Examiners* (Washington, DC: United States Department of the Treasury).

Comptroller of the Currency (1995) *Insider Activities: Comptroller's Handbook* (Washington, DC: United States Department of the Treasury).

Conrad, Joseph W. (1959) An *Introduction to the Theory of Interest* (Berkeley: University of California Press).

Copeland, Lennie and Lewis Griggs (1986) *Going International: How to Make Friends and Deal Effectively in the Global Marketplace* (New York: New American Library).

Drucker, Peter F. (1974) *Management: Tasks, Responsibilities, Practices* (New York: Harper Row).

Economist (1995) 'Shapely Curves: American Monetary Policy', *The Economist* (February 4–10) 67–8.

Economist (1995) 'The Insatiable in Pursuit of the Unquantifiable', *The Economist* (March 4–10) 71–2.

Falletti, Peter (1992) 'Financial Management', in Diana McNaughton (ed.) *Banking Institutions in Developing Markets: Building Strong Management and Responding to Change* (Washington, DC: The World Bank) Vol. 1, 64–83.

Federal Reserve Bank of Atlanta (1991) *The New Director's Primer: A Guide to Management Oversight and Bank Regulation* (Atlanta: Department of Supervision and Regulation).

Financial Accounting Standards Board (June 1993) 'Accounting for Certain Investments in Debt and Equity Securities', *Statement of Financial Accounting Standards* No. 115.

Flynn, T. (1978) 'Loan Profitability – A Method to the Madness', *Journal of Commercial Bank Lending* (March) 3–11.

Fundacion Mediterranea (1995) 'Argentina: Outlook', *Newsletter* Vol. 10, No. 2 (67), (February) 1–2.

Georgia, Richard C. (1978) 'Performance-Oriented Personnel Development Programs', in William H. Baughn and Charles E. Walker (eds) *The Bankers' Handbook* (Homewood: Dow Jones-Irwin) 154–163.

Giddy, Ian H. (1983) 'Eurocurrency Interest Rates and Their Linkages', in Abraham M. George and Ian H. Giddy (eds) *International Finance Handbook* (New York: John Wiley & Sons) Vol. 1, 3.3, 3–28.

Glen, Jack D. (1993) 'How Firms in Developing Countries Manage Risk', *IFC Discussion Paper* (Washington, DC: The World Bank) No. 17.

Goldstein, Morris and David Folkerts-Landau (1993) *International Capital Markets: Systemic Issues in International Finance* (Washington, DC: International Monetary Fund) Part II.

Guitian, Manuel (1993) 'From the Plan to the Market: Banking and Financial Reform Aspects', in D. E. Fair and R. Raymond (eds) *The New Europe: Evolving Economic and Financial Systems in East and West* (Netherlands: Kluwer Academic Publishers) 113–29.

Guttentag, Jack M. and Richard Davis (1964) 'Compensating Balances', in *Essays in Money and Credit* (New York: Federal Reserve Bank of New York) 57–61.

Hodgman, Donald R. (1961) 'The Deposit Relationship and Commercial Bank Investment Behavior', *Review of Economics and Statistics* (August) 262–3.

International Monetary Fund (1993) 'Monetary Policy, Financial Liberalization and Asset Price Inflation', *World Economic Outlook* (May) Annex I, 81–95.

Jesser, Jr, Edward A. and Hubert C. Mott (1978) 'Establishing Credit Policy: Criteria and Concepts', in William H. Baughn and Charles E. Walker (eds) *The Bankers' Handbook* (Homewood: Dow Jones-Irwin) 541–555.

Johnston, J. (1963) *Econometric Methods*, 2nd Edition (Tokyo: McGraw-Hill Kogakusha, Ltd.).

Kane, Edward J. (1985) 'Strategic Planning in a World of regulatory and Technological Change', in Richard C. Aspinwall and Robert A. Eisenbeis (eds) *Handbook for Banking Strategy* (New York: John Wiley & Sons) 725–44.

Kennickell, Arthur and Janice Shack-Maquez (1992) 'Changes in Family Finances from 1983–1989: Evidence from the Survey of Consumer Finances', *Federal Reserve Bulletin* (January) Vol. 78, 1–18.

Kuester, Kathleen A., and James M. O'Brien (1990) 'Market-Based Deposit Insurance Premiums: An Evaluation', *Working Paper* (Washington, DC: Federal Reserve Board Monetary and Financial Studies Section) (May).

Levich, Richard M. (1983) 'Exchange Rate Forecasting Techniques', in Abraham M. George and Ian H. Giddy (eds) *International Finance Handbook* (New York: John Wiley & Sons) Vol. 2, 8.1.3–8.1.30.

Libby, R. (1975) 'The Use of Simulated Decision Makers in Information Evaluation', *Accounting Review* (July) 475–89.

Liebling, Herman I. (1982) 'Forecasting Methods', in Douglas Greenwald (ed.) *Encyclopedia of Economics* (New York: McGraw-Hill, Inc.) 418–22.

Lindert, Peter H. (1986) *International Economics* (Homewood: Irwin) Eighth Edition.

Malkeil, Burton (1966) *The Term Structure of Interest Rates* (Princeton: Princeton University Press).

Mason, J. (1979) *Financial Management of Commercial Banks* (New York: Warren Gorhan and Lamont).

McNaughton, Diana (1992) *Banking Institutions in Developing Markets: Building Strong Management and Responding to Change* (Washington, DC: The World Bank) Vol. 1.

McNaughton, Diana and Clayton Townsend Dietz (1992) 'Managing Country Risk', in Diana McNaughton (ed.) *Banking Institutions in Developing Markets: Building Strong Management and Responding to Change* (Washington, DC: The World Bank) Vol. 1, 31–63.

Modigliani, F. and M. H. Miller (1958) 'The Cost of Capital, Corporation Finance, and the Theory of Investment', *American Economic Review* (September) 261–97.

Morris, Felipe, Mark Dorfman, Jose Pedro Ortiz and Maria Claudia Franco (1990) 'Latin America's Banking System in the 1980s: A Cross Country Comparison', *World Bank Discussion Paper* (Washington, DC: The World Bank) No. 81.

Muksian, Robert (1984) *Financial Mathematics Handbook* (Englewood Cliffs: Prentice-Hall, Inc.).

Nickerson, Clarence B. (1979) *Accounting Handbook for Nonaccountants* (Boston: CBI Publishing Company, Inc.).

Osius, Margaret E. (1992) 'Lending: The Essentials of Credit Risk Analysis', *Paper Presented at the Bankers' Seminar: Banking and Finance in Transition* (Moscow) (12–14 February).

Paterson, Richard L. (1985) 'Pricing Consumer Loans and Deposits', in Richard C. Aspinwall and Robert A. Eisenbeis (eds) *Handbook for Banking Strategy* (New York: John Wiley & Sons) 548–88.

Pindyck, R. S. and D. L. Rubinfeld (1976) *Econometric Models and Economic Forecasts* (New York: McGraw-Hill Book Company).

Prasad, A. J. (1982) 'Research, Development, and Technology Transfer', in Ingo Walter and Tracy Murray (eds) *Handbook of International Business* (New York: John Wiley & Sons) Section 36, 3–36.

Reed, Edward W. (1963) *Commercial Bank Management* (New York: Harper & Row).

Reich, Robert I. and Charles W. Sewright Jr (1989) 'The Bank Role', in Phillip L. Zweig (ed.) *The Asset Securitization Handbook* (Homewood: Dow Jones-Irwin) 385–415.

Roe, Alan, Nicholas Bruck and Marcus Fedder (1992) *International Finance Strategies for Developing Countries: An EDI Policy Seminar Report* (Washington, DC: The World Bank) No. 31.

Rosenthal, James A. and Juan M. Ocampo (1988) *Securitization of Credit: Inside the New Technology of Finance* (New York: John Wiley & Sons, Inc.).

Sahay, Ratna and Carlos A. Vegh (1995) 'Dollarization in Transition Economies', *Finance & Development* (March) 36–9.

Santomero, Anthony M. (1985) 'Pricing Business Credit', Richard C. Aspinwall and Robert A. Eisenbeis (eds) *Handbook for Banking Strategy* (New York: John Wiley & Sons), 589–605.

Scott, David (1992) 'Managing Foreign Exchange Risk', in Diana McNaughton (ed.) *Banking Institutions in Developing Markets: Building Strong Management and Responding to Change* (Washington, DC: The World Bank) Vol. 1, 124–37.

Scott, David (1992) 'Asset and Liability Management', in Diana McNaughton (ed.) *Banking Institutions in Developing Markets: Building Strong Management and Responding to Change* (Washington, DC: The World Bank) Vol. 1, 138–42.

Sinkey, J. (1983) *Commercial Bank Financial Management* (New York: Macmillan Publishing Company).

Siu, R. G. H. (1979) *The Craft of Power* (New York: John Wiley & Sons).

Small, Lawrence M. and Eugene J. Lake (1978) 'Manpower Planning and Management', in William H. Baughn and Charles E. Walker (eds) *The Bankers' Handbook* (Homewood: Dow Jones-Irwin) 101–9.

Snyder, Christopher L. (1989) 'Securitizing Middle Market Commercial Loans', in Philip L. Zweig (ed.) *The Asset Securitization Handbook* (Homewood: Dow Jones-Irwin) 440–76.

Study Group established by the Central Banks of the Group of Ten Countries (1986) *Recent Innovations in International Banking* (Basle: Bank of International Settlements).

Sweeney, Gordon P. (1978) 'Management of the Training Function', in William H. Baughn and Charles E. Walker (eds) *The Bankers' Handbook* (Homewood: Dow Jones-Irwin) 132–42.

Takeda, Masahiko and Philip Turner (1992) 'The Liberalization of Japan's Financial Markets: Some Major Themes', *Economic Papers* (Basle: Bank for International Settlements) (November) No. 34.

Thomson Corp. (1994) 'Project Finance Experts Expect Fruitful Year', *International Banking Report* (December) 363–4.

Uyemura, Dennis G. and Donald R. Van Deventer (1993) *Financial Risk Management in Banking: The Theory and Application of Asset Liability Management* (Chicago: Bankers Publishing Company and Probus Publishing Company).

Van Horne, J. C. (1978) *Financial Market Rates and Flows* (Englewood Cliffs: Prentice-Hall).

Vogel Jr., Thomas T. (1995) 'Bankers' Lament: "No Yield for Me, Argentina",' *The Wall Street Journal* (March 27) C1 and C19.

Wallich, Christine (1991) 'China: Financial Sector Policies and Institutional Development', *World Bank Country Study* (Washington, DC: The World Bank).

Walter, Ingo (1988) *Global Competition in Financial Services* (New York: Ballinger American Enterprise Institute).

Weisbrod, Steven R., Harold Lee, and Liliana Rojas-Suarez (1992) 'Bank Risk and Declining Franchise Value of the Banking Systems in the United States and Japan', *International Monetary Fund Working Papers* (June) 92/45.

Wheelen, Thomas L. and J. David Hunger (1989) *Strategic Management and Business Policy* (New York: Addison-Wesley Publishing Company).

Wolkowitz, Benjamin (1985) 'Managing Interest Rate Risk', in Richard C. Aspinwall and Robert A. Eisenbeis (eds) *Handbook for Banking Strategy* (New York: John Wiley & Sons) 407–56.

White, Alice P. (1989) 'The Evolution of the Thrift Industry Crisis', *Finance and Economics Discussion Series* (Washington: Board of Governors of the Federal Reserve System, Division of Research and Statistics) (December).

World Bank (1993) *The East Asian Miracle: Economic Growth and Public Policy* (New York: Oxford University Press).

Index

interest rates 1, 36–54
  asset–liability risk 156–8, 172–3
  averaging 40–43
  competition 37–40
  cost 270
  credit and deposit pricing 122–46;
    commercial loans 138–45;
    consumer loans 128–31;
    deposits 131–5
  fixed 147
  forecasting 48–53; conditional
    49–50; internal 49; official
    data for 280; unconditional
    49–50; variables 51–3
  risk management 149–52, 271–2;
    strategic 151–2; tactical
    151, 152; trading 151, 152
  yield curves and spreads 43–8,
    149–50, 172, 173
International Monetary Fund 279,
  291
Italy: bank regulation and supervision
  205, 208

Japan
  asset price inflation 4
  bank regulation and supervision
    205, 208
  credit, regulation of 3
  employment culture 284
Jenkins, G. M. 280, 290
Jesser, E. A. Jr. 282, 291
Johnston, J. 284, 291
Jorge, A. 289

Kane, E. J. 279, 291
Kennickell, A. 279, 291
Korea: credit, regulation of 3
Kuester, K. A. 286, 291

Lake, E. J. 284, 293
laws *see* regulation and supervision
Lee, H. 279, 294
Levich, R. M. 281, 292
liability risks 147–75
  asset–liability committees 148
  information 148–56
  liquidity 152–6
  policies 148–56

Liang, N. 286, 290
Libby, R. 282, 292
Liebling, H. I. 280, 292
Lindert, P. H. 281, 292
liquidity 7–8, 22, 274, 275
  asset–liability management 152–6
  capital adequacy and 225
  risk 70–1, 267–8
  runs 267–8
  supervision and regulation 204,
    212, 270
loans *see* credit

Malkeil, B. 292
management
  anticipation 265
  competent, principles of 2–10;
    collateral and economic shocks
    4–6; counterparties 8–10;
    credit 2–7; expansion 6–7;
    liquidity 7–8; maturity gap
    7–8; risk taking 6–7
  directors 266–78; boards 268–9,
    272–7; conflict of interest
    277, 278; duties 268–9,
    272–4; insider dealing 277,
    278; responsibilities; capital
    adequacy 269; costs 270;
    interest rates 270, 271–2;
    investment 270, 273;
    liquidity 270; reserves
    270–1; risk awareness 266–8,
    269, 270–2; risk monitoring
    and control 274–7; role
    272–4, 278
  financial planning and budgeting
    22–4; performance indicators
    22–3
  managers 31–3
  mission and objectives 17–19,
    33–4, 35; platforms and levers
    19–21
  strategic 16–35; budgeting 22–4;
    competitive strength, sources
    of 24–7; constraints 17–19;
    financial planning 22–4;
    importance of 16–17; levers
    19–21; markets 27–31;
    mission and objectives 17–19,